CREWE LOCOMOTIVE WORKS AND ITS MEN

CREWE LOCOMOTIVE WORKS AND ITS MEN

BRIAN REED

David & Charles
Newton Abbot   London   North Pomfret (VT)

TO

The Crewe 'premium' (1909–13) *Robert A. Riddles*
The Crewe 'premium' and pupil (1916–20) *Kenneth Cantlie*
The Crewe pupil (1920–22) the late *Donald H. Stuart*

who between them over many years
greatly warmed and enriched
the author's life

PUBLISHER'S NOTE
While this book was being set into type came the sad news of the death of the author. Brian Reed
had spent many years researching archive material and many record sources. This book will stand
not only as a tribute to the author, but also to one of the great railway works and the town it
serves.

British Library Cataloguing in Publication Data

Reed, Brian
  Crewe locomotive works and its men.
  1. British Rail Engineering – History
  2. Locomotive works – Crewe (Cheshire)
  I. Title
  338.7′ 62′ 52609427   TJ625.B/

  ISBN 0-7153-8228-4

First published 1982
Second impression 1985

Photoset by Typesetters (Birmingham) Ltd
and printed in Great Britain
by Redwood Burn Ltd, Trowbridge, Wilts
for David & Charles (Publishers) Limited
Brunel House Newton Abbot Devon

Published in the United States of America
by David & Charles Inc
North Pomfret Vermont 05053 USA

Contents

Acknowledgments

Of the many friends who over many years have helped the gradual formation of this book come first and foremost the three dedicatees, and after them the late Roland C. Bond and Dennis Dooley. Bond probably knew more about Crewe Works in its entirety than any other man, for additional to his two periods there as assistant superintendent and works superintendent he had the Works as one of his charges from 1946 until his retirement in 1968, as outlined in the Appendix, and until his death in December 1980 he kept himself informed of everything new at Crewe. Dooley, today the superintendent of ancillary shops at the Works, is a fourth-generation Crewe railwayman, and one whose great technical competence is supplemented by a well-developed historical sense. Apart from war service, he has been at the works continuously since 1934. The generosity and friendship of all five have provided much of any vitality this book may have.

John Edgington over two decades has been mentor on all matters to do with LNWR and LMSR locomotives; he, along with Philip Atkins, both at the National Railway Museum, have contributed much, and with a happy community of interest. In divers ways over the last dozen years unstinted help has come from the late Sir Reginald Terrell, J. W. Burrell, Brian Radford, Ernest Dutton, J. P. Richards, Harold D. Bowtell, Dudley Whitworth, George Barlow, the late G. H. Platt, Dennis Ollier, J. J. C. Barker-Wyatt, Clive Taylor, the present Crewe works manager Frank de Nobriga, and the chief technical officer of the borough of Crewe & Nantwich, G. A. Barnard, and his assistant K. I. Abram.

1
Origins

Fifty-five inside-cylinder locomotives from several makers, and 55 crank axles broken or replaced within the first 13 months, formed one of the unhappy records of the first main-line railway in England, the Grand Junction Railway (GJR), which was opened on 4 July 1837 throughout its whole 78 miles from Birmingham to Newton Junction on the Liverpool & Manchester Railway (L&MR), with the engines and trains running on a further 15 miles to Liverpool or Manchester. How such mass breakages, argued—nay, fought—about at the company's general meeting in 1838, *could* occur was highlighted by a subsequent remark of a well-known locomotive engineer of the time, Charles Todd, that he had once seen the leading wheel pair of a GJR six-wheel engine running at about 35mph on straight track suddenly rise some 18 inches in the air, drop back on the rails, and continue bouncing *decrescendo* for some distance.

All this was not good enough, and by the summer of 1839 the GJR board, then fully aware the system would grow substantially in the next ten years, was so disturbed by the locomotive costs and the personality of Thomas Melling in charge of the traction side, that Joseph Locke, the GJR engineer-in-chief, was ordered to re-organise the whole locomotive department completely. Melling clearly was unable to rise above foreman level, and because of the friction he engendered with other officials was given notice in December before a new chief was appointed. Concurrently Locke suggested the time had come to design "a new and improved engine of which as many parts as possible should be to one standard." On Locke's recommendation, William Barber Buddicom was appointed on 1 January 1840 as locomotive superintendent at £500 a year and took up office on the 15th. His first technical move was to try and improve crank axle performance and main frame strength, but from the start he was pushed by Locke to evolve a new type of engine that would eliminate the major troubles of the inside-cylinder Patentee engines.

At that time the GJR locomotive repair shops were at Edge Hill,

Liverpool. Uniquely, they were on ground and in buildings rented from the L&MR and were 15 miles away from Newton Junction, the nearest point of the GJR line; they were incapable of much enlargement. Locke knew a fresh works would have to be found to cater for an extended GJR and to suit the reorganisation of the locomotive department. In the negotiations for the take-over by the GJR of the Chester & Crewe Railway (CC) which was effected formally on 19 May 1840, the power of the CC to buy land around the junction at Crewe was noted, and its use appreciated because of the probable entry into Crewe at the same point of the Manchester & Birmingham Railway (MBR), then under construction. The CC already had purchased in 1838 a small amount of land near the junction on which it proposed to erect a workshop, and Locke realised that here might be a good location for a new locomotive works, as being near the geographical centre of the GJR system, though without coal or much water handy, and far from any iron workings.

How quickly the matter then had to develop is shown best by the succession of board minutes. First mention of Crewe for works was in 1840: *10 June*: "That Mr Locke be requested to prepare the estimates referred to in his report as to the removal of the Engine Shops to Crewe." *20 June*: "The chairman having read a letter from Mr Locke stating that his estimate of the cost of removing the workshops for engines to Crewe will be ready by the next meeting of the board and having stated that the powers of taking additional land under the Crewe Act [*ie* the CC incorporation Act of 30 June 1837] expires on 4th July next, Resolved: That Mr Swift [GJR solicitor] be authorised to purchase, at the junction at Crewe, additional land to the extent of 10 to 15 acres." *1 July*: "Mr Locke's report on the Removal of the Engine Shops to Crewe having been read and discussed, and Mr Swift having reported he can procure at the point of junction 30 acres of land at £100 per acre, Resolved: That Mr Swift purchase the land; and that Mr Locke prepare and lay before the board drawings and estimates for an establishment at Crewe which shall include the shops required for the building and repair of carriages and wagons as well as Engines." *12 August*: "Mr Locke also brought forward a ground plan of the buildings, etc for the workshops to be erected at Crewe, which was approved, and he to lose no time in forwarding execution of same."

Thus began the great Crewe works and town, which grew and grew until through many years of the 20th century the works employed 7,000 to 8,000 men and boys and the town housed over 45,000 persons, who until around 1940 were nearly all dependent on the

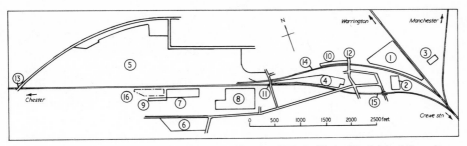

1 Old Works 2 Southern Annexe to Old Works 3 Grease works 4 Deviation Works 5 Steelworks 6 Gasworks
7 Carriage repair shops 8 Carriage storage sheds 9 Carriage cleaning plant 10 General offices 11 Flag Lane
Bridge 12 Chester Bridge 13 Merrill's Bridge 14 Old Chester Line 15 Deviation Line 16 Cooling ponds

Fig 1 General location of the three locomotive works, carriage works and gas plant at Crewe about the time of the end of the LNWR, 1922

railway for their subsistence. So was fulfilled the claim of John Moss, the GJR chairman, before the works was actually opened: "This grand manufactory will be the finest and most extensive railway workshop in the world."

The Works in its time has made and repaired not only locomotives, carriages and wagons, but also rails, chairs, keys, steel sleepers, points and crossings, signals and signalling equipment including interlocking frames, signal posts (wooden and steel tubular), signal gantries, electric staff and electric signalling installations, steel ladders for signal posts, signal and station lamps, chains, bridge material, level-crossing gates, platelayers' huts, portable huts, carts, barrows, foot-warmers, coal scuttles, soap, office furniture, marine boilers, parts for marine engines, canal boats, ships' anchors, grease, town gas, pipe mains for gas, water and sewage systems, iron hurdles, fences, bricks, wood and metal artificial limbs, machine tools, cranes, steelworks plant, dynamos, engine-shed frames, turntables, snowploughs, road transport trailers, rail tractors, cable drums, air compressors, armoured trains, and a wide range of armaments including tanks; and by its activities under the direction of a forceful railway chairman led eventually to the formation of the Locomotive Manufacturers' Association.

The Works is still in existence and operation, under the aegis since 1970 of British Rail Engineering Ltd (BREL), a wholly-owned subsidiary of the British Railways Board, to which it was transferred from the British Railways Workshops Division, that in its turn had been set up in 1962 when control of the 28 workshops of BR was taken away from the chief mechanical engineers of the various Regions. The Works today is the largest associated with BR. It handles major repairs to electric and diesel-electric locomotives, builds mechanical portions of electric locomotives and erects the whole machine, makes HST power cars, bogies, steel-castings, laminated springs, and mechanical portions of signal and telegraph equipment, and still employs around 4000 men. All work is now done at the west, or Steelworks, end (see Fig 1, frontispiece). Of the Old Works in the triangle between the Chester and Warrington lines scarcely a wrack remains, while the celebrated office block immediately west of Chester bridge is now empty, though for some years was leased by various private companies.

Following the GJR board authorisation of 12 August 1840, a contract was made in the September with Thomas Brassey for excavation and ground clearance at 9d [4p] per cubic yard, needed before the erection of the workshops could begin. In this ground preparation Buddicom and R. S. Norris, one of the assistant civil engineers, acted for Locke. In May 1841 Buddicom was instructed to prepare lists of tools and equipment, and to get quotations from makers, which he proceeded to do, but at the end of August that year he left the GJR with the blessing of Locke and certain members of the board to begin private locomotive building in France. Management of the locomotive department and of the Crewe scheme thereupon was given to Francis Trevithick, then resident engineer at the Birmingham end of the GJR.

An essential part of the whole project was a small town to house the workers and their families to be transferred from Liverpool, for at that time scarcely a score of persons lived in the area around the station, and which was known as Crewe in the parish of Barthomley, a parish located mainly around Crewe Hall and beyond. The Works and town were built mainly in the township of Monks Coppenhall, which in 1840 had some 200 inhabitants; Monks Coppenhall and Church Coppenhall were two divisions of the old parish of Coppenhall, and eventually some of Crewe town spread into Church Coppenhall. Strangely, the station was outside the boundaries of the new Crewe until 1936. The 30 acres of land acquired initially by the GJR was sufficient, when added to the small amount of CC land, only for the nucleus, and in the next five years another 50 acres and more had to be purchased. The civic and social history of the new settlement down to 1923 has been fully and delightfully recorded by W. H. Chalenor.[1]

A commonly-accepted tale is that the GJR had to pay £500 an acre for land after the railway projects came to the notice of landowners. From official contemporary records the only parcel of land at that figure was in the angle between the GJR Warrington line and the MBR line (fields 280 and 292 in Fig 2), which was not used for the

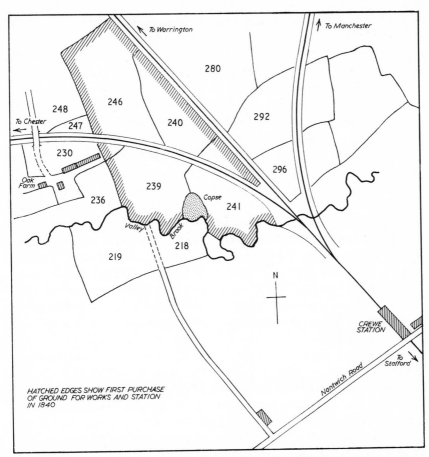

Fig 2 Tithe map of the area around Crewe junction just before the building of the works and town, *circa* 1842

locomotive works or the town, and which was not acquired until November 1846, and then not by the GJR but by the newly-formed London & North Western Railway (LNWR). Otherwise £100 an acre in 1840 and up to £300 in 1842–43 were the prices paid by the GJR, and in the 1860s much land was bought by the LNWR at £200 an acre.

Fig 2, based on the tithe map of the time, shows the two railway tracks in existence and the one (MBR) under construction in 1840–41. The town spread first north and west in fields 240 and 246 on which, and on field 241, the original shops were built. Over the next twenty years various adjustments in the boundary to the south were made; these included slight diversions and the eventual partial covering of the Valley, or South, brook, and the construction of a water reservoir and filter beds mainly in the area of the coppice and field 241. The layout here was influenced by the enlarged privately-owned flour mill pool (field 218). Further ground to the south of this was also taken, and came to be used in the 1860s for new engine sheds. Oak Farm was acquired in the second purchase of ground, and the present Oak Street is on its site. Some of the needed ground was bought from the trustees of the Edleston estate, and the family is still commemorated by Edleston Road lying between the station and the town centre.

Locke's final estimate submitted in February 1841 for the initial Crewe scheme exclusive of ground clearance and the cost of the machine tools was almost £70,000, made up of land £5,500, works buildings £35,800, cottages £25,000, extra allowance £3,300. First contracts were given to S. J. Holme of Liverpool: for main buildings £19,959, superintendents' houses £1,335, and £491 for each block of four cottages. Approximately 50 blocks were built at first. Within a month a revised price of £20,672 had been accepted for the main buildings. Another revision was needed before the end of 1841 because Trevithick found the planned height of the ground floor in the two-storey carriage shop was insufficient for a coach to be lifted well clear of its wheels.

Locke stated in July 1842 that he thought the move from Edge Hill could take place in another two months, and as a result of his report Charles Lawrence, the deputy chairman, told the shareholders in August: "The extensive workshops at Crewe being nearly ready for occupation, the company's establishment for repairing stock will shortly be removed there." However, not until the Spring of 1843 were the Works and houses sufficiently advanced for the initial transfer to be made. March 1843 is usually regarded as the month of the mass transfer, and a Crewe almanac issued in 1885 gives 10 March as the official date; but not until May did Locke announce to the board that removal was complete.

The money actually expended by May 1843 amounted to £90,396, made up of £4,335 for land, £77,611 for works and houses, and £8,450 for machinery, of which £28,967 had been spent on Works alone during the previous half-year, so that Locke must have had his tongue in his cheek in July 1842, or have been singularly ill-informed as to the true state. Trevithick's estimate for further expenditure to complete the sanctioned scheme was £12,936 Works and houses, £2,000 for a plant and town gasworks, and £3,950 for machinery, £18,886 in total. At the half-yearly meeting of the GJR in August 1845 Moss gave the value of land, Works and machinery at Crewe as £130,340.

Trevithick was in executive charge of both Works and town

building until February 1843, when the board minuted that the cottage department at Crewe be placed under Norris (then resident engineer of the northern part of the GJR), and that the workshops, yard, etc, and the regulation thereof be considered under the control of Trevithick. This restriction may well have been acceptable to Trevithick; that he was fussed by directors is suggested in a letter to him from Buddicom in France dated May 1843 when the Works was newly opened: ". . . Now, how are you going on? What are all the old devils doing? Mr Locke tells me you have had a weary time at Crewe, or rather with the Crewe works and old John Moss."

In February 1843 the board informed Locke, who by then was much engaged in France and elsewhere in Britain, that it still "relied on him not only to give minute and specific instructions on all the details, fix the new rates of wages, etc, but personally to superintend the organisation of the new establishment so that in all this important change the basis of an economical and efficient system for all time coming may be settled."

On 2 December 1843 the directors gave what became known as the 'Crewe ball and banquet' to the workers and their families to mark the completion of the scheme (Plate I). Alexander Allan, chief Works foreman, was in the chair at the two o'clock banquet, and his next in rank, Sykes, was vice-chairman. Later in the day Locke made artful references to Allan continuing in the chair against protocol, after Moss and other directors who were the hosts, and several higher officials had joined the party. The banquet was followed by a ball and then a supper. The main functions were held in the main repair and coach shops, which were cleared as much as possible for the purpose. At that time the wagon shop was being used on Sundays for religious services, after being duly consecrated, and this continued until the completion and consecration in December 1845 of the railway-built Christ Church. Not until October 1845, after repeated deferments, did 200 directors and shareholders visit the Works, at a time when around 340 men were employed on the locomotive side and 370 on carriages and wagons.

By December 1843 the locomotive repair and erecting shop already was in full swing and, additional to repairs, two new engines had been built and despatched while a third was on the point of completion. First of the three, and the first new engine to be built at Crewe, was *Tamerlane*. The old records show it to have been completed in October, and one verse of a poem written by a Crewe wheel-shop workman, David Atkinson, for the 1887 Jubilee celebrations, claimed the exact date to have been 20 October. The other two of the first three engines were *Merlin* and *Prospero*. That *Columbine*, now in the National Railway Museum at York, was the first Crewe-built engine is a complete fable, though repeated in new publications nearly every year this century up to the present time.

At the time of the banquet the area allotted to the works and yard, the gasworks and the water supply was around 15 acres, of which 8 to 8½ acres were in the triangle between the Warrington and Chester lines, and the remainder south of the Chester tracks. This group eventually became known as the Old Works. Roofed shops aggregated only some 2½ acres at the end of 1843. The engine repair shop was 300ft by 100ft and its roof was in two bays covering three and two tracks respectively. A narrow arcade, into which were put various machine tools, was arranged along the dividing line of the two bays; this long-standing Crewe feature, traces of which may be seen to this day, may well have been initiated by Locke himself.

The two-bay carriage and wagon shops, 240ft by 87ft and 240ft by 74ft respectively, had a ground floor and a first floor, as had the office-and-stores block. Additional were a smithy with a steam-driven fan for most of the fires, a forge, a fitting shop with about ten small planers plus slotters, lathes and other tools, tiny iron and brass foundries and a small spring shop, all laid out as shown in Fig 3. The buildings were of substantial brick construction with stone facings, and roof beams and joists were of wood throughout. By the arched gate there was also a two-bay four-track engine-in-steam shop 140ft by 84ft which could be used as an engine shed, into which could be brought from Crewe station any engine needing quick light repair, and in which steaming tests of new or repaired engines could be made.

According to contemporary published references, 161 men were employed in December 1843, which suggests that all men had not yet been transferred from Edge Hill; maybe the 161 referred to the opening of the Works in March/April, for at the end of the year the population of the town approached 2000, of whom 1150 were dependent on the railway and lived in over 250 railway-owned houses. These cottages were of four different types with respective weekly rents of 2s 9d [14p], 3s 9d [19p], 4s 3d [21p] and 6s 6d [33p], which sums included parish rates, water and gas-lighting fixtures, but not the gas, which was charged at 2d [1p] per burner. The cottages were rightly considered as models for their time, even though those with the lowest rent had no tap water, the residents having to go to one of the street pumps.

The well-known clock tower at the Works entrance from the railway, which remained until 1976, latterly in dilapidated condition,

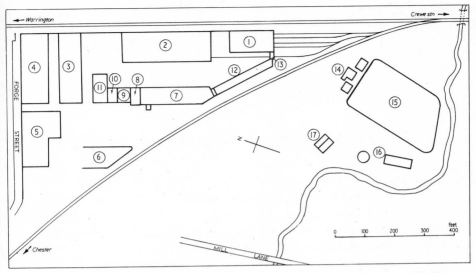

1 Engine-in-steam shop 2 Engine repair and construction shop 3 Wagon shop 4 Coach shop 5 Smithy
6 Forge 7 Fitting-machine shop 8 Spring shop 9 Brass foundry 10 Dressing shop 11 Iron Foundry 12 Stores
and general offices 13 Clock-tower arch 14 Water-pumping plant and two filter beds 15 Water reservoir
16 Gasworks 17 Gasworks cottages

Fig 3 Plan of Crewe Works as at the end of 1843

was not part of the original plans of the architect John Cunningham,
but was authorised by the board in August 1843 and was complete by
the time of the banquet. This was not the workers' entrance, which
was in Forge Street close to all the houses; above the entrance was the
bell that was rung for starting and stopping times, and which lasted
until a steam whistle was substituted in 1861. That first winter of
1843/44 must have been uncomfortable, for in January 1844 the board
was complaining that Jones & Potts still had not finished the heating
installation ordered in December 1842, and which was specified to
keep the engine repair shop to 60°F and the carriage shop to 65°F.
This heating system was advanced practice; most engineering shops of
the time had none.

2

Direction and Administration

In the primitive early stages all matters concerning the line were dealt with by the whole GJR board in session, but with the growing business important decisions were delayed by incessant discussions at irregular intervals and without any proper agenda for each meeting. By 1841 certain affairs had to be delegated to small committees of board members. The first mention of a Crewe Committee is in the minutes of 22 December 1841, but the wording suggests that such a committee with a fluid membership had already been meeting with the station, operating-staff cottages and the ground clearance for town and works as its subjects. Not until 2 February 1842 came a minute: "that Mr Ripley, Mr Bold, Mr Gilfillan and the chairman *ex officio* be named a committee for superintending and carrying out arrangements at Crewe and making from time to time such modifications as shall appear necessary." Town, Works and station came within the authority of this committee, which lasted until 14 June 1845, when a board committee was formed "to take charge of the Locomotive, Carriage and Wagon Departments, also the general management of the town: Mr Earle, Mr Booth, Mr G. R. Lawrence, Mr N. D. Bold. To meet at Crewe every other Thursday as at present."

This was the body generally known in its time and later as 'the Crewe Committee'. Its formation was due first to the consolidation of the GJR with the L&MR and the Bolton & Leigh Railway as from 1 July 1845, and to the projected extension of the Works and town needed to centralise the coming additional repair work and supervise the bigger three departments; secondly to the large extension of Crewe station and adjacent lines to suit the merger and to cater for the forth-coming completion of the trunk line to Scotland; and finally to the growing size of the town, for the company, rich and powerful for the time, was perforce taking-on the management and amenities of the new settlement, the existing 'local authorities' being based on a quiet agricultural area and quite incapable of dealing with the sudden influx.

With the formation of the LNWR by the fusion of the enlarged GJR

Three successive locomotive superintendents: Trevithick (centre), Ramsbottom (right-white beard), and Webb (left-wearing hat) at Chester Place in 1875. Mrs Trevithick at far right

An epitome of Crewe works in its first 40 years as published in the *Crewe Guardian* 1882, showing at the bottom corners the Crewe banquet in December 1843, and at the top centre the girders for the new Llandulas viaduct ready to go off to site, 1879

The only known view of the Old Works wheel shop, which was changed over to general machine work in 1882 and later became the valve motion shop. This view is dated 1872–73 and shows one of the rope-driven single-rail cranes

Millwrights' shop in the Deviation Works *circa* 1873, when about five years old, and before it was extended to absorb the Deviation iron foundry

with the London & Birmingham Railway (LBR) and the MBR as from 16 July 1846, came from the end of November that year a General Merchandise and Locomotive Committee which was supposed to co-ordinate locomotive and rolling stock activities of the three divisions into which the LNWR was arranged, and which had to sanction any substantial financial commitments recommended by the continuing ex-GJR Crewe or Locomotive Committee of what had become the Northern Division (ND) of the LNWR, and by the corresponding ex-LBR or Southern Division (SD) and MBR committees. The SD continued to run its own locomotive and carriage works at Wolverton and Euston, and the MB division its much smaller repair establishment at Longsight, Manchester. The MB Division was changed to the North Eastern Division (NED) to incorporate the Huddersfield & Manchester and the Leeds, Dewsbury & Manchester Railways as soon as those two lines were opened in 1849. The two railways themselves had been absorbed into the LNWR in 1847 before any of their lines were opened. In 1857 the ND and NED were amalgamated into an enlarged Northern Division.

For locomotive purposes the ND included from 1846 the Wigan–Preston line of the North Union (NU), from 1846 to 1857 the Lancaster & Carlisle (LCR), and from 1849 the Chester & Holyhead Railway. From 1848 to the end of 1859 the Trent Valley line from Rugby to Stafford was worked by ND engines; for some four years from 1851–52 to the end of 1855 the working of the Shropshire Union and South Staffordshire Railways also came within the ND orbit, but was then transferred to the Southern Division. Chester & Holyhead uncompleted locomotive orders were taken-over by the LNWR, but only the NU (five engines) and the South Staffs (21 engines) brought actual locomotives of their own into the Northern Division pool, and all at first were repaired at Crewe.

The needs and extensions at Crewe—both town and works—continued to be sanctioned by the Crewe Committee until April 1858, when the board put the two locomotive divisions (Northern and Southern) under a General Store and Locomotive Expenditure Committee, and the two superintendents reported direct to it, as did the carriage and wagon superintendents. Nevertheless the Crewe Committee continued to look after town affairs, and also sanctioned many matters connected with the Works and made suggestions for wider locomotive-department matters.

In 1862 the Northern and Southern locomotive divisions were amalgamated under one superintendent with headquarters at Crewe, under the circumstances related in Chapter 4. Shortly after this consolidation board supervision of the single department was transferred to the LNWR Locomotive Committee, but from January 1864 authority was assumed by a new Locomotive & Mechanical Engineering Committee to "take the supervision of the Locomotive, Carriage and Wagon Departments and also the Company's steamboats." This arrangement continued until the end of the LNWR on 31 December 1922, but the Crewe Committee also continued for some years after 1864, and not long before this had recommended to the board the building of the steel works.

As to management as distinct from direction, Trevithick was in charge on the Northern Division until 1857, being followed by John Ramsbottom who, as related in Chapter 4, became the first all-line locomotive superintendent in 1862. His official title was just that, though he was often known loosely as the mechanical engineer. He retained his headquarters at Crewe. His successor in 1871, F. W. Webb, was appointed with the same title, and though in his later years he was often styled chief mechanical engineer both on and off the railway there is no record of him being given that title formally, though it would have been apposite in view of the work that he handled. Webb himself continued to use the title locomotive superintendent in all departmental notices until he retired, and he also used that term in his will. Nevertheless his successor, George Whale, was appointed by the board "to succeed Mr Webb as chief mechanical engineer", and he used that title and signed departmental notices as such. *His* successor, C. J. B. Cooke, was appointed chief mechanical engineer, but signed departmental notices without a title appended, assuming that every recipient would know who and what he was. Under Ramsbottom and Webb the Crewe Works manager officially was styled the indoor assistant to the locomotive superintendent. He had under him the steel plant and gasworks with an assistant for those activities, and a senior assistant for the locomotive works—Old and New.

For 75 of the 76 years of life of the LNWR as a corporate body locomotive running was under the locomotive superintendent or chief mechanical engineer, though over the final two or three years the internal organisation changed a little. On the consolidation of the Northern and Southern Division locomotive departments in 1862 Ramsbottom retained the two divisions for locomotive running purposes and crew control, with Crewe as the dividing point. He had a separate superintendent for each, but when Thomas Wheatley, the Southern Division running man, went to the North British Railway in 1867, John Rigg, hitherto running chief of the Northern Division, was given general supervision of the whole line. When he retired in 1877 the two divisions were resuscitated, with George Whale as ND superintendent and A. L. Mumford as SD chief. When Mumford retired in 1898 Whale was appointed to take charge of the whole line, but still responsible to Webb. On his own accession as chief mechanical engineer Whale reverted to the old arrangement, and had Southern Division (Cooke) and Northern Division (J. O'B. Tandy) superintendents responsible direct to him. This organisation remained when Cooke became chief mechanical engineer in 1909, but in 1916 W. H. B. Jones was appointed as all-line running superintendent; when he retired in 1919 that position was abolished in favour of two divisional superintendents—Bowes, Southern and Black, Northern— but with the addition of an all-line mechanical superintendent of motive power, F. W. Dingley.

Over the first eight years of Crewe production those valve motion constituents that depended upon the actual dimensions, particularly the frame dimensions, of each engine as it came forward to the erecting shop, were often stamped with the name of the engine, for under Trevithick and Allan the variations could be considerable. In 1851 numbers were substituted for names on the vital motion parts, and thus began the well-known Crewe 'motion number' series that lasted through the remaining 70 years of the LNWR and for some 15 years afterwards.

Though these numbers simplified the stamping of individual motion parts, the reason for their introduction was something entirely different. At the end of 1847 John Gray began to claim royalties from the LNWR (as the successor of the L&MR) on the grounds that the Stephenson link motion infringed his patent No 7745 of 1838, which in essence was for infinitely-variable expansion motion and the proportions of lap and lead, though tied more particularly to his 'horse-leg' motion. Erratic correspondence and opinions then spread over some years, and not until 1851, after Gray had been adjudged bankrupt and the patent rights re-assigned to him, was the matter brought to a head by a Court action and ensuing arbitration. It was in preparation for this that Trevithick was instructed to check how many locomotives in his charge would be liable to a *per capita* royalty if Gray should win his action. At the end of 1847 Gray had mentioned 110 LNWR engines as infringements, and these presumably would include both ND and SD stock and also any fitted engines from any absorbed lines on which fees had not been paid.

The number of North Division engines that had run or were

Table 1   Milestones in Crewe Works steam locomotive production

Locomotive	Class or Type	Wheel arrangement	Date of completion	Running number	Crewe motion number	Name
First	Early Crewe[1]	2-2-2	10/1843	GJR 32	None	Tamerlane
	First Standard Single[2]	2-2-2	7/1845	GJR 49	None	Columbine
1000th	DX	0-6-0	12/1866	LNWR 613	1000	
2000th	4ft 6in, passenger tank	2-4-0T	24/5/1876	LNWR 2233	2000	
3000th	3-cylinder compound, passenger tank	2-2-2-2T	7/1887	LNWR 600	3000	
4000th	Jubilee 4-cylinder compound	4-4-0	3/1900	LNWR 1926	4000	La France
5000th	George V	4-4-0	5/1911	LNWR 1800	5000	Coronation
6000th	Horwich Crab	2-6-0	6/1930	LMSR 13178	6000	
7000th	Class 2MT	2-6-2T	9/1950	BR 41272	None	
7331st	Class 9	2-10-0	12/1958	BR 92250	None	

[1] With gab motion   [2] With Stephenson link motion

running against which Gray might press a claim were judged in the late Spring of 1851 by Trevithick to be 182. To simplify matters thereafter, motion No 183 was allocated to *Glyn*, the first direct-action Stephenson link motion 2-2-2 bearing running number 267, which fortuitously happened to provide a convenient current point at which to start the new series. In the event, the arbitration went against Gray in December 1851. The motion number series, however, was perpetuated as a convenient base of reference and identification, though it had nothing to do with Crewe production totals.

The series was continued up to No 6101 in the year 1931, long, long after the originating reason had been forgotten. Then a new series beginning at No 1 was introduced with LMSR Class 7F 0-8-0 No 9620, and was carried on to No 340 (on 5XP 4-6-0 No 5742), though No 321 appears to have been the last marked number, on 5XP No 5723. From around 1926 certain motion details from time to time were stamped with the engine running number despite the continuing book allocation of motion numbers. Steam locomotives subsequent to No 340 were not given motion numbers.

Though these motion numbers were tied to a special motion purpose, and so must have included the 14 Crewe-type engines erected at Edge Hill, they came erroneously to be regarded as Crewe works or progressive numbers even before the end of the 19th century, and led to mistakes inside and outside the LNWR, LMSR and BR as to Crewe production totals. The milestones in Crewe production included in Table 1 are those always given over the last hundred years or so by the railway authorities; but all are around 20 out, and for a few years up to 1926 the motion numbers were approaching one hundred out compared with actual production, until a correction was applied which eliminated 111 engines built outside over the period 1916–22 that wrongly had been allocated Crewe motion numbers.

Each locomotive order placed on Crewe works from GJR days was denoted by letters, at first by a combination of two letters, eg OP, TH and so on, and certain combinations, eg BO, were repeated after a few years. These were only for locomotive accounting purposes, and were forgotten outside the books when the order and costing were completed, with the exception of the Ramsbottom standard 0-6-0 engines built 1858–75, the first five of which were built to order DX, a notation that was perpetuated on and off the railway as a class designation, probably because it applied to a completely new design quite different from anything Crewe had done before.

These twin-letters combinations lasted until the end of 1861. At the beginning of 1862 an A series was introduced, but after running from

A1 to A73 was changed in 1869 to an E series which ran from E1 to E113, after which in 1883 a new series beginning again at E1 was adopted and ran up to E504, which was in BR diesel days. Since that time numbers in others groups have been used. In LMSR times a few of the prefixes in this series were changed to T for tenders and B for boilers when only those components were being built. In orders for complete steam locomotives the boilers and tenders were built to subsidiary B and T numbers the same as the E number. Outside this range, the engine portions of the eight steam railmotors of 1905–06 were built to Q numbers (Q819 and Q822); the ninth engine, built in 1909, was given an E number.

For 60 years from 1843 Crewe works and its products went through three great stages that corresponded closely to the tenures of office of three successive superintendents, each of whom was affected profoundly by one director, Richard Moon. In the ensuing 45 years until nationalisation Crewe came under nine chief mechanical engineers and six works managers or works superintendents, and the position was always more fluid than through Victoria's reign (Table 2). Much of the rise and development of Crewe works and of LNWR motive power built and repaired there can be covered well in the three stages from 1843 to 1903, but first the carriage and wagon activities may be cleared off.

The stated purpose of the original establishment was the repair and construction of GJR locomotives, carriages and wagons. With the increase in locomotive work consequent upon an ever-increasing stock, wagon building and repair became a nuisance, and on 9 February 1847 the Crewe Committee decided to remove the wagon department to Edge Hill repair shops belonging originally to the L&MR and to put it under the independent supervision of Owen Owens, hitherto wagon foreman, who had joined the GJR in 1841. The locomotive department was ordered to vacate Edge Hill gradually and turn the shops over to Owens, but this did not go smoothly, for in 1847–48 erection of 14 new locomotives had to be transferred to Edge Hill to ease the pressure on Crewe, and Edge Hill gave up space reluctantly and tardily.

When the wagon department began to move out of Crewe in 1847 its shop was taken over gradually by the locomotive side, and all that Owens had to supplement his efforts at Edge Hill was the small ex-L&MR wagon shop at Ordsall Lane, Manchester, to which some new wagon construction already had been transferred, but some space in the Crewe shop was retained by 'wagons' for a few years. With developing route mileage and traffic, and corresponding increase in

Table 2 Leading Officers over and at Crewe Works 1843–1981

Locomotive Superintendent or Chief Mechanical Engineer	Works Manager[1]	Chief Draughtsman
Francis Trevithick (1843–57)	Alexander Allen (1843–53)	Charles Wayte (c. 1848–54)
John Ramsbottom (1857–71)	Thomas Hunt (1853–61)	Wm. Williams (1855–59)
Francis William Webb (1871–1903)	F. W. Webb (1861–66)	F. W. Webb (1859–61)
George Whale (1903–09)	Thomas Stubbs (1866–70)	Thomas Stubbs (1861–66)
C. J. B. Cooke (1909–20)	H. W. Kampf (acting 1870–71)	H. W. Kampf (1866–71)
H. P. M. Beames (1920–21)[2] (1922–30)[3]	Thos. Wm. Worsdell	Charles Dick (1872–77)
George Hughes (1922–25)	Charles Dick (1882–88)	H. W. Norman (1878–88)
Sir Henry Fowler (1925–30)	Henry Douglas Earl (1888–1903)	J. N. Jackson (1888–1919)
E. J. H. Lemon (1931)	A. R. Trevithick (1903–10)	F. M. Grover (1920–32)
Sir Wm. A. Stainer (1932–44)	W. W. H. Warneford (1910–16)	T. F. Coleman (1932–35)
C. E. Fairburn (1944–45)	H. P. M. Beames (1916–20)	*After 1935 the Crewe drawing office took a subsidiary part in locomotive design to the headquarters office at Derby*
H. G. Ivatt (1946–51)[4]	F. Arnold Lemon (1920–41)	
R. A. Riddles (1948–53)[5]	Roland C. Bond (1941–46)	
R. C. Bond (1954–68)[6]	James Rankin (1946–47)	
	Irvine C. Forsyth (1948–60)	
	Ellis R. Brown (1960–62)	
	J. C. Spark (1963–64)	
	J. J. C. Barker-Wyatt (1964–67)	
	George Oldham (1967–74)	
	C. H. Garratt (1974–77)	
	F. O. de Nobriga (1977–)	

[1] From 1853 to 1910 the official title was chief indoor assistant to the locomotive superintendent or chief mechanical engineer. [2] cme of the LNWR. [3] Divisional mechanical engineer of the LNWR (1922) and of the LMSR 1923–30. [4] cme of the LMSR 1946–47, and of the London Midland Region 1948–51. [5] As Member of the Railway Executive. [6] As cme BR 1954–58, Technical Adviser to BR 1958–65, and as general manager Workshops Division 1965–68.

the number of engines, heavy and light locomotive repairs done at Edge Hill increased. Eventually, in January 1853, Owens in his turn was directed to give back to the locomotive department whatever space he could.

A complete change was then made, for in January 1853 the LNWR agreed to rent as from March the Jones & Potts locomotive and general engineering works at Newton-le-Willows. These shops and their machinery had been offered to the LNWR in 1851 for sale at £14,450 or on a lease of three or seven years, but the offer had been refused. Early in 1853 the LNWR re-opened the matter and took a seven-year lease at £600 a year. On the expiry of the lease in May 1860 the LNWR purchased the property outright for £15,000, but extensions had been made at LNWR expense prior to that date. Only with the beginning of the lease was the Crewe wagon shop completely vacated.

The lease was really the beginning of the Earlestown wagon works. First use of that name dates to January 1855 before the establishment became LNWR property, and was a tribute to Hardman Earle, one of the most forceful of GJR and early LNWR directors, who always had a particular interest in locomotives and rolling stock. The Jones & Potts eight-acre nucleus, which included 33 workers' cottages and a gasworks, was known previously as the Viaduct Foundry from its proximity to the celebrated Sankey viaduct on the L&MR. Owens took charge at Earlestown and remained as the wagon superintendent until June 1867.

Carriage building and repair at Crewe continued in the original triangle of ground until in 1848–49, to cater for the increasing number of carriage repairs a new coaching stock repair and painting shop some 450ft in length was built on the east side of the Warrington line on that ground which had cost the LNWR £500 an acre in 1846, mainly fields 292 and 296 in Fig 2. Here also was put a smithy, a timber yard and a grease works for axlebox lubricant. New carriage construction then spread into the two bays of the original shop of 1843; previously one bay had handled repairs and the other did new working, smithing, etc. From around 1852–53 the North Division coaching department employed 600 to 700 men, some 90 percent of whom were concentrated at Crewe, building and looking after 650 to 700 vehicles.

To get more locomotive repair capacity at Crewe after the fusion of the ND and NED in 1857, the board decided at the end of 1859 to transfer ND coach building to Saltley, Birmingham, where some new coaches already had been constructed in a small new factory built by the LNWR, and in 1860 R. Bore was made manager there. The coaching shop in the original triangle at Crewe was given-up only very gradually to the locomotive department, and some coach work was done there until the end of 1860 and possibly later. Reduction in the number of men employed at Crewe was not drastic, because heavy repairs, running maintenance and re-painting continued in the shops on the eastern side of the north main line for another 18 years or so, when a new carriage repair and storage establishment was built well to the west on the south side of the Chester line. The grease plant remained on its original site.

On the amalgamation of the Northern and Southern Divisions in 1862 the board decided to give up Saltley gradually and to concentrate coach building and major repairs for the whole line at Wolverton. No further new locomotives were put in hand at Wolverton, but SD locomotive repair work continued *decrescendo* until 1865, when a substantial transfer to Crewe began, but a small and decreasing amount of locomotive repairs and parts manufacture was done until 1876. Saltley was closed in 1865 and the machinery transferred to

Wolverton, and at the same time Bore went to Wolverton as the first all-line carriage superintendent.

Despite the separation of the locomotive, carriage and wagon departments, the plums at Earlestown and Wolverton during the first quarter of the 20th century usually were given to prominent Crewe officers, sometimes as compensation on failing to be selected for the highest posts in the mechanical engineering department. This practice did not bring failures for, above all, Crewe men in senior positions were well experienced in organisation and administration.

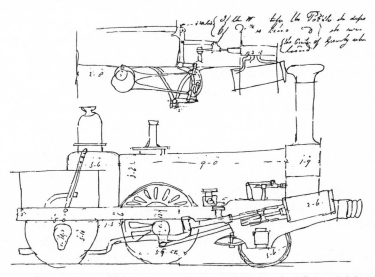

Fig 4 David Joy's sketch of *Hecla*, made at Crewe in 1844, the first Crewe 2-4-0 and the first Crewe-built engine of any kind with Stephenson link motion

3

The Time of Trevithick, 1843–57

Trevithick had two major non-routine matters awaiting him when he took up office at Edge Hill on 1 September 1841. First was the supervision of the layout, erection and equipment of Crewe shops and town, 30 miles away from his headquarters, and he it was who carried Locke's plans into effect, as Buddicom could do little before he left. Second was the development of Locke's new standard locomotive from the prototype 2-2-2 *Aeolus* introduced just before Buddicom went to France.

After *Aeolus* had run for some months, Locke suggested in February 1842 the conversion of two more engines at Edge Hill and the ordering of four similar engines from Jones & Potts, working in any old parts practicable. Board approval was given, and all six 2-2-2s were completed during 1842. Few if any parts were re-used from the old Patentees, whereas *Aeolus* seems to have retained at least the Patentee boiler. This was the design that became known as the Crewe type, and a full history of its initiation, development and construction at Edge Hill and Crewe was published in 1971.[2]

Through the winter of 1844–45 the designs were revised into the 'standard' Crewe 6ft 2-2-2, and in 1846 into the 'standard' 2-4-0 with 5ft wheels. *Columbine* was the first of the standard singles and the first single with Stephenson link motion; the preceding 19 Crewe-built engines were, except for *Hecla* (Fig. 4), 2-2-2s with gab motion. The last-named was the first 2-4-0, completed October 1844, and was the first GJR engine of any type to have Stephenson link motion. *Columbine* was the first engine with 14½in cylinders and 75lb/sq in boiler pressure; its forerunners had 13/13½in cylinders and 50–55lb/sq in pressure.

Modifications to the original wheelbase spacings were made in the 2-2-2s in 1846 and 1853, and in the 2-4-0s in 1849, 1851 and 1853. The 1853 modifications in each case were associated with bigger boilers and fireboxes, and the engines built thereafter became known as the LFB (large firebox) types, the older ones them being dubbed

SFB (small firebox). Until 1848 the inside frames of standard engines were splayed out towards each end; engines built from that year had straight frames, and the older ones then came to be described as of crooked-frame form.

The importance of these design factors to Crewe works procedure was that from 1843 to the Spring of 1858 over 400 new locomotives were completed there and another 14 assembled at Edge Hill from parts manufactured mainly at Crewe, and with eight exceptions all were standard Crewe-type 2-2-2s and 2-4-0s, though 15 singles plus one conversion had 7ft wheels. Moreover, more than 75 percent of all general repairs in that period were to Crewe types.

Of the eight exceptions, five were 2-4-0Ts that had most parts standard with those of the tender engines, though three of the four tanks built in 1856–57 had 16in cylinders and were the only Crewe-type engines bar *Cornwall* ordered in Trevithick's time to have a cylinder bore above 15¼in, but two of them were for the NED. The other three exceptions were the three 'specials' of 1847–48: *Cornwall* with a contorted boiler slung below the axle of 8ft 6in driving wheels; *Courier*, a 2-2-2-0 Crampton with alterations by Trevithick; and *Velocipede*, with 7ft wheels and outside eccentrics, and which was suggested by Allan, the chief works foreman. The first and last of these had framing based on the Crewe type.

Though Crewe production through Trevithick's time was strictly concentrated in types, the modifications noted earlier were supplemented by an important change from indirect rocking-shaft valve motion to direct-action motion in 1851, and by continuous development of details, particularly in regard to slide valves, steamchest and valve location, boiler feed-pump drive, and experiments such as the Routledge double-expansion valve motion; two dimensions remained among all standard 2-2-2s and 2-4-0s built, namely the boiler barrel diameter of 3ft 6in and the transverse spacing of the valve stems, the former presumably so that the outer firebox could always have vertical sides that would drop between the frames, and the latter so that the lateral location of the eccentrics on the driving axle was always the same whatever the valve arrangement.

Locke's original idea had been to have as many parts as possible the same in different engines, because the 55 Patentees had infinite variations; but his policy of parts standardisation was never really accepted. Reversing gears varied as to position and lever movement. Boilers and fireboxes of 2-2-2s and 2-4-0s in each category (SFB and LFB) were different. Modifications in 2-4-0 SFB boilers occurred according to wheelbase, and dome practice was not standard; all

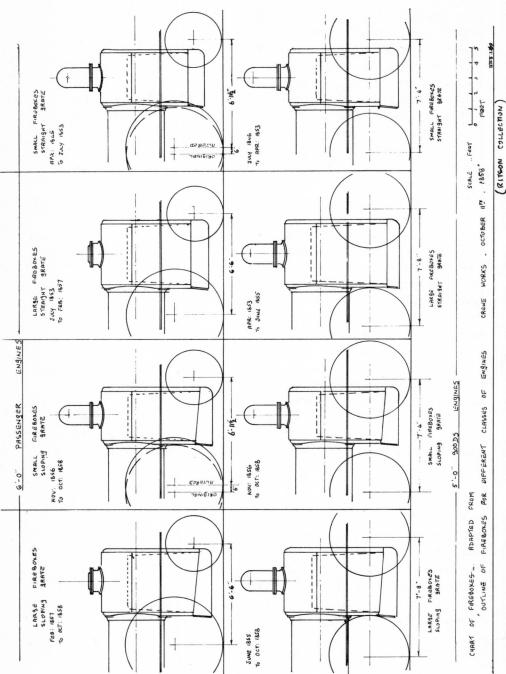

Fig 5 Boiler and wheelbase chart of Crewe-built 2-2-2s and 2-4-0s 1845-58 (traced from original drawing)
(RIXSON COLLECTION)

except LFB 2-2-2s had a dome on the firebox. Boiler and wheelbase variations of Crewe-type 'standard' locomotives through Trevithick's time are well shown by the chart reproduced in Fig 5. This drawing is dated October 1858, and seems to have been drawn up to give Ramsbottom an idea of what he had to cope with in repairs, reconstruction and re-boilering of Crewe-type engines after he had succeeded Trevithick.

Despite the statements in the *Dictionary of National Biography*, thoughts of interchangeability could not have arisen in Locke's mind in view of the primitive manufacturing facilities available in 1840. 'Interchangeable parts' cannot be read into his brief report to the board or into the minuted statement as given in Chapter 1, which form the only contemporary evidence. Ample evidence 'against' is provided by Figs 6, 7 and 8. At the end of his own time in 1857 Trevithick stressed the standardisation principle of Locke's when writing to the LNWR company secretary, C. E. Stewart, but through his period as chief it was not pressed, and few measures were taken to incorporate the same parts in various classes or to get exact manufacture, though lip service was paid to these ideas when dealing with outsiders.

Crewe engines of 1843–57 were really hand-made; everything had to be adjusted and hand-fitted to the actual measurements of each frame assembly as it was put together, and that assembly was not machined or erected to template. This, not the take-up to counter wear in service, was the primary reason for so many parts having wedge adjustment, and was also the reason why no centre-to-centre distances were given on connecting- and coupling-rod drawings. It is quite possible that the dimension of 6ft 11½in between driving and trailing axles in the SFB 2-2-2s arose simply from the first frame set being wrongly marked-off for 7ft 0in.

With only trifling additions to the December 1843 layout and equipment Crewe Works carried on until April 1845, when the GJR board brought under consideration the extension of the roofed shops and the alternative of re-equipping the ex-L&MR shops at Edge Hill to undertake heavy repairs additional to those of the 50 or so existing engines of the L&MR that were about to come within Trevithick's charge.

This question arose because the GJR board in March 1845 agreed in principle to provide the motive power and rolling stock for the Lancaster & Carlisle Railway (LCR) then under construction, and the alternative of Edge Hill L&MR works was about to become possible by the absorption of the L&MR. The decision was for a Crewe extension, and the enlargement and new equipment needed to build and

Fig 6 Crewe erecting shop as it was in 1848 according to the artist of the *Illustrated London News*

then keep in repair engines needed for the LCR working, at that time estimated as only 16, was carried through quickly. The plant was supplemented by some machine tools already ordered for LCR running sheds, then a long way off completion. The extension was recorded as permitting a 2½ times increase in the yearly production of new locomotives over the 1845 total, but that year's figure of 12 new engines was nothing like up to the new-building capacity of the works. In any case, no increase was made in repair shop or erecting-shop floor area.

How necessary was some increase in machining capacity and general equipment to cope with the construction and then repair of even 16 or 20 additional engines can be judged from Figs 6, 7 and 8. At that time repair of old Patentees and miscellaneous 2-2-2s and 0-4-2s of 1837-41 construction still accounted for some of Crewe's activities. A non-technical visitor to the works early in 1846 recorded that all machinery was driven by one 20hp steam engine, but this was a mechanical impossibility unless the erecting, engine-in-steam, carriage and wagon shops were without power-driven tools. The record may refer just to the fitting-shop block.

In September 1847 Trevithick told the Crewe Committee that he was building new engines as fast as he could. That year's total was 34, but partly because of the then urgent need for new locomotives and partly because of the board's vacillation in sanctioning new construction and then instructing Trevithick to retard the work, nine engines had to be assembled at Edge Hill in 1847 and five in 1848.

Fig 7 Crewe fitting shop in 1848 as seen by the artist of the *Illustrated London News*

The year 1848, with further shop equipment installed, saw the peak of new construction in Trevithick's time, with 55 tender engines turned out of Crewe. This fulfilled that engineer's report in March 1847 that eventually he would be able to complete one new engine a week. This production represented only a fraction of the total work. Contemporary records of the number of general repairs given in the 1840s are scanty, but well over 200 a year would be done in 1848–49, and to well-mixed constructions.

At this time opposite the clock-tower entrance, and on the other side of the Chester line, was a boiler house containing the main pumping engine that currently was lifting up to 80,000 gallons of water a day from the Valley brook and passing it through adjacent filters and a reservoir into a tower, from whence it was supplied to both works and town, and to watering locomotives at Crewe station. In later days, as the town and works grew, a much larger and better supply was obtained from Whitmore, ten miles to the south.

By 1850 a further boiler house and several engines provided more power for the shafting in the erecting, fitting and boiler shops north of the arch, and provided steam for the hammer and fans in the smithy. Around 1850–52 one or two old locomotives overdue for withdrawal were taken off their wheels and installed as the power source for various shop and equipment extensions, supplementing but not supplanting the existing stationary engines, and introducing decentralisation with completely independent units.

In 1849 the engine-in-steam shed (or engine-waiting room as it was named in one account) was still being used as such. To the north of it was the main erecting shop with five sets of rails inside; within its 3,300sq yd of floor space were done all major repairs, new engine construction and all tender work, a combination that stretched the shop facilities to the limit, for at that time there were only one or two fixed but swivelling cranes. About 220 men then were employed in the shop, and they must have got much in each other's way. Around 1848–49 efforts were made to finish any new engine by Friday night, paint it on Saturday in the erecting shop, let it dry over the week-end and despatch it on Monday morning. Just how the boiler painting was finished off is not clear, for the outer covering over the lagging in those days was oil-cloth or tarpaulin.

One end of the fitting ship abutted onto the Chester tracks. That shop originally was rectangular, nearly 300ft long and 60ft wide. To the north of it by 1848 was a narrow T-shaped boiler shop and then a large smithy. Spread over the rest of the limited area were the small iron foundry, still with only half a dozen moulders, a small brass foundry, a wheel forge, a wheel-and-axle shop, a coppersmiths' shop and a pattern shop, but some of these were sections of a shop rather than separate buildings. The stores shop was just inside the clock-tower entrance, and upstairs above it were the offices.

Through 1848–50 the locomotive side of the works had 80 to 85 shapers, slotters, punchers, shearers and planers, 35 to 40 lathes, and about 60 forge fires and anvils, of which a dozen were engaged more or less full time on wrought-iron wheel centres. At that time there was only one steam hammer – a Nasmyth of the early type in which control was exercised by a man on top. Despite this machinery and power, much of the production in 1848–50 was still achieved by primitive methods, with much handwork. Lathes, shapers and slotters of simple form were the major tools; planing machines were still small. Not many lathes were occupied in screw cutting, and several men were engaged almost wholly in screwing bolts and studs by hand dies, while nuts were threaded in similar fashion by hand taps. Cylinders were bored one at a time on a lathe fitted with a boring bar and head for the purpose. Frames were of plate sections forged together end-on, and after rough slotting were finished by hand.

Slide bars were entirely a hand operation, with chipping and filing from the black bar or forging. Ramsbottom was one of the first to improve on this, and from 1854 he used at Longsight a grinding machine of his own devising for slide-bar machining, but this was not adopted at Crewe until 1857–58. Coupling- and connecting-rods were

One of the several brick-making plants and huts put up in the Steelworks yard while extensive building construction was going on in 1869–75. Behind the shed are the three bays of the then new boiler shop (to the left) and the even newer boiler-yard smithy (to the right)

The steel rail mill under construction in 1874. Behind the building are the original chimneys of the steel-melting plant of 1864–65; to the left of the yard is the original west-end boiler plant, and even by that time a water tank had been put over part of the roof. The swivelling crane in the stone yard was of Haigh Foundry make

Centre bay of Ramsbottom's new boiler shop of 1870 at the Steelworks end. The photograph probably dates from early 1872, and shows some of the first Webb chimneys and a Napier-type boiler for one of the 14in 0–4–0STs built to replace those sold to the LYR

Looking north from the old Crewe North signalbox in 1881. Manchester line going off to the right. Old carriage repair shops (then largely disused) between Manchester and Warrington lines, and connected by Birdswood bridge to the Old Works. Main erecting shops flanking west side of north main line, with power station chimney between Nos 1 and 2 shops. Old office and stores block prominent to left of clock tower. To the left the northern abutments (still standing) of the then new Midge Bridge

held in two vices while a couple of fitters worked at the two ends with files and scrapers. Smiths' work was left just as it came from the smithy except for any drilling to take pins or bushes, and went back to the smithy to be jumped or up-set to exact length when the particular engine was well forward. Monthly consumption of files was enormous, and there is a record that in a month in 1847 files were bought at 57 different prices. The few simple fixed swivelling cranes were used to lift frame assemblies and other parts from one track to another, but much lifting was by block-and-tackle, which needed several labourers to manipulate them. At that time the erecting shop was without pits.

Normal working time was 58½ hours a week, from 6.00am to 5.30pm with two breaks totalling 1½ hours a day Monday to Friday, and from 6.00am to 4.00pm with the same breaks on Saturday. Payment was fortnightly on Saturday afternoon. C. E. Stewart, the LNWR secretary, considered the method of keeping the timesheets at Crewe was simple and satisfactory, and it did not (1847) involve the Longsight practice of the workers first writing details of their day's activities on slates. In any system there was always at that time liability to errors in that many of the workmen could not read or write, nor were stores and accounting practices much more than primitive (see Chapter 4).

In spite of growing experience and improved equipment and increased production, the ten years from the formation of the LNWR in 1846 were a decade of instability and frustration in the whole direction, administration and production of Crewe Works. This came from two main causes. First, the directors had no experience in the steady financing and control of so large an enterprise as the LNWR—railway finance and accounting themselves were passing through an unstable phase. Second, there was the personality and capacity of Trevithick.

One effect of the board's wavering actions was repeated abrupt alterations in sanctioned new-building programmes to suit temporary financial scares and short-time lulls and booms in trade. Particularly between 1847 and 1852 there were also ups and downs in accord with variations in accountancy methods, for these affected even the existence of depreciation, reserve and suspense funds to cover locomotives and rolling stock. Often members of the General Finance Committee were in disagreement as to how many engines should be charged to revenue and how many to capital. This was of some importance, for LNWR dividends fell steadily year by year from 10 percent in 1846 to 5 percent in 1850. On several occasions building of

Fig 8 Another view of the Crewe fitting-machine shop in 1848 from the *Illustrated London News*

engines to capital account was stopped without notice; any engines within ten days of completion were then finished, greased, and put into store so that they did not at once have to be entered into the stock list. Such actions occurred two or three times over the years 1848–51 when the LNWR board was trying to close the capital account, an idea that was not given up until 1853.

Such variations, continued for almost a dozen years from the foundation of the LNWR and from time to time thereafter, supplemented the general insecurity of employment at Crewe resulting from the lulls and booms in railway traffic. In fact, this insecurity was a feature of Crewe all through LNWR years except during the period of expansion under Ramsbottom in the 1860s and the years of World War I, for the board policy was always to dismiss men at the slightest recession, though from the 1870s putting the whole works on short time reduced, but did not eliminate, actual dismissals.

On 3 December 1848, after record production throughout most of the year and much overtime worked above the basic 58½hr week, the Crewe Committee ordered work on orders DD and EF to be stopped forthwith, and "that no more engines under any circumstances to be laid down." At the same time the wages of many men were reduced. A fortnight later Trevithick reported that as a result of this instruction 142 men had been dismissed at Crewe and 20 at Edge Hill additional to the 40 previously laid-off at the latter place, and that during the next three months a further considerable reduction would have to be made. Earlier in 1848 over 800 men had been employed in the locomotive shops and several hundred in the coach department, but by the end of the year the total number was under 800 and sank lower during the next two years.

Yet as early as its next meeting, on 19 December, the Committee minuted that engines were wanted as fast as they could be repaired and "the directors must look to the building of new engines [which was going on at the rate of two a month] for the displacement of dead stock." Here was an impasse between a crying need for new engines and a desire not to have an extra £1 charged to capital account, or even to revenue account, at a time when ND operations were expanding by the opening of the Trent Valley and Chester & Holyhead lines, and by the general increase in traffic on the newly-opened Anglo-Scottish trunk line.

In January 1850 came another injunction to Trevithick to stop all building on capital account, and to try and make up the needed number of locomotives by applying to the Southern Division for ten engines being held in store at Wolverton, but as many of these would be too heavy for most Northern Division routes they were to be set to work on the LCR, which had newer and better track. At that time over 50 miles of the ND proper were still laid with the original 60lb iron rails on stone blocks of 1837 and were without fishplates.

Throughout 1851 the works had to soft-pedal on new production, particularly on 23 passenger engines and to a lesser extent on ten of the 2-4-0 goods engines being built to revenue account, so the whole works and town remained in a depressed state. Only 23 new engines were turned out that year, seven of them in the last two months, after Trevithick had drawn the Committee's attention to the long-standing directed delay and the effect he thought it would have during the ensuing 12 months on traffic operation and on Crewe works.

Heavy repairs continued most of the time more or less in correspondence with the number of engines in ND stock, which rose from about 140 in the first half of 1846 to around 360 at the end of 1851. Increasing traffic through 1852 ended the three-year depression and necessitated further works extensions and full-time working. Here Trevithick took the lead, and he wrote to Mark Huish, the general manager, early in November to get his support: "In October 1850 we had 451 men employed at Crewe; we have at the present date 827—and the men are working overtime. . . . Miles run and stock of engines in May 1851 show average miles per engine in the quarter was

9187, and in the quarter ended August last was 9976, a 10 percent increase, whereas on the Southern Division in May 1851 the average was 8023 miles per engine, or 10 percent less than on the Northern Division."

Mileages quoted must have been those of engines actually running, and not the average of all those in stock; even so the figures are suspiciously high. Also, the quoted number of 451 men at Crewe was far below the normal Crewe locomotive department average, and resulted from the last of the numerous pay-offs. Well over 600 men had been employed on the locomotive side even at the end of 1848. These were the years that really began a "floating population", for many of those paid-off left the town in search of other employment and never returned. By the end of 1851 the population of Crewe had fallen to 4,600; three years earlier it had been nearly 8,000.

Norris brought before the Committee plans for the 1853 proposed shop enlargements, with estimates of £5,000 for new buildings and £5,000 for more tools. These sums were exclusive of a much-needed increase in the number of houses in the town, a complete reversal of the state little more than twelve months back, when many houses were unoccupied and even boarded-up. The full scheme was approved by the board in November 1852. The urgency for new capacity was such that lathes, shapers and slotters to a total cost of £2,700 had to be acquired quickly and installed at Edge Hill so that more repairs could be done there pending the Crewe enlargement, with the proviso that these tools should later be transferred to Crewe. This Edge Hill re-equipment was possible because of the transfer of the wagon department to Viaduct Foundry as outlined in Chapter 2.

New machine tools put in at Crewe during 1853 exceeded the £5,000 estimate, and a further £5,000 expenditure under this head was sanctioned in October 1853. The new equipment included two wheel lathes at £700 each to take 6ft diameter, and one at £200 to take 3ft 6in wheels; wheel slotters for 6ft wheels at £258 each; and numerous drilling machines, general slotters, planers, shapers and lathes, also, at a cost of some £600, a further large steam hammer. At that time planing machines cost £150 to £250 according to size, drilling machines £140 to £200, large slotters up to £300, small ones about £120, and screw-cutting 10in lathes £120.

Part of the extension and 'modernisation' in 1853–54 was the construction of pits along the length of the existing erecting shop, and in the engine-in-steam shop that was now lengthened and converted into a second erecting or repair shop. The extension was in a southward direction that brought half the shop outside the clock-tower gate.

Previously the outer end had been level with the clock tower. The fitting shop area also was extended – the first of several piecemeal additions over many years that eventually brought it to a fantastic shape. An extension also was made to the southern end of the boiler shop, and to one or two other buildings and more machinery was installed in the old wagon shop. The original areas of ground north and south of the Chester line were not extended.

With the help of these facilities 50 new engines were completed during 1854, and all being of LFB form they were rather larger than the 55 engines built in 1848. In 1854 general repairs were given to 322 engines and their tenders, an average of above one each working day, while in the first half of 1855 the number of tender engines passed through was 198. At that time there was only one tank engine that had been built new as such for the Northern Division.

According to *Bradshaw's Industrial Guide 1854*, the number of men employed was 1,500, but this figure included the coach men. A reflection of the times was the weekly wage bill of scarcely £2,000. Local-traffic engines were considered to average 68,000 miles between Crewe repairs and the repair cost averaged £720, equal to 2½d [1p] a mile. A first class passenger engine cost only £400 for repairs, but mileage between repairs was much less.

Thomas Brassey, the well-known railway contractor, asked the Committee in March 1854 if Crewe could build 10 large engines for his Newport–Birkenhead coal traffic, but the new capacity was needed entirely for repair and renewal of ND stock. This inability to help came at a time when Brassey already was setting up the Canada Works at Birkenhead in conjunction with Peto and Betts, and which turned out its first locomotive at the end of May 1854.

The 1853 extensions at Crewe necessitated one hundred further cottages in the town, built at a cost of £94 for one of the No 1 type (see Chapter 1) and £120 15s 0d [£120·75] for one of the No 2 model; later the same year another 75 had to be built to house workers at the new rail mill. Contracts for all these were given to Thos Stone of Newton.

Until the 1853 extensions the works lay almost entirely within the 8½-acre triangle bounded by the Warrington line, the Chester line and Forge Street. In the additional seven acres to the south of the Chester line (referred to often in this book as the 'Southern annexe') there were only one or two small huts, the baths, and the waterworks and gas plant; the 1853–54 enlargements necessitated further development of this ground, first by the erection of a new tender shop, secondly by the transfer of joiners and carpenters to a building end-on to the tender shop, and later by use of adjacent ground for a large timber stack.

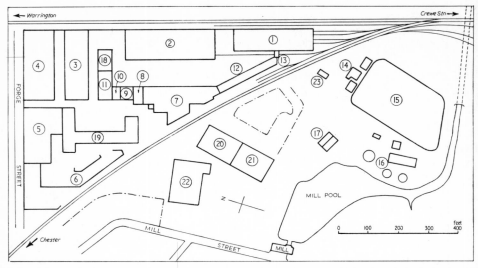

1 Engine repair shop 2 Engine repair and construction shop 3 General machining shop 4 Coach shop
5 Smithy 6 Forge 7 Fitting shop 8 Spring shop 9 Brass foundry 10 Dressing shop 11 Iron foundry
12 Stores and general offices 13 Clock-tower arch 14 Water-pumping plant and two filter beds 15 Water
reservoir 16 Gasworks 17 Gasworks cottages 18 Wheel shop 19 Boiler shop 20 Tender shop 21 Joiners and
patternmakers 22 Iron rail mill 23 Bath house

Fig 9 Plan of Crewe Works and Southern Annexe, December 1854

In July 1853 a new iron rail mill close to the tender shop began production. It had been sanctioned the year before because, according to Mark Huish[3] "of the deteriorating quality of iron rails supplied from outside." Thus by the end of 1854 the works had grown to the extent shown in Fig 9. The main business of the rail mill for some 20 years was the production of iron rails in 21ft lengths, along with fish-plates, which the LNWR began to use generally at the same time, and by 1854 production of these two items attained 90 tons a week. That rate then had to be stepped up to 150 tons a week to keep pace with the extensive relaying of old 60lb track, a difficult matter, for tyre bars also had to be rolled for the locomotive department and necessitated a change in rollers whenever tyre bars were needed.

The first mill manager, Talbot, was not considered as under the locomotive department and reported direct to the board, but in March 1854 the mill was put under the Crewe Committee, and Talbot was given an increase of £50 to £350 a year as a suitable company house could not be found for him. When he left LNWR service in April 1856 the mill was put in charge of John Ramsbottom, in addition to his duties as head of the NED locomotive department at Longsight. This must have hurt Trevithick deeply, though he and Ramsbottom maintained friendly personal relations until the former's death. By the mid-1850s one or two directors led by Richard Moon were becoming critical of Trevithick's lack of system and his unwillingness to enforce

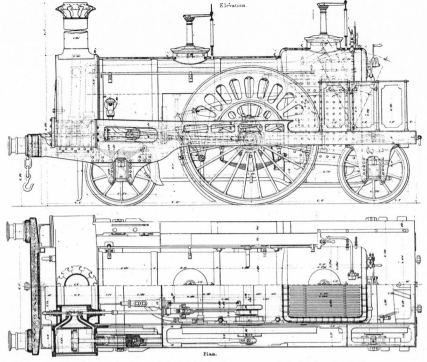

Fig 10 General arrangement of Trevithick Crewe-type 7ft single of 1857

discipline. Nevertheless, the production of new and repaired engines per unit of covered shop area from 1848 onwards was creditable to Trevithick and to his head foreman Alexander Allan.

When Ramsbottom was given charge of the combined ND and NED locomotive departments in 1857 the rail mill remained under his authority, and from that time the mill and its successor, the steel rail mill, were regarded as an integral part of the locomotive department and of Crewe locomotive works. From 1856 to 1866 the day-by-day running of the mill was under the foreman, E. Stott.

In 1856 steam-driven rivetting machines were introduced in the boiler shop; eventually they proved reliable and able to give good rivet heads and tight joints, and their use was extended. Years later Webb inferred that the consistency of these power-driven machines influenced him in adopting hydraulic rivetters as soon as these were brought to his notice.

South of the rail mill and tender shop was the gas plant that provided for works and town needs. It began operation in 1843 and was enlarged from time to time. In 1849 it was generating 30,000cu ft of gas a day and in 1856 over 40,000cu ft. In the latter year it was supplying around 4,600 open-flare lights (there were no incandescent mantles or gas cookers in those days) of which over 1,100 were for the locomotive department, over a thousand for the coach shops, and 1,670 (including 385 meter lights) in the town. After the administration of the town was taken over in 1860 by a new local board fresh supply tariffs were arranged, and from 1864 the local authority paid the LNWR £2 10s 0d [£2·50] a year for the gas for each street lamp, the authority finding and fixing all new street lamps and using the company's standard size of burner. Domestic supply continued only to the company's own houses.

Towards the end of Trevithick's time the annual production of new locomotives decreased somewhat, partly because traffic increase slowed down. A statement (Table 3) given to the Committee in February 1855 led to a resolution that after the 40 engines therein were completed the rate of building further new engines was to be dropped from one a week to one a fortnight, and that this would just about meet the wear and tear of existing stock. Actually from October 1855 until May 1858 only eight engines were built at Crewe to capital account and all were for the NED, so that the Committee's instruction was kept exactly for the remainder of Trevithick's time. As before, this restriction led to dismissals, and the work force was reduced until 1858 when the amalgamation of the ND and NED led to more activity at Crewe.

Table 3   Locomotive construction programme at Crewe, February 1855

Locomotives building	Date commenced	Money expended £	Money required for completion £	Probable time of completion
10 goods [2-4-0]	June 1854	14,500	1,500	March 1855
10 goods [2-4-0]	Sept 1854	4,200	11,800	July 1855
10 passenger [2-2-2]	Oct 1854	8,200	8,100	May 1855
10 goods [2-4-0]	Jan 1855	200	15,800	Oct 1855
40 ⬅——— Totals ———➡		27,100	37,200	

Throughout his years as chief, Trevithick as a locomotive engineer was conservative. Design scarcely progressed from 1847 to 1857, and increase in power and capacity in that decade was little more than 10 or 11 percent. Boiler pressure did not get above 100lb/sq in, and even the rise to that figure from 90lb/sq in in 1854 had to be pushed by Parker, the foreman of the ND running shed at Rugby that provided engines for the Trent Valley line. The figure of 120lb/sq in often quoted for Crewe-type engines was obtained only in the reboilerings

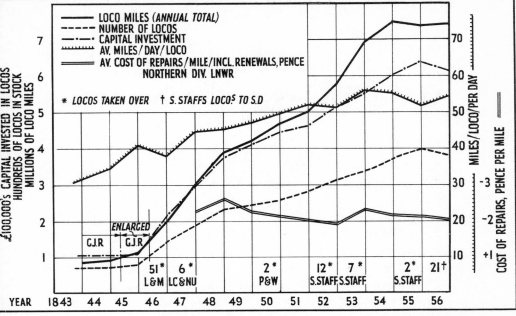

Fig 11 Graph showing rise in locomotive performance on the GJR and Northern Division of the LNWR, 1843–57

and rebuilds by Ramsbottom from 1858.

The increase in responsibilities shouldered by Trevithick are shown succinctly by the 71 GJR locomotives making 821,646 miles in the year Crewe works opened and the 376 ND engines running 7,482,249 miles in his last full year, 1856, and by the repair costs of 3d [1½p] a mile in 1845 and 2·1d [1p] a mile in 1856. The locomotive works had grown to employ around 1,150 men, seven times the number that had come over from Edge Hill. Fig 11 shows the gradual rise during the Trevithick period in the number and value of the locomotive stock and its performance in mileage and repair costs with which Crewe works was so closely asssociated. At the time Trevithick went the works under his methods was just adequate for repairing the number of small 20/21-ton engines in hand, and by 1857, with the works layout still as shown in Fig 9, the time was ripe for a change and for a major alteration in outlook.

4
The LNWR Locomotive Department
1846–62

The rise of Crewe Works as the principal locomotive repair and construction establishment of the LNWR was due primarily to the almost unwilling centralisation policy of the directors, and to the activities of one man – Richard Moon – who became a member of the board in 1851, though not until 1855 did he become a member of a sub-committee dealing direct with locomotives, in this case an *ad hoc* group on accounts. Before that he had brought forward occasional matters on the locomotive department and on Crewe through his pre-occupation with ordered management in all branches of the railway.

From its inception in 1846 the LNWR had been saddled with three locomotive and operating divisions as detailed in Chapter II, with separate superintendents and committees of directors, partly because of residual mistrust between the old constituent companies, and partly because the primitive communications systems of the times and the lack of business experience made difficult the central control and handling of such a large organisation. The predilection of some board members for the area of their previous company lasted long, and even as late as 1859 Moon was writing to the chairman, the Marquis of Chandos, that, at least until recently ". . . whereas nothing previously could be had for the Northern Division, money was ordered to be spent like water for the South. You yourself suggested the money to be spent on Wolverton should be treated as capital whilst that for Crewe is to be revenue."

Amalgamation of all three locomotive departments was considered by the board in the winter of 1854–55 and a special committee, of which Moon was not a member, reported in May 1855 that consolidation was desirable and recommended the board to affirm the principle, but suggested that the means to be adopted be referred to a sub-committee. In July this sub-committee reported that ". . . the three divisions be consolidated under one general superintendent whose personal services should especially be directed to the working of the engines in concert and co-operation with the general manager. That the workshops at Wolverton, Crewe and Longsight be under the control of the general superintendent with an assistant at each who shall have charge of the repair and building of the engines and shall have all necessary authority over the workmen." However, the sub-committee, composed of Lord Chandos, Hardman Earle, Admiral Moorsom, H. W. Blake and M. Lyon, was not prepared to recommend an immediate change.

In March 1856 the same sub-committee reported that as the board had just decided not to continue the working of the Lancaster & Carlisle Railway after the summer of 1857 there would then be a big change in the operation of the Northern Division, and though no sudden or violent change in the all-line organisation was recom-mended it thought advantage should be taken of any opportunity towards consolidation. When this was considered at a board meeting in May 1856 Moon moved that the ND and NED locomotive depart-ments now be placed under the single management of John Ramsbottom, but this was defeated. The chairman was left to bring the subject forward again whenever he thought propitious. This he did in March 1857, and the re-appointed sub-committee's motion that the ND and NED should be combined under Ramsbottom was carried, though not without strong dissent from certain directors. Trevithick was given notice, and the new arrangements came into force on 1 August 1857, when the LCR working was terminated, Ramsbottom transferring his headquarters from Longsight to Crewe.

How strongly Moon felt at this last stage is shown by his letter of 5 May 1857[4] to Chandos when the critical decision of consolidation and the removal of Trevithick, though only a few days off, was by no means certain. This letter also indicates the deficiencies of Trevithick as manager of a large concern, defects that had contributed earlier to the indisciplinary outburst of Alexander Allan, chief works foreman, which had led in August 1853 to acceptance of his resignation after a strong reprimand by the Crewe Committee.[5]

Moon wrote: "It is not that Trevithick is not clever or honest, but we want more than that, and from all our experiences of him I am sure both you and I are satisfied we shall never have any vigour or strength in his management – if a difficulty comes he will not take the responsi-bility, he will not speak to his foremen or order his accountant or give notice to his men, but we shall extend wider the laxity of system on his division by adding the North Eastern to it. We shall never know what our engines are doing or what they might do if they were most scientifically disposed."

During the 1855 investigations the three superintendents were consulted by the sub-committee, and naturally the knowledge that at some future date two of them, if not three, would have to go or become subservient unsettled them. Trevithick seems to have taken no action, though previously in August 1853 at the time of the trouble with Allan both he and the latter applied for the vacant locomotive superintendency of the Scottish Central Railway and Allan got it, probably because he could accept a smaller salary. Ramsbottom in 1856 considered applying for the vacant locomotive superintendency of the Eastern Counties Railway and even consulted Chandos on the matter,[6] then he inclined strongly to going back into industry. McConnell at Wolverton made attempts to get enhanced status for the Southern Division and himself to bring him eventually to the top position.

Early in 1857 Ramsbottom let it be known to Moon and Lyon that if he *was* chosen for the combined Northern and North Eastern Division he would want a salary of £1,200 a year. This was £200 more than the board had in view, but Moon stressed to Chandos: "I hope you will not let £200 p.a. stand in the way . . . a trifle in salary is nothing to get the men you want . . . I look upon the labour for any one taking Crewe to put in order as herculean. It is the man, not the system, on which we must depend. No system would work with Trevithick's weak hand, and I shall despair of any good to our concern if he is retained."

Ramsbottom's demand was not at once met; he and McConnell were each paid £1,000 a year until 1860, when their salaries were raised to £1,200. Trevithick in 1857 was given an honorarium of £3,000 in view of his long service, honourable personal character, and the good opinion of him held by two or three members of the board.

As early as 1847 C. E. Stewart, the LNWR company secretary, had been directed to make a survey of the locomotive and stores accounting on the three divisions. He lighted not merely on three different systems but on several remarkable features. At Crewe he found impossible any check that would show whether the store-keepers' figures were right *or* wrong; moreover, he realised that Trevithick had no means of finding out weekly or monthly what he had used or what he had in hand; and the works storekeeper was not strictly a member of the locomotive department. At Longsight the storekeeper was also the locomotive accountant. Stewart made certain recommendations, but these were carried out half-heartedly. When several years later Moon realised how little had been done, and that much confusion still existed, an *ad hoc* sub-committee was appointed under his chairmanship in 1855 to try and unify and then consolidate the system of locomotive department accounts in the three divisions.

The recommendation for an eventual single locomotive accountant for the whole line could be taken a stage further at the change-over of superintendents in 1857. Bell, the Northern Division locomotive accountant at Crewe, who had been on the GJR even in Edge Hill days, was asked to leave at the same time as Trevithick, and was paid a year's salary as an honorarium, for the board had agreed to treat generously any who had to go as a result of the consolidation. In his place George Wadsworth was appointed as locomotive accountant of the enlarged Northern Division.

Up to that time Moon had not been a member of the Crewe Committee nor of the standing Locomotive Committee, but he was chairman of the Stores Committee, and in April 1858 the two last-named bodies were combined into a General Stores & Locomotive Expenditure Committee, so that Moon came to have more say in loco-motive matters.

Though the three locomotive divisions were replaced by two in 1857, the recommendation of the 1855 committee for full consolida-tion had been accepted by the board and remained on the table for action at a suitable moment. Moon was not content to let the matter rest, particularly when he saw how well Ramsbottom shaped at Crewe. Nevertheless, that in itself would not have been sufficient for an early final consolidation, but after August 1857 McConnell began to blot his copybook in the eyes of Moon.

McConnell was ambitious, and on the board calling in 1859 for reports on locomotive arrangements and on the boundaries between ND and SD largely to try and diminish non-effective locomotive mileage and idle time of crews; he favoured an extension of the SD and put forward estimates mainly based on cost per ton-mile statistics of substantial savings that would accrue if the SD boundary was moved further north. The separate reports of McConnell and Ramsbottom were by no means in accord, and Ramsbottom had to tell Chandos, on the latter's request, that he was unable to understand how McConnell arrived at some of his figures.

Nevertheless a special board committee, of which Moon was a member, decided on a revision of the boundaries and working of the two divisions more or less in agreement with McConnell's ideas, and on this decision McConnell and Ramsbottom agreed in a brief joint report in December 1859: "(1) that Stafford be the limit of both divisions; (2) that an independent engine shed be erected at Stafford for the SD; (3) that the length from Stafford to Bushbury be worked jointly as it may best be found to suit the time bills; (4) that the SD receive a proportionate number of engines for this work." The actual transfer of motive power in January 1860 to the Southern Division, which then had the Trent Valley line to operate, comprised 34 Northern Division engines, of which two were actually delivered new to the SD by Beyer Peacock; the other 32 were made up of three 7ft singles, 20 6ft singles and nine 5ft 2-4-0s, all of Crewe type.

Moon had never believed in McConnell's estimates nor, after coming into closer contact with him from 1858, had he believed in the man himself. On 31 December 1859, after the board had accepted the new SD/ND boundaries and working, Moon had written to Chandos: ". . . having no confidence in McConnell's upright truthfulness, and disbelieving his statements and reports, which I am certain are misleading . . . McConnell's ambition to go to Crewe is still keeping up the old irritation."[6]

More important, when the board accepted the special committee's majority-decision report to revise the working, Moon resigned his chairmanship and membership of the General Stores & Locomotive Expenditure Committee for, as he told Chandos, it would be quite out of order for him to retain these positions in a body that had to supervise a major change of which he thoroughly disapproved. Some months passed before Chandos prevailed on him to return to the committee.

By 1861 the board was dissatisfied with the results of this altered working, also with the economy, and McConnell's own statements of November 1859 were invoked. A board committee appointed in April 1861 reported towards the end of the year that the results of the divisional boundary change suggested by McConnell in 1859 did not bear out his claims. Though McConnell protested that other circumstances such as increase in traffic and necessary further new locomotives to handle it had nullified his estimates, the committee stressed in January 1862:

> We find that the expenditure incurred exceeds Mr McConnell's largest estimates to the extent of £44,275, and we regret to state that no part of the anticipated saving of £12,080 3s 9d yearly, as set forth in his report of 30 November 1859 has been realised. Whilst as regards the question 'how far Mr McConnell's statements have been affected by other circumstances', we do not see that any change has taken place in the policy of the board, nor has extension of traffic ensued which can with propriety be assigned as the cause of the failure of these statements. We are therefore reluctantly led to the resolution already submitted to the board on the 21st ult; 'That this committee is unwilling to impute to Mr. McConnell an intention to mislead the board, but find his statements of the probable outlay on capital account have been so much at variance with the real facts of the case as seriously to shake that confidence which the board ought to have in the reports and statements of an officer holding so responsible a situation'.

After delaying action by two directors, G. C. Glyn and R. Benson, specially interested in the Southern Division, the board accepted the committee's report. There was nothing left for McConnell to do except resign, and his resignation was accepted on 20 February 1862, to take effect on 31 March. He was granted £1,000 on account of a half-year's salary and his "additional expenses by reason of the sudden removal of his present residence;" he received £200 worth of plate from staff and workers at Wolverton.

Moon at the beginning of 1862 was in a much stronger position, for he had been elected chairman of the board on 22 June 1861 after the sudden death at the end of May of Admiral Moorsom, who had succeeded Chandos only a few months earlier, and of course all Moon's prognostications had been proved to the hilt. Thereafter Moon's word was LNWR law for 30 years until his retirement.

On 22 March 1862 Ramsbottom was appointed locomotive superintendent of the whole LNWR as from 1 April at a salary of £2,000 a year, and headquarters were concentrated at Crewe. New locomotive construction at Wolverton was given up after completion of the engines in hand, but repairs to Southern Division engines and odd machining work for Crewe continued *decrescendo* until 1876. From then on all LNWR motive power activities and many other matters were centred firmly at Crewe. The locomotive department accounts also were consolidated, and by 1865 Wadsworth was acting as the all-line locomotive department accountant. In that year Stewart made another examination of stores and locomotive accounts, and objected strongly to the Crewe stores practice of adding overheads for articles sent outside the locomotive department, and said this was entirely a matter for the accountant. From his comments Crewe must even before that date have been supplying parts to the Lancashire & Yorkshire Railway.

At the time of the consolidation of the ND and SD, or more strictly at the end of 1861, the ND had 581 engines (392 goods and 198 passenger) with a book value of £1,135,972. The SD stock was made up of 368 engines valued at £828,629, the enhanced value per engine in SD stock being due to the number of large engines introduced by McConnell from his arrival at Wolverton in 1847. This combined power, totalling 949 locomotives, made an aggregate mileage of 9,580,567 in the half-year ending May 1862, and in the same period handled a gross ton-mileage of 745,842,174 in passenger and goods traffic. Average daily mileage of 52.6 per engine in 1862 was lower than in any half year after 1858, as was the average daily ton-mileage per engine of 4,098.

5
The Ramsbottom Period, 1857–71

An entirely different competence and outlook, suited to vast extensions in size and capacity that continued unbroken to the end of the LNWR, began when Ramsbottom assumed charge of the enlarged Northern Division at Crewe on 1 August 1857. He came to a works reasonable in its equipment, but crying out for release from Trevithick's easiness and conservatism to bring it back into the van of current mechanical engineering practice. Ramsbottom gave the whole works and department a jolt similar to that applied 85 years later by Montgomery in the Western Desert, and like the latter he ensured that he got the *materiél* needed. Over the 65 years from 1857 his ideas were simply extrapolated, the LMSR in 1923 absorbing what was really a Ramsbottom works and Ramsbottom locomotives enlarged, but a department that had declined almost to the same comparative level as it was in the first half of 1857.

Ramsbottom's first job was to tighten-up discipline and improve the standards of manufacture. The latter had got out of hand as a result of the lack of control and in 1857–58 numerous detail drawings, old and new, were given a revealing inscription in black ink: "Work to dimensions" or "Dimensions must be worked to." Only from January 1859 did centre-to-centre distances appear on the drawings of connecting and coupling rods. Moreover, many drawings were now signed by Ramsbottom, or in 1859–61 by Webb as chief draughtsman. Drawings signed by Trevithick or anyone else were rarities up to 1858.

Being almost certain from 1856 that he would succeed to Crewe, and being quite familiar with the tools and personalities at that place from his friendship with Trevithick and his weekly visits to the rail mill, Ramsbottom probably was clear in his own mind just what he would do, and from the beginning all his moves were directed to the re-casting of Crewe operations to make and repair a greatly increased stock of new standard locomotives accurately, cheaply and quickly, and gradually to do away with the types of 1843–57.

Above: Reputed to be the 3,000th locomotive completed at Crewe works, and bearing the special numberplate for this photograph. It was the Webb 3-cylinder compound 2–2–2–2T of 1887 having the running number 600

Below: The carriage works girder bridge being given its test load of six 0–6–2T engines in 1882. Carriage repair sheds beyond; Eagle Bridge adjoins the embankment to the right

Bottom: Single-ring slightly-tapered steel boiler shell built at Crewe *circa* 1874; it is shown on the traverser of No 7 shop. Stamped steel dome cover on fixture used for holding while scraping the joint   *(NRM, York)*

Steelworks boiler shop centre bay in the 1890s

Putting copper side stays into the firebox of a Jubilee 4–4–0 in May 1900. Note the water-bottom firebox. The "bowler hat" is Henry Cooper, chief boiler shop foreman. Behind the smokebox tubeplate is the old wall engine giving tool power at the east end of the shop

Soon he was ordering new machine tools of advanced types and making others, and revising shop procedures to get greater accuracy and approach to interchangeability. By the mid-1860s templates and simple gauges were in use for the machining of many parts, and to an extent then scarcely practised in other locomotive works except perhaps Gorton Foundry, while a series of graduated sizes had been adopted for the renewal of worn parts.

Concentration on organisation and administration had to take priority over Ramsbottom's inventive faculties, and the displacement lubricator and water pick-up, both in 1860, were the only 'locomotive' inventions of his Crewe period. The water troughs were at first cast as iron sections 6ft 3in long in Crewe Works foundry, but a dozen years later Webb changed the material to Bessemer steel plates. By the end of Ramsbottom's time as chief, water scoops had been fitted to seventeen 2,000-gallon and 201 1,500-gallon tenders of Crewe make and to 174 of Wolverton type.

To Ramsbottom's appreciation of the enhanced capacity needed to deal with the normal increase in stock, to handle the ex-LCR engines that came back into the LNWR fold in 1859 and the ex-Birkenhead Railway engines acquired in 1860, was added the knowledge of the board's principle eventually to consolidate the ND and SD – when this was effected a still further major increase in Crewe capacity would be required. For the better part of a decade from 1857 actual extensions of covered shop area in the original triangle were small, though vital rearrangements were made. Working times were changed in 1858, when a 12.50pm closure was introduced on Saturdays, but the weekly hours remained almost the same in that work was carried on until 6.00pm Mondays to Fridays.

To effect the policy of standardisation and efficiency that made Ramsbottom so acceptable to Moon, suitable locomotive designs had to be evolved, and as Ramsbottom preferred inside cylinders (probably because of his experience at Sharp Roberts) works discipline and procedure had to be improved for that reason alone irrespective of any general benefits, for up to that time the only crank axles fabricated at Crewe had been small replacements for old Patentees with a piston thrust around 8,500lb. Moreover, the shops had never built a six-coupled locomotive, nor with the exception of the three 'specials' of 1847, dealt with locomotives heavier than 21 tons.

Ramsbottom had no intention of enlarging or perpetuating the Crewe-type outside-cylinder designs, and told the Committee in 1858 that he would do as little major repair work as possible on those engines so that they could be phased out gradually. As they were of such sturdy construction, and so many of them were under ten years old, he got sanction in 1858 to rebuild ten and then another 40 of the SFB 2-4-0s into 2-4-0Ts; eventually over one hundred were converted at Crewe at the rate of five to twelve a year through the years 1859–71.

To check the condition and strength of the old Crewe-type boilers an experiment was conducted in 1864 on the boiler of 2-4-0 No 57. The No 1 erecting shop book reads: "*June 28.* Tried to burst boiler with hydraulic pump, the boiler being 16 years old. Got 220lb. *June 29.* Again got 250lb, when roof of firebox came down ½ inch. It had six split stays and two solid ones. *June 30.* Got 230lb only. Roof of box cracked at lead plug. Could get no more and gave it up at that."

As discipline and works methods improved some of the numerous adjusting devices on the locomotives could be eliminated, particularly at the rod ends. First modification recorded is of case-hardened solid eyes with bushes in the small ends of No 53 in March 1860, and a few years later Hunt, the works manager 1853–61, claimed that the idea was due to him. In 1863 solid-bushed coupling-rod ends were adopted for the 14in 0-4-0ST shunters, and in August 1864 solid ends with steel bushes were put into Nos 511, 1035 and 1040. By 1866 standards of manufacture had advanced sufficiently for the Newton class express 2-4-0s to be given solid-bushed coupling-rod ends as normal practice.

New locomotive construction to orders placed under Ramsbottom began with the DX class 0-6-0 weighing 27 tons and having 17in by 24in cylinders and 120lb/sq in boiler pressure. Though not a big engine for its time, compared with the 2-4-0 Crewe goods that it succeeded it showed 65 percent advance in adhesion weight, 48 percent greater cylinder capacity, 25 percent higher boiler pressure, and 95 percent greater starting tractive effort, concentrated within a frame only 10 percent longer and on an axle load 9 percent higher. The most up-to-date Smith & Beecroft slotter was bought to machine the frame plates and other massive parts, but many other parts needed special tool fitments and procedures as the engines were completely different in concept and details from preceding Crewe practice. Design work was begun in 1857, and the first locomotive was completed in September 1858.

The next design was for an express passenger 2-2-2 and as large wheels, here 7ft 6in, were then still deemed necessary for high speed, outside cylinders perforce had to be adopted. In a sense a try-out, for this wheel diameter had been made in 1858 when the almost useless old *Cornwall* had been rebuilt at Crewe into an outside-cylinder 2-2-2 retaining much of its framing and the original 8ft 6in wheels, but acquiring a boiler-firebox assembly and a few other details standard with those of the first five DX goods engines going through the shops at the same time. The 60 Problem class 2-2-2s of 1859–65 were the last outside 2-cylinder standard gauge locomotives built new at Crewe until after the end of the LNWR on 31 December 1922.

Through Ramsbottom's insistence on parts standardisation, the 7ft 6in outside-cylinder Problems had the boiler-firebox assembly, smokebox door, slide valves, and most valve gear components built to the drawings of the 5ft inside-cylinder DX 0-6-0s, while after the first few pump-fitted engines of each class both had the same injectors, huge Giffard equipment carried on the sides of the firebox.

The succeeding 6ft 3in 2-4-0 Samsons, begun in 1863, were sanctioned specifically to replace Crewe-type 6ft singles on secondary passenger services[7] and were *not*, as suggested by many writers over the last 80 years, main-line engines effete and under-powered. These engines had several details similar to those of the DX, including a 16in by 24in cylinder pattern that had been used for a few non-standard DX engines in 1860. Original ideas had been to use only 15¼in bore. The express 6ft 7in Newton 2-4-0s introduced in 1866 had boiler-firebox, 17in by 24in cylinders, slide valves, crank axle, driving and coupled axleboxes, connecting-rods and big-end bearings standard with those of the DX; the 0-6-0ST 'Special Tanks' of 1870 onwards had the same boiler, cylinders, valve motion and other parts.

Thus by Ramsbottom's retirement in 1871 numerous parts had become standard, even if not strictly interchangeable, between over 750 DX, 50 Samson, 76 Newton, 60 Problem and 20 0-6-0ST locomotives, which brought great simplification and cheapening of Crewe construction and repair work, and eased the spares and stores positions. Allied to the programmed allocation of certain types to certain shops, this standardisation enabled 130 general and intermediate repairs to tender engines to be effected in a calendar month, a remarkable total considering that the four new erecting shops were a mile away from the main fitting and machine shops.

Of Ramsbottom engines with generally non-standard parts, the most important were the 0-4-0ST shunters introduced in 1863, with which were originated the cast-iron wheel centres so much used in later years. With them also came the first Bessemer steel boilers and fireboxes; both shell and firebox were cylindrical. Possibly the first six in 1863 had iron construction, but the next 20 were of steel, so that Ramsbottom began at the bottom end of the scale and felt his way upwards with the new material.

On 11 August 1859 the General Stores & Locomotive Expenditure Committee minuted: "To keep the most important part of the business, viz. repairs, under the immediate eye of Mr Ramsbottom, it is necessary to enlarge the present shops at Crewe. At that place the works area including stores and yards is 28,800sq yd, or deducting the open area 15,723sq yd by locomotive shops plus 4,486sq yd at Longsight, or 20,209sq yd total to maintain 464 engines. At Wolverton, to maintain 316 engines the area is 28,450sq yd, of which 22,000sq yd are covered by shops, plus 2,100sq yd on upper storeys." These figures for Crewe represented only part of the triangle; they did not include the carriage shop, the upper floors, or the southern annexe. The last-named by that time had the tender and woodworking shops, plus the rail mill.

No extension or alteration of buildings in the original triangle of ground followed immediately on this minute, largely because at that time the differences between various members of the board as to the relative importance of Wolverton and Crewe were coming to a head, as touched on in Chapter 4. In 1859–60 the transfer of coach-building to Saltley resulted in the much-needed coach shop at Crewe being made available to the locomotive department, and this also eased matters in the yard, for there was then only one department concerned.

However, the transfer was very gradual and was merged into a larger scheme for dealing more comprehensively with the coach shop and the adjacent former wagon shop which had been used over some ten years for miscellaneous general machining and wheel work, and to mill-wrights and stores. Ramsbottom considered that with the growing size of the railway much more repair and erecting capacity was needed. The first alteration to be completed in the summer of 1861 was the conversion of the former wagon shop to locomotive repairs; despite the narrow width of around 74ft four lines of pits were got in to the two bays, but even with small 2-4-0s and 0-6-0s a very cramped shop resulted. This shop was the first erecting shop to get rope-driven travelling cranes. At this time the upper storey was removed to get the height needed to lift locomotives by crane, and new circular-section cast-iron supporting pillars were inserted and ventilating skylights put in.

Early in January 1861, months before this work was complete, a *soirée* was held to initiate the whole new scheme, and was open for all works employees and their wives and daughters over 16 years of age. The chair was taken by Hardman Earle, and the function was attended by many directors and leading officers. In the speeches was a statement that the new extensions and alterations would cost £25,000 and would give employment to another 500 in the locomotive department. This *soirée* was held in the almost empty carriage shop. During 1861–62 small surface additions were made to the main machine shop, the foundries and the smithy, the last-named being given more steam hammers.

A new situation was created in 1862 by the board decision to transfer all Wolverton's new locomotive building to Crewe forthwith, and gradually all locomotive repairs; and then to move all the carriage work from Saltley to Wolverton and give up the first-named premises. This threw a great strain on Crewe over the years 1863–65, because more engines were sent there for repair and were of quite different types, with no parts even similar to those of Trevithick and Ramsbottom engines. But the already planned works alterations were not accelerated—if anything they were retarded, probably because an altogether greater scheme was then envisaged, and at the same time the question of steel manufacture was under way. The work on further erecting-shop capacity was delayed, but other improvements were made, and the small iron foundry was worked intensively on parts for the new shops and tools as well as on locomotive castings. A large engine-boiler house also was built alongside the Warrington main line between Nos 1 and 2 shops; its tall square chimney was a landmark even among Crewe chimneys for 40 years.

An additional strain came through 1863–65 when three or four hundred Wolverton workmen (amounting with families to about 1,700 persons) were transferred to Crewe and had to be housed, and the workmen trained in Crewe methods and discipline. They may not have retained their wage rates, for Wolverton's average at that time was about four percent higher than that at Crewe. The men transferred included such future 'giants' as George Whale, and many who did not rise above the level of artisan or charge-hand, but who kept alive a certain 'Wolverton spirit' in their new surroundings. Even in the 1980s a few veterans still gave tongue to the belief that nothing out of Crewe had equalled the Wolverton products of 1860–62.

Some of the production improvements of 1861 came from the first applications of Ramsbottom's rope-driven cranes that stemmed direct from his early textile-engineering experience. These were of two types: first, a travelling jib crane running on a single rail and guided above by two I-beams, second, an overhead traversing type. Two of the first pattern, of four tons lifting capacity and with a radius of 8½ft, were put into the then small wheel shop in 1861 and saved £300 a year in piece-work prices by the elimination of about two dozen sets of block-and-tackle and the many labourers needed to manipulate them. The two cranes and two men handled all the shop lifting and transfer quicker and more cheaply. Travelling speed was up to 80ft/minute and hoisting speed up to 9ft/minute.

Additional to the cranes in the new converted erecting shop of 1861, by the end of 1862 20/25-ton overhead traversing rope cranes had been put into each bay of the main erecting shop, and by the end of 1864 others were working in the old engine-in-steam shop, one of six tons in the boiler shop, and one of four tons in No 2 turning shop. All these needed new cast-iron pillars and girders for the crane runways, and in general new roofs at higher levels were put in. All the pillars and girders were cast in the small Old Works foundry, and some at the west end are still in service. In succeeding years more of the rope cranes were installed in other shops, and they were put from the beginning into the shops at the far west end.

They were driven by endless cotton ropes of ⅝in diameter weighing 1½oz/yd, which travelled at speeds up to 5,000ft/minute, and which had a working life of about eight months. By looping round grooved and accurately balanced pulleys of various diameters a leverage up to 3000 to 1 could be provided for heavy lifts at low speeds with a very small force applied. These endless ropes ran alongside the top of the shop walls close to the roof ties and gave a distinctive noise when in operation; the initial drive came from a steam engine. The body of a traversing crane was of timber beams with bar-iron trussing, and spans were up to 40ft. The crane man sat on a platform attached to the crab; for the jib type he walked alongside. These cranes were a Crewe feature until the general electrification of the works, and even then they left a low-speed legacy that remained for the life of the LNWR.

Before dealing with the further re-arrangement and re-equipment of the shops within the original triangle and its southern annexe, a brief account is desirable of five distinctive Crewe developments sponsored wholly or in part by Ramsbottom over the years 1861–66, that not only influenced the alterations but lasted through the independent life of the LNWR and well into the time of its successor, the LMSR.

First was the manufacture of non-locomotive and non-track items, beginning with brick-making, sanctioned in 1861 and started in 1862 with clay from the cutting between the south end of Crewe station and Whitmore, a scheme agreed when Ramsbottom submitted that he could make bricks at 16s 2d [81p] per 1000 against the 24s 0d [£1·20] per 1000 the company was then being charged by outside makers. Thenceforth all new shops to the south-west and away to the west, enlargements in the Old Works, and many Crewe houses were made of 'company bricks'.

The first brickworks was south of the Chester line and west of what later became Eaton Street. By 1869 this site was absorbed by new wood-working shops and a timber mill, and a temporary brickyard was made on waste ground between the new Chester line and Wistaston Road. Around 1871 brick-making was transferred to the far north-west of a large parcel of ground beyond Flag Lane acquired over the years 1863–66 by the LNWR. Most of the erection of the 100ft diameter Hoffman kiln and its steam power plant was undertaken by Webb in 1871–72, and costs were cut to 15s 0d [75p] per 1000. Eventually this plant came to have a moulding house for making tuyeres and pipes for the steel plant, also machines for clay mixing; by the 1880s its capacity was five million bricks a year. The circular kiln with its central 115ft chimney was a landmark in the west of Crewe for some 60 years. With the big extension of shops at the west end from 1866 to 1879 several small temporary brick plants were dotted about the yards close to the erection sites.

Brick-making seems to have widened Moon's views as to what might be done at Crewe, and though no further important sidelines other than steel-making were undertaken in Ramsbottom's time, others were considered. There is still in existence a note dated 15 October 1869 from Ramsbottom to Moon: "It appears to me you may safely encourage the establishment of a foundry and agricultural implement manufactury at Crewe." Around this time also were introduced such side lines as waste cleaning and grease manufacture in the southern annexe, which supplemented the grease plant of the carriage department east of the northern main line.

The second development was the southward deviation of the Chester line from its junction with the northern main line to a point about one mile west, for which further property had to be bought, though much of the route was over land already in the company's possession. This was done specifically to counter the inconvenience of a growing number of production shops to the south being separated from the principal works by a main line with increasing traffic, and to improve rail transport within the works area. It led to a re-arrangement of the southern shops and, away to the west end of the 'island' between old and new lines, to the construction of a number of new shops that came to be known as the Deviation Works. The old Chester line was retained for standard-gauge works transport, and later to give connection with the big west-end extension beyond Flag Lane.

A deviation line was recommended by the Crewe Committee in January 1863. The necessary Act was 27 & 28 Vic. cap. 226 of 25 July 1864, obtained so that the land could be bought forthwith at reason-

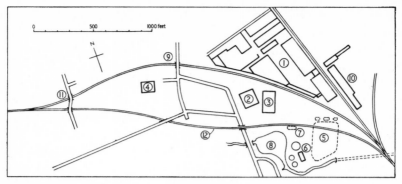

1 Old Works 2 Iron rail mill 3 Tender shop 4 Brickworks 5 Water reservoir 6 Gasworks 7 Gasworks cottages 8 Mill pool 9 Chester Bridge 10 Carriage repair shop 11 Flag Lane Bridge 12 Deviation Line

Fig 12 Map of Deviation line as planned in 1864 and completed 1868, showing the cut across the waterworks and streets

able price, but construction was deferred deliberately until well on in 1866, and the new line (see Fig 12) was not opened until 26 July 1868. It ran between the tender shop and the gasworks in the southern annexe necessitating some re-arrangement of the approach tracks to the locomotive shed erected on Horse Pasture in 1865, and the moving further south of the proposed site for another shed, built in 1867.

The Deviation Line also cut across the town reservoir and pumping house. A cholera epidemic a short time before had accelerated work on the new water supply from Whitmore initiated in 1861, and by the beginning of 1863 some 280,000 gallons a day were being supplied, so that when the Deviation-line work began in 1866 the local reservoir could be filled-in and the pumping house dismantled. From 1863 Whitmore water was delivered by the LNWR to the new Local Board at 6d [2½p] for 1000 gallons.

A likelier promoter of cholera than the water was the primitive sewage system put in by the GJR in 1843 and extended piecemeal by the LNWR as the town grew. For public purposes the town nominally was under existing local sanitary and highway authorities until 1860, when town services and administration came under a new Monks Coppenhall Local Board. Only in 1865 was the sewage problem tackled seriously, and a main drain laid jointly to take away all town and works sewage. Before that both sewages went to the south brook direct, and the town and works fresh water was taken from the same stream a little higher up. Yet a long time elapsed before the whole system became satisfactory, and in the meantime further outbreaks of cholera and smallpox occurred in the town in 1870–72.

The long narrow site between the old and new Chester lines was divided into two by a portion of the town made up of High Street, Oak

Street, Exchange Street, and the short cul-de-sac Wistaston Street (later Eaton Street), see Fig 13, but the eastern end was never considered as part of the Deviation Works and remained an annexe of the Old Works throughout its various changes. Not until the Deviation line was complete was Edleston Road extended south from Oak Street to the new Nantwich Road.

The third development was the beginning of a comprehensive internal works railway of 18in gauge to facilitate inter-shop transport. When sanctioned in October 1861 only 550yd of track were needed in the Old Works, and Ramsbottom estimated he could provide this and build one 3-ton locomotive for it at a cost of £500. Eventually over the three works this transport system had five miles of track. Along with its seven steam locomotives, and the standard-gauge rail system in the whole works area, it is of sufficient interest and importance to warrant a separate section. (Chapter 11).

The fourth development was the initiation of steel manufacture. Steel came first to the LNWR in the late 1850s through Alfred Longsdon, the English representative of Krupp, who prevailed on the company to try some straight and cranked axles and some tyres of crucible-cast steel, and these were followed by a few of South Yorkshire manufacture applied at various times from 1859 to 1864. From early 1860 Crewe itself was casting some driving hornblocks for DX and Problem engines of a steel mixture in the works iron foundry. The development to commercial requirements around 1861 of the Bessemer process, patented in 1855–56, put an entirely new aspect on steel for railway purposes. Bessemer recorded in his autobiography that when he first put mild-steel rail proposals to Ramsbottom that engineer was almost horrified, but by his experience at the Crewe iron mill and foundry, and the acquisition from outside of a few axles and tyres of Bessemer steel, Ramsbottom soon realised the great advantage steel could bring to the LNWR, and that it would be 'safe'.

After close reflection on his detailed proposals and estimates the Crewe Committee agreed, subject to board approval, in February and March 1863 to the construction at Crewe of a Bessemer plant capable of producing up to 1000 tons of ingots a month. There was at that time no other method of getting steel in the quantities, qualities and continuity Ramsbottom foresaw would be desirable. Allied with Bessemer in the licence negotiations was his brother-in-law Robert Longsdon, brother of Alfred, for Bessemer worked much through the Longsdons, and Krupp took up the Bessemer ideas early and developed the Continental side.

As no room was available for a steel plant in the Old Works or

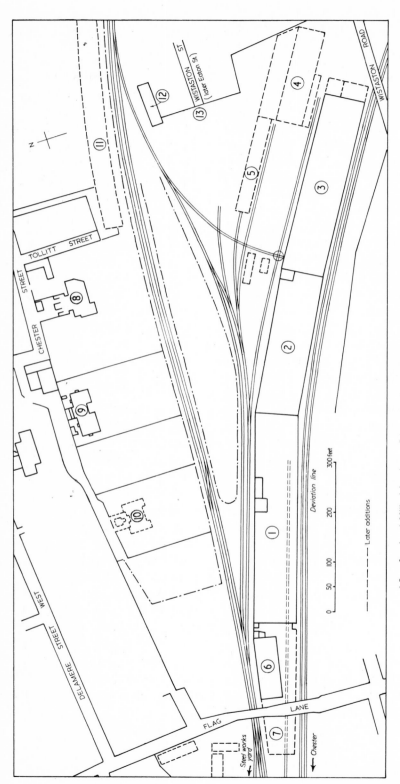

Fig 13 Layout of the Deviation Works and surrounding area in 1874, with subsequent additions and alterations shown in dotted lines

1 Iron foundry 2 Millwrights shop 3 Joiners and patternmakers shop 4 Sawmill 5 Timber stack 6 Brass foundry 7 Chain shop (post-1874) 8 Chester Place 9 Deva Villa and West Bank 10 The Grove and Windycote 11 General offices (built 1876) 12 Workers' dining room 13 Works entrance

southern annexe, a cast had to be made for land away to the west of Crewe town as it then existed, and this led to a unique feature of the steel plant: it was built on land presented to the company free! John Hill, on learning of the proposals, offered the LNWR in February 1863 eight acres of ground free, on the condition that the company would erect a works upon it, and that if and when the company required further land for works extensions it would buy the extra land from him at £200 an acre. To this the LNWR agreed – if the eight acres could be in the shape of an oblong.

Hill, the first chairman of the Monks Coppenhall Local Board in 1860, was an ex-railway contractor, an astute business man, and a general benefactor of Crewe, as was in later years his son, A. G. Hill. Probably he divined Ramsbottom's developing idea eventually to transfer the whole production and repair work of the locomotive department to obviate the inconvenience of separate works and the already congested triangle. Though this idea was never accomplished in the years of steam locomotive building, much of the new locomotive factory away to the west was on land acquired from Hill or his executors at various times at the agreed figure, as were several streets of houses. Hill was given a contract for some of the construction work at the west end, and as a venture of his own he built a few streets of houses to accommodate the extra workers.

The new steel plant was erected alongside the Chester line some 500yd west of Flag Lane, and formed the embryo of what later became the principal locomotive building and repair establishment, and which as a whole just bore the name of 'the Steelworks' (see Fig 1). In this book that term is used for the whole west end, and 'steel works' or 'steel plant' for the actual steel melting and making portion, usually known colloquially as 'the melts'. The new locomotive factory west and north of the steel plant is to be accounted as the fifth major development at Crewe initiated by Ramsbottom.

Through 1867–68 the joiners and pattern makers were transferred from the southern annexe to new buildings at the east end of the Deviation site, and a year or two later these were supplemented by a saw mill, timber store and all woodworking activities; the old shops were altered to give an extension of the tender shop. New iron and new brass foundries were built at the west end of the Deviation area adjacent to Flag Lane; the old small iron foundry in the triangle was absorbed into the No 2 turning-and-wheel shop, which already had been given an additional bay butting on to the end of the main erecting shop. The old brass foundry became an extension of the spring smithy. The new Deviation iron foundry came into full operation in

Fig 14 Visit of Prince of Wales (later King Edward VII) to Crewe Works in January 1866 showing circular saw at the new steel plant and the then new tram locomotive *Pet*

1868 and had two large cupolas for the heaviest castings, and was given one 30-ton rope crane and another of 10 tons capacity; power in the shop was provided by a vertical steam engine. Between the new iron foundry and the new pattern shop was located a commodious millwrights' shop, and this had to deal not only with works and machine tool maintenance but also with jobs coming in from out-stations. The Deviation layout around 1871–74 is shown in Fig 13.

While all this new construction was going on the reorganisation of the Old Works proceeded, and by 1866 the old coaching shop was at last in full function as an engine repair and erecting shop, and despite its awkward situation the construction of the majority of new engines was given to it. At the same time the long narrow open space between it and the old wagon shop was roofed and became the frame shop. The Old Works smithy and forge were enlarged by some 50 percent by taking in open yard space, and they came to have 15 steam hammers from 6cwt to 50cwt; of the 100 smiths' fires about 20 were employed full time on wheel centres. The fitting shop was extended in ground area by taking in the southern end of the boiler shop, and an upper floor was put over part of the existing shop. Part of this upper floor was the beginning of 'the nursery'. (see Chapter 6). The long narrow ground floor and first floor stores and office building just inside the clock tower arch was given an additional floor over the whole of its length around 1864–65.

The boiler shop, reduced in size by 30 percent, remained for some three years until a new boiler shop was put into commission away to

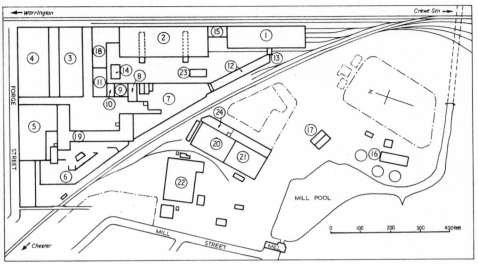

FORGE STREET

MILL POOL

MILL STREET

← Chester

0   100   200   300   400 feet

1 No 1 Erecting shop 2 No 2 Erecting shop 3 No 3 Erecting shop 4 No 4 Erection shop 5 Smithy 6 Forge
7 Fitting shop 8 Spring shop 9 Brass foundry 10 Dressing shop 11 Iron foundry 12 Stores and general offices
13 Clocktower Arch 14 Copper shop 15 Boiler and engine house 16 Gasworks 17 Gasworks cottages
18 Wheel shop 19 Boiler shop 20 Tender shop 21 Joiners and patternmakers 22 Iron rail mill 23 Stores
24 Grease works, Fire engine, etc.

Fig 15 Layout of Old works and Southern Annexe after the 1866 alterations but before
the Deviation Works was opened

the west of the steel plant in 1869–70, but the reduced capacity came
to have a serious effect on engine repairs by the end of 1869, and a
dozen engines under heavy repair were noted in the works for six to
nine months awaiting new boilers in 1870, while *Phalaris* was in for 16
months, 13 of which were waiting for a new boiler. For some years
from 1871 the residue of the Old Works boiler shop was used for
repairs to small boilers.

For some years in the 1860s the old engine-in-steam shop was
known loosely as No 2 repair shop, but from 1866–67 the then four
erecting shops were definitely numbered from the south, the old
engine-in-steam shop became No 1 erecting shop, the old main repair
shop No 2, the old wagon shop No 3, and the old coach shop No 4.
Nos 3 and 4 were at right-angles to Nos 1 and 2 and were alongside
each other, whereas Nos 1 and 2 were in line. In these re-arrangements
of the 1860s the traverser that had been put alongside the tracks of the
Warrington line to get engines in and out of No 3 was extended to
cover No 4 shop as well. The small copper shop begun around 1861
was extended in 1866. The layout of the Old Works after the 1866
alterations is shown in Fig 15.

As to steel works and steel production, the first steel rails were laid at Crewe station in November 1861 and taken-up the next year to go on show at the London Exhibition; further steel rails were laid at Chalk Farm in 1862. No authentic contemporary record can be found as to where these rails were made, but it is likely they came from trial production in the iron rail mill in the southern annexe.

Most of the erection of the new steel plant was completed by the end of 1864 from parts mainly made at Crewe, but the plant was not properly opened that year, though the first 'blow' of steel was made on 22 September 1864. Some months of 1865 were occupied in installing further equipment, trial working, and acquiring knowledge of heating-up, charging, ingot-handling and other processes. Ramsbottom recorded in 1866 that he had followed Bessemer's instructions for the plant itself, but had put in some unusual equipment to work on the ingots produced, and he took out eight patents over the years 1863–65 covering improvements in steel manufacture and handling. Bessemer himself had the agreed royalties of £1 to £2 a ton of steel produced according to its character and purpose until his principal patents ran out in 1869–70, and for some time he had an extra 2s 6d [12½p] a ton on steel for wheels and crank axles made according to his patent No 670 of 1859.

Steel keys for rails and a few steel boiler and general plates were the first normal productions in the winter of 1864–65, but Ramsbottom was keen to get safe and reliable tyres from the new plant, though at that time he still preferred the old fixing method of deeply-counter-sunk rivets through tyre and rim. The first useable steel tyres were not rolled until September 1865, and on 4 October were put on the 3ft 6in leading wheels of engines Nos 73 and 363. By the end of 1865 278 steel tyres of various diameters had been made, and production in 1866 was over one thousand. More than one hundred steel axles also were made in 1866.

The first steel boiler shell other than the cylindrical small ones of the 0-4-0ST shunters was completed near the end of 1865; about a dozen more were made at times up to the end of 1871, but not until January 1872 did Ramsbottom's successor get the agreement of the Locomotive Committee to build steel boilers generally thereafter, and quoted the good condition of the 1865 boiler as evidence. Production of iron boilers on a decreasing scale continued until 1875, what time the number of steel boilers manufactured at the new west-end shop increased.

By the end of 1868 Crewe-produced steel was being applied to some of the heaviest parts of valve motion, reversing gear, brake gear, and to some frame plates, and cast steel continued for some hornblocks. Until

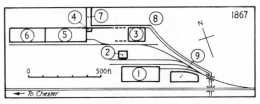

1 Bessemer converting plant 2 Boiler house 3 Tyre mill, Plate mill, Steam hammer 4 Workmen's entrance
5 No 5 Erecting shop 6 No 6 Erecting shop 7 Hill Street West 8 Footpath 9 Pig bank

Fig 16 Layout of original Bessemer steel plant 1867, west of Flag Lane

around 1870 the frame plates of DX and certain other engines were still in two lengths forge-welded together, for the frame-plate rolling mill could not take plates longer then 17½ft.

Solid steel rails (*ie* rails entirely of steel) were not produced in any quantity for the first ten years of the steel plant operation, and during that time there was no rail rolling mill at the west end. The steel plant had been sanctioned particularly for locomotive parts, but when the question of steel rail making was introduced early in 1863 Ramsbottom and Baker (the LNWR chief civil engineer) were told to report on costs. When in March they estimated one mile of double track could be relaid with steel rails at a cost of £3,301 and with iron rails at only £1,879, the Crewe Committee decided that only ingots surplus to locomotive requirements should be used for rails, and that these should be put first on new lines or in relaying existing stations. This was the reason why few solid steel rails were laid in Ramsbottom's time, and was also the cause of Webb's invention in 1864 of steel-headed iron rails, so that most effective use could be got out of the small surplus of steel. The 1863 relaying estimates included the Bessemer royalties. With increased experience and greater demand, and the elimination of royalties from 1871, the cost of steel fell from £14 or £15 a ton in 1865 to £12 or £13 a ton in 1867 and to £10 a ton in 1872, whereas the price of iron rails kept steady at about £7 a ton.

Iron rails up to 6,000 or 7,000 tons a year were rolled at Crewe until the end of 1874 at the existing mill in the southern annexe, and from 1865 many of these were steel-headed. Iron rail production then dropped sharply and the last of such rails was rolled in February 1876. First serious production of all-steel rails began near the end of 1875. The old rail mill was then cleared and the building used as a rail store. Iron rails remained in 21ft lengths until the end, but steel rails began at 30ft.

The Bessemer plant of 1864–65 was concentrated mainly within a space of 272ft by 106ft (see Fig 16) and comprised two twin converters

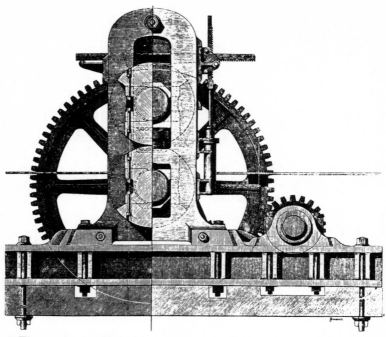

Fig 17 The cogging machine with two 5ft rolls put down at Crewe in 1864 to deal with large ingots

with a total capacity of 24 tons, three furnaces (one, at least, of which was a Siemens gas-fired furnace by the end of 1865), a cogging mill, blowing engine and steam hammer, all on the north side of the Chester line. The cogger (Fig 17) was formed of two large rolls about 5ft dia with hydraulic adjustment and driven by a pair of standard 17in by 24in locomotive cylinders with direct reversing, and fed with steam at 60lb/sq in pressure. There was an open pig bank to the east of the steel plant and a separate boiler house and chimney to the north. Further north again was a tyre mill and a circular saw. Within four years this plant had been given hydraulic hoists and cranes working at 350lb/sq in pressure to handle coke, metal and ingots to and from the firing stages. In January 1869 two 5-ton open-hearth Siemens furnaces were built, following the developments of C. W. Siemens from 1863, in particular his patents for furnaces and processes in 1867–68. In 1869 around 375 men were employed in this new west-end area of steel plant and two erecting shops, the weekly wage bill being just short of £450.

Tyre ingots were cast as cones 22in dia at base and 22in high for a 5ft tyre, a form suggested by Webb. The bloom was brought down under a duplex hammer to 34in dia by 5⅜in thickness with a 11in hole

All photographs
on this page are
by courtesy of
J. P. Richards

Iron foundry of 1882
as it was in 1892;
beam with
commemorative
plate is still in use
today

Below: West-end signal shop – today the brass foundry – looking east *circa* 1896, and showing a large mechanical signalling frame. *Right:* Part of the Steelworks forge, with an old locomotive boiler and cylinders providing tool power. In the foreground is an 18in gauge tramway track

Bottom: One end of the steel foundry, *circa* 1893–94; this shop began operation in 1884. *Right:* A corner of "the melts" in 1894, with "pigs" just brought in for the furnaces

Old Works from Midge Bridge, 1882. Through the arch of the bridge are the two Deviation Works chimneys. Deviation line in foreground and centre. Christ Church tower and roof beyond fitting shop and smithy. Two chimneys in foreground are in "the southern annexe", then occupied by signal shop, rail stores, sponge-cloth cleaning plant, etc *(NRM, York)*

Making up standard iron fencing in a corner of the Old Works forge *circa* 1872; note shade for large gas burner

Fig 18 Rolling a Bessemer steel tyre at Crewe on the occasion of the visit of the Prince of Wales, 1866

in the centre, and then finished in a circular mill evolved by Rothwell Jackson of the Salford Rolling Mills, which by rolling on inside and outside at the same time brought the bloom to the form and dimensions of the finished tyre at one heat, with no more than 5½ minutes in the rollers. From running the melt into the casting ladle from the Bessemer converter, a batch of six tyres could be completed in 5¼ hours.

The duplex hammers were a development by Ramsbottom under a patent of 1865. He had found the tup and anvil weights of certain large vertical hammers in the Old Works to be too great for convenient installation and regular operation, and therefore he laid two large hammers on their sides to act horizontally in opposite directions with the bloom placed between them. A 30-ton ensemble of this form with steel hammer blocks was adopted in 1866 after some months of experience with a 10-ton size, and like much of the steel plant equipment was made in the Old Works and erected on site. The smaller hammer remained in service until November 1896 and the 30-ton unit until September 1898.

When the steel plant was opened the workmen's entrance was put on the north side of the ground and Hill Street West, soon to be renamed Goddard Street, was extended southward to reach it. Along the north wall was laid the short Bessemer Street, which had nothing in it except a new workers' dining room and a shunting track down the centre,

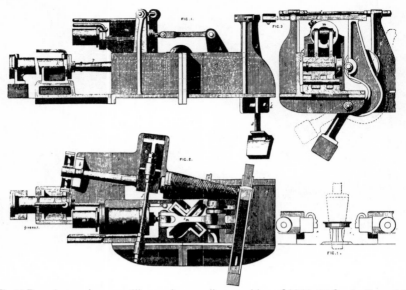

Fig 19 Ramsbottom's tyre rolling and expanding machine of 1864–66 for dealing with annular tyre blanks as they came from the steam hammer

though at the corner of Bessemer Street and Hill Street West was built the necessary public house, the Bessemer Vaults (Fig 20). All this was well away from the main blocks of company houses, which had been built first to the north of the Old Works and then had extended some distance west and north of Chester bridge and Coppenhall Road with Delamere Street, Victoria Street, Hightown and their offshoots.

After the steel-making nucleus was in full function the construction of several new locomotive repair shops and a new boiler shop was begun as part of the Wolverton replacement programme already outlined. First of all stripping and erecting facilities were provided by a line of shops near the Goddard Street entrance, which were planned in an extending east-west line. No 5 was built first, and was in partial use by the end of 1866. No 6 was functioning by the end of 1867, No 7 in the winter of 1869–70. No 8 erecting shop came into partial use in 1870 and into full production in 1871, when the layout at the west end was as shown in Fig 20. In construction and external appearance these shops followed the lines of the 1843 buildings, and No. 7 is believed to have had at its west end a Ramsbottom traverser moved by endless chains on toothed drums. Much of the shop construction at the Steelworks end in 1871–72 was in charge of John Aspinall, many years later chief mechanical engineer and general manager of the LYR.

By the end of his time Ramsbottom had all these shops fully organised to handle different classes of engines, apportioned as shown

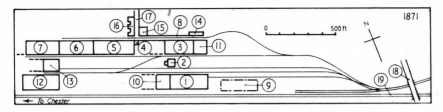

1 Bessemer steel plant 2 Boiler house 3 Forge 4 Workmen's entrance 5 No 5 Erecting shop 6 No 6 Erecting shop 7 No 7 Erecting shop 8 Bessemer Street 9 Pig bank 10 Spring mill 11 Plate mills 12 Boiler shop 13 Boiler-shop smithy 14 Workmen's dining room 15 Bessemer vaults 16 Houses 17 Goddard Street 18 Flag Lane 19 Deviation Line

Fig 20 Layout of west-end works 1870–71, showing steel plant, new repair shops and Bessemer Street

in Table 4. The rigid allocation of specific classes to specific shops was in advance of practice in other large railway workshops. The new shops at the Steelworks end were laid out particularly to repair the large and ever-growing number of DX 0-6-0s. Shop procedures and locomotive parts were highly standardised to get efficient production, and repaired locomotives from the Old and Steelworks rose from an average of 15 a week in 1865–66 to 21 a week in 1867 and to 35 in 1870. Of these, 30 to 33 percent were intermediate repairs.

The west end shops Nos 5 to 8 with their greater space, newer equipment, and their virtual concentration on the DX class, were rather more efficient than the Old Works, averaging 1·95 engines a year per man employed in them, whereas Nos 1, 2 and 3 in the Old Works averaged 1·7 to 1·8. That the west-end average was not higher probably resulted from the time absorbed in parts transfer between old and new works. No 4 shop had a lower value because after 1867–68 most of the new-engine building was concentrated there, and its repair output varied with the amount of new construction in hand. The repair performance in the final years of Ramsbottom's regime is summarised in Tables 5 and 6.

During 1870 and the first half of 1871 parts of the new boiler shop and boiler-shop smithy were put into commission away to the west in line with the steel plant, but not until the end of 1871 was full production attained. This was a great relief, for the T-shaped boiler shop in the Old Works had become quite inadequate for the growing stock of engines.

When the steel-plant nucleus was opened in 1865 the track lead-in

Table 4   Allocation of locomotives for repair 1870–72[2]

Erecting shop	Pit capacity locomotives[1]	Classes	Total allocated
No 1	30	Wolverton 7ft passenger; old L&C Rothwell 2-2-2; Crewe 6ft 2-2-2; Old Clwyd, Cockermouth, Birkenhead, etc.	287
No 2	35	106 Wolverton goods; 75 Fairbairn goods; 116 Crewe-type tanks, etc.	316
No 3	24	*Cornwall*; 60 7ft 6in Problems; 17 7ft Crewe passenger; 40 Large Bloomers; 30 Small Bloomers; 76 Newton 2-4-0s; 22 ex-L&C 2-4-0s; 7BP tanks; various 6-wheel STs, etc.	315
No 4	25		
No 5	29		
No 6	28	785 DX 0-6-0s; 36 0-4-0ST; 50 Samson 2-4-0s; 6 Bury 6ft passenger; 2 Bury 0-4-0s nos. 1148 and 1154; any 6ft 6in Newtons not taken by shops Nos 3 and 4	895
No 7	29		
No 8	28		

Additional capacity: Longsight erecting shop holds 25 small locomotives, mainly ex-NED types; 52 allocated; Wolverton erecting shop holds 12 locomotives; 17 ex-SD locomotives allocated.

[1] Actual numbers could be greater if many locomotives in were 4-wheelers or small 6-wheelers

[2] In October 1871 the actual numbers in were: No 1–32, No 2–35, No 3–24, No 4–16, No 5–36, No 6–35, No 7–33, No 8–31; in paint shop–28; outside awaiting repair–79; total in Crewe works area–349. Under repair at Longsight–24 (all ex-NED); under repair at Wolverton–19; at Carlisle–10. Total stock 1882 engines; total under repair 402; percentage under repair–21.36

Table 6   Average number of engines repaired per week at Crewe Works

Year	No 1 shop	No 2 shop	No 3 shop	No 4 shop	No 5 shop	No 6 shop	No 7 shop	No 8 shop	Lying in paint shop	Total average repairs per week	Total locomotives in the year
1867	4·8	5·0	4·4	2·0	5·0	–	–	–	6·6	21·2	130
1868	5·25	5·15	4·8	2·7	5·13	4·7	–	–	8·55	27·74	104
1869	4·6	5·0	4·6	4·0	5·8	5·7	–	–	9·5	29·7	62
1870	5·18	5·53	4·2	3·0	5·46	5·11	4·26	2·8	10·0	35·54	70
1871	5·0	5·4	3·92	2·48	4·88	4·64	3·8	3·0	10·52	33·12	88
1872	4·82	5·55	3·57	0·67	5·65	5·78	4·69	1·73	9·32	32·46	147
1873	4·16	4·11	1·72	0·16	4·22	5·0	3·88	0·38	10·05	23·63	–

from the Chester main line was close to the east end of the melts as shown in Fig 16, but the 1868–71 extensions were made after the Deviation line had been built, and the track lead-in to the works areas then was moved some 1000yd further east and was a prolongation of the old Chester line, which then had no through traffic. A junction between the old and new Chester lines just west of Flag Lane was never made, so no mishap on the Deviation line could be overcome by temporary use of the old Chester line. The original Flag Lane bridge over the old Chester line was only 16ft wide; its 1868 southward extension over the Deviation line was 24ft wide. By the end of the century both these widths were inadequate, but the LNWR was unwilling to stand the cost of widening.

A feature of Ramsbottom's first ten years at Crewe was the number of machines devised to do various jobs more quickly and accurately. They began with the slide-bar grinder and a portable tool for truing-up port faces that had been in use at Longsight since 1854–55. Within a couple of years were designed and made at Crewe tube cutters, tube cleaners, tube expanders, connecting-rod borers, and a spring-buckle stripper. The reorganisation of 1861 brought further machine-tool developments such as the nibbling machine with 160 small tools round a large disc to cut out the slots between crank webs in crank-axle forgings, and a crank-axle roughing lathe with seven tool points in operation at once. Others included Webb's ferrule-making and finishing machine, Ramsbottom's triple-roll straightening and centering machine for firebox stays, a drifting machine for squaring bolt holes in cylinder covers and gland faces, a machine to produce snap-heads of any form on bolts by the use of a template, a hammer-handle producer guided by a cast-iron former, a Jobson turn-over table for casting buffer housings, a double-plate moulder to cast fusible-plug housings, and a steam-operated spring tester with a 26¾in diameter cylinder. Nameplates were cut out on a twin-spindle borer operating on Blanchard's copying principle. A pair of shearing machines in the yard, worked by boys, cut iron scrap to lengths convenient for scrap piles.

Of particular interest was the frame plate grinder, in operation by 1865, that saved some eight to ten man-days in the complete dressing of a pair of frame plates. In its original form with four 20ft cast-iron bedplate girders this machine was used to grind not only the edges after rough punching and slotting, but also the two faces so that the numerous brackets and hornblocks could be attached to dead flat surfaces. That was in the days when a frame plate was forge-welded of two or three sections. When in the early 1870s rolled plates of suitable

Table 5   Average annual Crewe Works repairs and new construction,
1866-67 and 1871-72

Shop	Locomotives repaired		Locomotives rebuilt		New locomotives built		No of locomotives repaired per annum per man in shop	
	1866-67	1871-72	1866-67	1871-72	1866-67	1871-72	1866-67	1871-72
No 1	245	221	8	23			1·7	1·7
No 2	247	300	8	16			1·66	1·85
No 3	228	195	3	10			1·44	1·53
No 4	100	88	3	19	100	116		
No 5	249	253		9			1·46	
No 6		241		6				1·98
No 7		215		3				
No 8		152		8				

lengths became available, dressing of the surfaces was no longer required and the machine was then confined to dressing the plate edges; the frame plates and a 4ft diameter vertical-spindle grinding wheel were then laid in a shallow trough of water. On similar principles was a template-controlled rope-driven horizontal grinder that reached across the frame assembly and dressed the faces of the hornblocks on each side at one time; the frame was set up on jacks. This machine was in operation in No 3 shop as early as 1862.

Smithy ventilation was improved by letting in some of the air from the large blowing fan. In the new Deviation brass foundry the furnaces had an opening in the top part near the mouth, and the opening connected with the main flue at the back, so that the induction current carried off the fumes of the metal before they could contaminate the shop atmosphere. In the forge was developed, first to aid wrought-iron wheel making, a circular hearth with a form of cap or deflector shaped like the roof of a house and lined with firebrick. This could be made also in semi-portable form, and a remarkable demonstration of its use outside was made on the Birmingham–Shrewsbury line, where an experimental two miles of rail was welded up in one length in 1866–the first long-welded rail of all.

Unequal tread wear on the tyres of a pair of 3ft 6in leading wheels on a Problem 2-2-2, caused by out-of-balance wheel rims, led to Webb's invention in 1863 of the so-called curvilinear slotting machine, devised to machine the curved inner surface of wheel rims between the spokes. By 1866 three of these machines were made and installed at a cost of £420. Webb claimed that three hours were occupied in going round the rim of a 5ft DX wheel and that one man could easily look

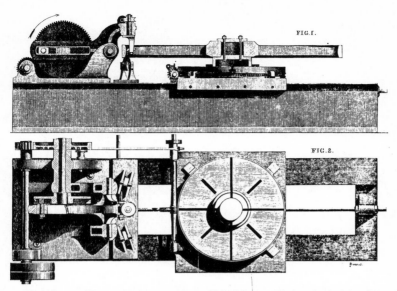

Fig 21 Webb's curvilinear slotting machine of 1864 for machining the inside of the rim of wrought-iron wheel centre

after two machines at one time, and that the incidental saving of files was enormous.

Crewe bossed-up wheel centres under 10cwt steam hammers which were used also for iron plate-frame forging. Two such hammers were engaged almost entirely in these operations in the late 1850s, and in 1861 were supplemented by two more bought from Kitson. Partly to make full use of the rolling mills present in one form or another in various shops from 1853, Ramsbottom changed over to wrought-iron for firebars, and by the mid-1860s around 800 tons a year were being rolled in a mill located in the forge.

A chemical laboratory was set up in 1865, first to develop the application of a spectroscope to the Bessemer converters, and to try and determine the best mixtures of cast-iron for cylinders and other parts. Ramsbottom sent one of the young draughtsmen, Reddrop, for training in this work under Professor Roscoe at Manchester, and he became a well-known Crewe personality, eventually handling a wide range of duties including weekly coal and oil analyses and testing of steel compositions, with the photographic department from the mid-1870s as a pleasant offshoot.

From 1866–67, when nearly 4,000 men and boys were employed in the three works, special means were introduced to issue the fortnightly pay quickly on alternate Fridays. That day itself had been chosen in preference to the Saturday afternoon of the early days in the hope

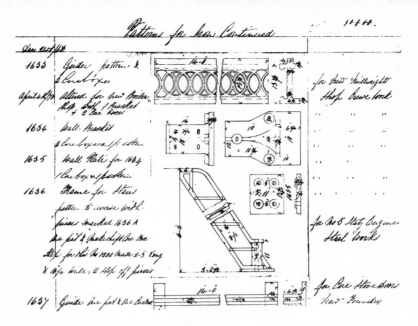

Fig 22 Page from Old Works pattern-shop book showing crane-run beams, frame for stationary engine at Steelworks, and other details cast in the Old Works iron foundry, 1868

there would be less tendency and opportunity to squander money as soon as it was received. The men were divided into two lots; one was paid on leaving for the mid-day break and the other at 5.30pm. In the morning four small wooden cabins were put up in the yard close to the various exits, and each had two pay windows at diagonally opposite corners, with a pay clerk at each. Every man passed in his number check, receiving his money in exchange, and each mass pay-out was over in 20 minutes. The money was first made-up into packets at a central pay office close by Chester bridge.

A primitive fire service existed in Trevithick's day, but Ramsbottom developed and disciplined it along two avenues. First he acquired two steam fire engines fitted to wheeled frames that could travel over the works standard gauge tracks. With attached hoses, goose-necks and so on they were valued at £490 apiece, and a third was built in 1861 and mounted on an old tender frame and wheels. Secondly, on the fire precaution side, a system of recording or telltale clocks was installed throughout the works so that the actual patrols of the night watchmen could be checked.

In the last full year of the Ramsbottom period, 1870, the whole establishment of reorganised Old Works, Deviation shops, and the one boiler and three repair shops at the west end gave general repairs to some 1,200 locomotives and 1,092 tenders, intermediate repairs to another 400 engines, rebuilt 89 engines including over a dozen tender

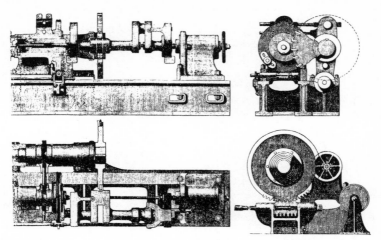

Fig 23 Ramsbottom's rose-cutting multi-tool crank axle roughing lathe of the 1860s

engines into tanks, and built 70 new engines and 90 new tenders. Average number of hands throughout the year was just 4,000 including men engaged in the construction of new west-end shops, in the steel plant, gasworks and inter-shop and inter-works transport. Crewe was then responsible for the upkeep of some 1,750 locomotives valued at £3·5 million contrasted with about 600 engines valued at £1·25 million early in 1862.

Nevertheless Moon was still not satisfied, and in August 1871 suggested that spare boilers should be kept in hand to expedite repair times. This idea probably arose from the boiler-shop impasse already recorded, and from Ramsbottom's then recent practice of building new DX engines on capital account without wheel-and-axle sets, for these were repaired so quickly that a float of them was always lying about the works waiting for the rest of the engines being finished. This practice itself was a development from the tender 'negative float', which arose from a Locomotive Committee minute of 10 May 1867: "that a portion of all engines built in future to capital account should not have tenders built with them." and over the remainder of the Ramsbottom period only 10 or 11 tenders to every 15 locomotives were constructed.

According to Woodehouse, the Stafford-division civil engineer, speaking at a dinner to Ramsbottom on his retirement, the cost of operating the Northern Division locomotive department including all locomotive repairs was 10·75d [4·5p] per locomotive-mile in 1857; by 1870 the cost of the whole LNWR per locomotive department had been reduced to 7·75d [3p] per locomotive-mile. The former is a hoary figure, for GJR muniments show it as the cost, including general charges, for 1845, and it was also the actual rate charged to the LCR

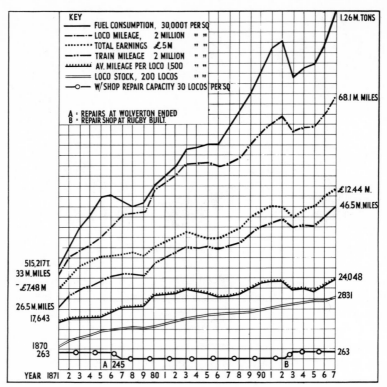

Fig 24 Rise in locomotive performance and traffic on the LNWR over the period 1871 to 1897

by the LNWR for locomotive power over the years 1855–57. In Ramsbottom's years the cost varied from 7·75 [3p] to 10·5d [4·3p] according mainly to coal prices. When Ramsbottom retired the value of machines, tools, stationary engines and boilers at Crewe was around £215,000, four times the figure for 1862.

The real measure of Ramsbottom's competence as engineer, administrator and disciplinarian was not just his build-up of the locomotive department and Crewe Works to twice their size in ten years; rather was it that by the end of 1866 the Old Works and its southern annexe, with a total works and yard area of 11¼ acres (the area of the annexe had been reduced by the transfer of several acres to the running department), and a covered shop area of about 6¼ acres, was repairing 15 engines and tenders each week, turning out a new DX every 2¼ working days, rebuilding a score or more older engines and scrapping many more in a year, making 6,000 tons of iron rails in a twelve-month, and undertaking a great deal of new shop construction, a *tour de force* of production that on the basis of output per square yard was never equalled in British steam locomotive works.

6
The Years of Webb, 1871–1903

When F. W. Webb succeeded to the top position on 1 October 1871 he had been away from Crewe for five years. He returned to a first-rate department and a well-organised tripartite works suffering somewhat from Ramsbottom's absences through illness, and from the works having been run for a twelve-month by an 'acting' works manager who was also the chief draughtsman. He tightened things up at once, but his return to Crewe brought him straight away into three situations more pregnant than that of just handling a large factory.

In 1871 the boards of the LNWR and LYR proposed to amalgamate the two systems, but Parliamentary committees of 1871–74 refused to sanction the merger as being too monopolistic. During the preliminary discussions the two boards decided to work together closely, and one method agreed was that Crewe should build LNWR-type locomotives for the LYR, partly because the latter company's works at Miles Platting was inconvenient and ill-equipped, and partly because common standard types were envisaged.

Richard Moon had led the amalgamation talks and he, not Webb, was the sponsor of the locomotive-building suggestions, which were under way when Webb took over. Within a month Webb was authorised to let the LYR have at a price of £2,100 per engine-and-tender six of the DX class just completed at Crewe, to build another 20 for the LYR as soon as possible, and to help LYR maintenance by turning-up wheel-and-axle sets at Longsight. In January 1872 Moon agreed also to let the LYR have five of the Ramsbottom-type 0-4-0Ts quickly, Webb being authorised to build five replacements.

During the next month Moon and Webb went over the whole Crewe enlargement and production programmes, and felt that by putting on some overtime the LYR locomotive requirements could be met, and 20 more DX engines for that railway were sanctioned. However, when the production question was remitted down to Worsdell, the works manager, he found that to make an additional 20 DX engines and tenders by November, followed immediately by 20 more and five extra 0-4-0Ts on top of Crewe's normal new construction programme, all the wheel fires and 20 others in the smithy would have to work the equivalent of 1¼ days a week overtime, all the foundry men would have to work the equivalent of two days a week overtime, 200 men in the fitting shop 1¼ days, 100 erectors one day, the flangers and machine men in the boiler shop 1¼ days, and the coppersmiths just could not do the extra work at all. Further new machines required would be one 10cwt steam hammer, one multiple driller, one firebox tapping machine, two radial drills, a slotter of 12in stroke, one cylinder planer and one general planer. Actually the number of men employed had to be increased.

Up to that time all the engines concerned had, or were to have, iron boilers; when later in 1872 the LYR wanted 40 more DX engines and 10 Newton-type 2-4-0 passenger engines, they were given steel boilers, and the selling price then became £2,250 per engine-and-tender, rising to £2,400 for 1873 deliveries.

These matters remained almost unnoticed until 1875, when at the instance of A. L. Sacré, manager of the Yorkshire Engine Co, several of the private locomotive builders got together on 29 April 1875. At a second meeting on 4 June they formed what was at first the ad hoc Locomotive Manufacturers' Association, a body that succeeded in getting a court injunction preventing the LNWR building locomotives for any other railway or user. Perhaps it was significant that the instigator was the newest of the locomotive builders of any size, and had been set up largely with capital from the South Yorkshire iron and steel industry, which already looked askance at the rapid development of steel manufacture by the largest railway. Of significance also was an order for a dozen 0-6-0s placed by the LYR with the Yorkshire Engine Co early in 1875, for probably during the negotiations the builders heard for the first time the extent of Crewe construction for the LYR.

The expenses of the legal action and of the Association over its first year were met by a levy of 9d [4p] per employee, totalling £360 from the 13 member firms, which at that time employed 9,600 men. Not all builders joined the Association. After the successful action the LMA was continued on a permanent basis with a secretary "at the nominal salary of £10."

Up to the time of the court action Crewe had supplied the LYR with 86 DX engines, 10 Newtons and five 0-4-0Ts at a total cost around £225,000, an acquisition of new engines more than usually valuable, for a fire at Miles Platting in April 1873 had disorganised the LYR's meagre facilities for construction and repair, and led also to the supply of some coaches from Wolverton.

The second major situation confronting Webb was the movement for a nine-hour working day, originating on the North-East Coast but with strong moral support and a weekly financial contribution from the men at Crewe Works. Just a month after Webb took over he was asked by the workmen to transmit a memorial to the directors asking for shorter hours. This was granted, and from 1 January 1872 the 58½-hour working week was reduced to 54 hours by closing the works at noon on Saturday and at 5.30pm Monday to Friday. This necessitated a close study of works activities by Webb and Worsdell in order to maintain production without any increase in work force, and almost immediately came the complication of the LYR business. From that time Webb's daily interest in the works was unremitting. Already he had advanced the first warning buzzer in the morning from 5.40am to 5.30am to give an extra ten minutes before the 6.00am start. In 1882 Webb ruled that no worker should live more than 2½ miles from the works gate, a restrictive measure that may have been wise, for there was no transport, not even bicycles, and some men spent an hour or more walking from home and the same time going home in the evening. Despite the shorter hours, efforts were made in a few months to gain higher wages, but with only small success.

A third matter imposed on Webb during 1872–74 was the soaring cost of coal. Price paid by the LNWR rose from 7s 0d [35p] a ton in 1870–71 to a peak of 15s 0d [75p] a ton for a month or two in 1874; this had a decided effect on the cost of locomotive running and of the whole locomotive department, putting at least £15,000 a year on to Crewe Works costs. Though the rise was a general industrial matter, Webb felt keenly the increase in the department's costs soon after he assumed charge. The rise was temporary, and by 1876 the price was down to 8s 0d [40p] a ton and remained below seven shillings a ton from 1879 to 1889. The bitter experience of 1872–74 was a main reason for Webb's adoption of compound propulsion after Mallet brought this forward in 1878, and for the perpetuation until his retirement.

As if all these matters were not sufficient in addition to the daily administrative task, ten weeks after his appointment Webb began the re-arrangement and re-numbering of all engines in duplicate stock, including the transfer to capital stock of one hundred duplicates. This was the move that initiated the appalling complexity of LNWR locomotive numbering that existed through the remainder of the company's existence. The complexity was intensified when additional scrapping numbers were introduced, and when the locomotive capital account was closed for years at a fixed number of 2,323 engines, and the duplicate stock went up and up. From 1886 all duplicate-stock engines were renumbered from 3001 upwards.

Over the whole 31½-year period of the Webb régime the LNWR constantly expanded in route mileage, train mileage, ton mileage, and in general traffic and the facilities needed to handle it. (Fig 24). As a result, the number of locomotives increased by 60 percent, and in general the new construction was larger than the old. Nevertheless, under a chairman with a decided bent for ordered economy and moderate schedule speeds there was no encouragement for large loco-motives, particularly as men and coal were cheap; Webb, like Trevithick and Ramsbottom before him, followed a small engine policy for his first 20 years.

As soon as Moon retired in 1891 Webb began to supplement the universal 6-wheel engines with larger 8-wheelers for top-class passenger and freight services, but like many locomotive engineers before and after him he was unable to move successfully into larger sizes and outputs. He added to the natural difficulties by retaining compound propulsion with ill-proportioned ratios and steam circuits, and by retaining until 1897 uncoupled wheels for his passenger compounds. Despite their defects, nearly all the compounds main-tained excellent annual mileages while Webb was chief, and at no time did they throw any extra stress on Crewe Works except in details such as the handling of 30in pistons and cylinder covers. In the 1890s Teutonic compounds ran up to 80,000 miles between heavy repairs at Crewe, whereas the earlier and smaller Experiments and Dread-noughts managed only 45,000 miles and the 2-cylinder simple Precedents 56,000 to 60,000 miles.

Whatever the new locomotive production, the major operation at Crewe was always the number of locomotive overhauls. From 1873 to 1903 that number ranged from 1,350 to 1,650 yearly. In Ramsbottom's time anything up to 30 percent of repairs were intermediate or light repairs, but Webb diminished that proportion though he never eliminated intermediates. The figures of around 2,000 repairs at Crewe in a year claimed by Findlay[8] in 1889 and by Cooke[9] in 1893 were rounded-off exaggerations based on the early years when many intermediates were being done, and they included rebuilds. The figure of 300 engines under repair at one time given by both authors included engines standing outside awaiting repair space and others that were completed but in the paint shop or in the weighbridge area. The engines to which repairs were given rose from a maximum weight of 36 tons in 1870 to 57 tons in 1897 and 60 tons in 1903, and maximum frame length went up from 24ft in 1870 to 32ft

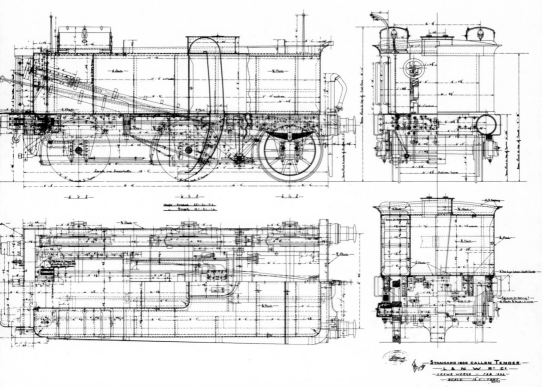

Fig 25 General arrangement of LNWR 1800-gallon wooden-framed tender as built from the 1870s to the 20th Century

6in in 1891. Moreover, from 1893 increasing numbers of 8-wheel engines were built and came in for repair.

The scale on which work was done at Crewe throughout Webb's time shown in Table 7. This includes the number of engines scrapped, for cutting-up old locomotives was a continuous activity in Nos 1 and 2 erecting shops at the Old Works, proceeding alongside the stripping and re-erection of repaired engines. The degree of scrapping as distinct from sale of old engines was influenced by the needs of the Crewe steel plant for good-quality scrap, and a total of around 1,500 obsolete engines was scrapped under Webb.

The No 1 erecting shop book kept by foreman A. Roberts for 30 years from 1860 shows that in addition to rebuilding and scrapping numerous old engines this shop also did the conversion of the first Webb compound, the altered Crewe-type single then numbered 1874 but later bearing duplicate number 3088. The No 1 shop book entry is: "16 August 1878. No 1874 Passr. Reduced LH cylinder to 9 inches and put valve box in smokebox to work compound." The Met-type 4-4-0T No 2073 also was converted to a 3-cylinder compound in this shop in February 1884 under erector J. Oakden, while the ex-LCR

2-4-0 (originally with a Beattie boiler) then numbered 1866 was fitted with Westinghouse brakes to engine and tender in 1872 at a cost of £34 6s 7½d [£34·33] for trials on the Euston–Watford trains.

Engines shown in Table 7 as rebuilt did not give such a heavy work load as might be thought from the numbers, for in the Webb years an engine was considered as rebuilt if it was given a new boiler, new boiler and cylinders, or new boiler, cylinders and valve motion, perhaps with the addition of a cab. Of the real rebuilds the most important were the 26 conversions of Crewe-type LFB 2-4-0s into saddle tanks, and the 500 DX engines altered to Special DX over the years 1881–98, for which cabs, new steel boilers working at a higher pressure, steam brakes on engine and tender, vacuum equipment for train brakes, hooped-web crank axles, and different smokeboxes and trailing springs were provided, while the bronze axleboxes were changed to cast-iron with bronze crowns and whitemetal inserts. From the mid-1890s many Special DX engines on conversion or heavy repair were given built-up crank axles.

All the tenders included in Table 7 had wooden frames made up of two inside baulks 15in deep by 3½in thick and two outside baulks 11in deep by 4⅜in thick, with wooden transoms and buffer beams. This type (see Fig 25) continued until 1904 in new construction in tank capacities of 1500 to 2500 gallons, and it brought many joiners into the tender shop. Many of these tenders lasted until LMSR days. The number of new tenders built did not correspond to the number of new tender locomotives, for after suitable repair many old tenders were allocated to new engines, and from 1867 there was always a tender 'negative float' as described in Chapter 5.

The number of men employed, as shown in the bottom line of Table 7 is that at Crewe Works as a whole, and includes those engaged in steel and signal manufacture, at the brick yard, gas plant, in the out-station shop, and in works transport, but not the 600 to 700 men (drivers, firemen, cleaners, fitters, clerks) of the locomotive-running department at Crewe sheds, nor the men employed in the carriage repair, cleaning and storage sheds away to the west. The figures are the averages for the years listed; within any year the number might vary by several hundred according to dismissals because of shortage of work. In quite a number of years after 1876 short-time working was in force for months at a stretch.

On the other hand, the works areas which have from time to time been given without explanation in various LNWR, LMSR and BR handouts and publications, are inclusive of the gasworks and tip, the carriage establishment, and two cooling ponds between the

Two new 14in 0–4–0STs coupled back-to-back for special trials in 1865; handled by one crew

Below: Coal engine and the gang that erected it in $25\frac{1}{2}$ working hours in 1878. Foreman George Dingley on the footplate; Bowen Cooke is the third figure in white from the left-hand side   (*NRM, York*)

Bottom: Ramsbottom's *Newton* in the standard green when new in 1866. No 1 erecting shop to right; office-stores block to left

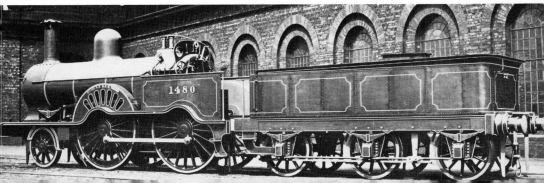

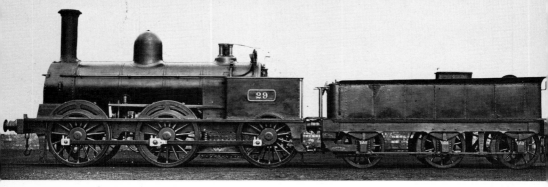

Standard DX completed in 1871, photographed in 1879 with Webb chimney. Over the years 1858–75 a total of 943 was built at Crewe, of which 86 were for the LYR

Below: 3-cylinder compound 2–2–2–0 when new in September 1884, against the south wall of the Old Works fitting shop; Webb is in the cab

Bottom: The 10-ton duplex steam hammer. After some months' trial service in 1866 it was supplemented by a 30-ton duplex; both operated for 30 years

Chester line and Victoria Avenue. The carriage ground eventually amounted to some 27 acres. Nor was all the remaining land devoted to works purposes; it included much spare ground such as the football field and the waste land between that and the brick yard. The published total did not include Crewe North depot and its approach lines, or the ground between the Warrington and Manchester lines that was used successively by the carriage department, permanent-way department, and the grease works, some of which eventually was taken by the freight line fly-unders of the Crewe station re-arrangement scheme of 1896–1906.

Two factors in Crewe engine-repair work and LNWR locomotive-running performance under Webb have remained generally unnoticed. First, for an increase in locomotive stock rising steadily to 60 percent over the 31 years, the number of heavy repairs undertaken at the works did no more than equal the combined total of heavy and intermediate repairs effected annually in 1870–71, but more rebuilding and reboilering were done. Very approximately, the weight of repaired engines (exclusive of tenders) increased from about 38,000 tons a year in 1875 to over 50,000 tons in 1900. Annual mileage per engine in stock rose from 17,120 in 1871 to 24,800 in 1900, and the increased ton-mileage per engine was reflected in a further 15 percent in fuel consumption above the pro-rata mileage figure. These last factors in general were what determined the need for and extent of heavy repairs. Distance run between heavy repairs increased, but time between repairs did not alter markedly.

Second, for 27 years of Webb's 31½-year régime the total under-cover pit length for engines (exclusive of tenders) remained the same at around 7,125ft. LNWR charts considered this as equal to 245 six-wheel engines (see Fig 24), which meant an average of 29ft per engine and the space between it and the next. However, from the early 1880s No 7 erecting shop was diverted much to boiler-mounting and boiler-test work. In No 1 shop engine scrapping accounted continuously for a portion of the pit length, while up to half of No 4 could be engaged in new construction, so that not more than 205 to 210 engines actually could be under repair on the pits at a time. Throughout the year Crewe invariably had that number on the stocks, plus others standing outside awaiting pit space, with others completed but in the paint shop or on the outgoing tracks, so that 290 to 310 engines were always in the works area. In 1898 erecting shop No 8 was lengthened, increasing the effective repair capacity to around 240 engines, and 320–340 locomotives were then in the works area. The number of engines awaiting repair on the works tracks then sometimes rose to one hundred.

Table 7 Crewe Works production through Webb's period as chief

Year	1870	1875	1880	1885	1890	1895	1899	1900	1901	1902	1903
New locomotives built	69	110	93	89	70	91	110	100	90	105	95
Locomotives rebuilt	89	56	136	83	109	93	84	134	148	113	100
Locomotives cut up	5	20	39	38	45	59	50	68	68	48	36
Locomotives sold	–	9	6	1	3	4	1	7	4	9	2
Locomotives given heavy repairs	1770[1]	1291	1477	1564	1325	1205	1373	1257	1304	1355	1459
Locomotives painted	521	606	497	400	303	579	420	434	466	351	344
New tenders built	90	84	–	–	7	7	38	30	20	35	25
Tenders rebuilt	–	–	73	52	57	67	114	93	37	35	69
Tenders repaired	1092	1008	1024	1123	960	876	849	832	847	973	1039
Crank axles manufactured	211	260	218	174	106	235	182	218	175	166	234
New boilers built	–	–	–	182	175	246	211	211	226	219	197
Boilers repaired	–	–	–	129	158	224	195	197	204	255	339
Average staff employed	4093	5460	5617	6224	6295	6990	7357	7376	7460	7634	7842

Including about 28% intermediate repairs

Though the actual time of overhaul was as short as in most other railway shops, say 40 days on the pits, the time out of traffic was long, and resulted during the later years of the 19th century in 11 to 13 percent of the whole stock always being at Crewe. This in itself was an improvement over the 15 or 16 percent in the early 1870s and the 19–20 percent in the late 1860s, but in the last-mentioned period the guiding rule still was to work engines easily. In fact, the measure of Crewe performance under Webb was that by 1900 the works could maintain in good order a stock of 3,000 hard worked engines as against 1,800 easily worked units 30 years earlier.

Contributing to the sustained repair output of ever longer and heavier engines was the frequent acquisition of new and better machine tools bought out or made at Crewe, to revised procedures, and to the commissioning of new forges, foundries, wheel shops and the like, but there was by no means a clean sweep-out of the old. A visitor to Crewe in 1884 notes: "The tools in Crewe shops are all of good kind, but a large number are old-fashioned." In fact, a prominent Crewe characteristic up to the 1960s was always the perpetuation of the very old among the very new. Axlebox brasses of 7½in by 13½in to suit the Greater Britain and John Hick classes of 2-2-2-2 compounds were still being skimmed up in 1902 and after on a Whitworth lathe of pre-Crewe vintage, bearing the date 1842. Several machines of Trevithick's time lasted in both Old Works and Steelworks until LMSR days, while some men active today have worked on machines bearing the initials 'GJR'. One old Whitworth lathe of 1847 lasted in the tender shop until the very end of new steam construction in 1958.

On beginning design of his own engines in 1872 (the 0-6-0 coal engines and 2-4-0 Precursors that appeared first in 1873) Webb adopted many of the wearing parts and other constituents of Ramsbottom's freight and passenger engines, though more details were of steel in place of iron. Precursor parts built to DX drawings included pistons, piston rods, crossheads, slide blocks, eccentric straps and bolts, nuts and cotters, eccentric sheaves and bolts, reversing wheel, connecting-rods, small-ends with strap, gib and cotter, big-end strap, gib and syphon, safety-valves and casing. The big-end brasses, dome, trailing springs, firedoor handle, ashpan, smokebox door, and coupling pipes were the same as those of the new coal engine; the steel coupling rods and bushes were the same as those of the Samsons; delightfully, the blastpipe was the same as that of the old Large Bloomer 2-2-2s of Wolverton type.

Similar principles were applied to the 6ft 6in 2-4-0 Precedents built from 1874, and to the 5ft express goods 0-6-0s and later passenger

0-6-2Ts with the same size of wheel. In the final Webb stages the 4-cylinder compound 4-6-0s of 1903–05 had the same boiler, cylinders, valve motion, reversing gear, axles and axleboxes as the 4-cylinder compound 0-8-0s and the same front truck as the Jubilee and Alfred 4-4-0s. By the late 1890s the same pattern of connecting-rod at 5ft 11in centres was being used in over 2,000 simple expansion engines, and boiler shells were standard among over a thousand 2-4-0s, 0-6-0s and 0-6-2Ts. The degree of standardisation then was higher than in any subsequent time to the end of steam.

Following Ramsbottom's practice in the 0-4-0Ts, the same pattern of cast-iron wheel centre, with a rim diameter of just under 4ft to suit tread diameters of 4ft 3in to 4ft 5½in according to the thickness of the tyre applied, was used in the unbalanced form, but with 12 spokes in place of the 10 in the 0-4-0ST and 0-4-2ST types, eventually in a total of about 1,100 engines of 2-4-0, 0-6-0, 0-6-0ST and 0-6-2T types, and later, with balance weights cast between certain of the I-section spokes, also in numerous main line 0-8-0s. This extensive use resulted from a cost analysis of 1872 that showed a wrought-iron centre of 4ft diameter cost £16 16s 0d [£16·80] to make and machine, whereas the cast-iron centre cost only £3 9s 7d [£3·48] of which merely 8s 8d [43p] was charged to machining. This detail alone meant in Webb's time a total saving in construction costs above £100,000.

The close discipline Webb imposed was needed to get unswerving adequate production from a widespread area in which some erecting shops were separated by a mile from the main machine shop, and in which many large parts had to travel two miles between fabrication and being dropped into the frames. Alongside this strict discipline trade unionism grew but slowly until the late 1880s, although as early as 1843 there was in Crewe a branch of the Journeyman Steam-Engine Makers' Society, a workman member of which was William Allan, later well known as secretary of the Amalgamated Society of Engineers from 1851 to 1874. To some extent the rise of trade unionism in the town was influenced by the bitter political war in the town council 1885–91 resulting from what was seen as railway rule; but the absolute authority of foremen to engage or sack workers without higher appeal often led to resentment, and to fear because of the instability of employment at the works. From time to time letters in the Cheshire press described life within the works as "a reign of terror."

Insecurity of employment was the most disturbing feature until World War I, for substantial pay-offs were the rule whenever work was slack, though mitigated as such by short-time working from 1876 onwards, either five-day or four-day. Slack periods of this kind in

Webb's day occurred in 1879, 1885, 1888, and above all in 1893–94, when a general miners' strike brought on a long-drawn depression. Against these a workman's main protection was to belong to the same sect, have the same political colour, or to be in the same company of the Volunteers as his manager or foreman. Though foremen could impose discipline without resort to higher authority, they were themselves under close control. While all this was considered normal in large industrial areas, Crewe was in an agricultural district and many of the workers had a rural background and continued to live outside the town. The outlook was always different from that in, say, South Yorkshire and the Black Country.

Strict control at all levels was imposed not because Webb was a natural tyrant but because he realised absolute discipline was needed to get sustained orderly production from a far-flung works with over 5,000 employees, otherwise the system of Trevithick would return with disastrous results. Webb and Worsdell let nothing pass. One day Capper, the yard foreman, received a note from Worsdell beginning: "This morning Mr Webb and I noticed for a length of time all the platelayers in these sidings standing doing *nothing – every one.*" Again, Martin the steel plant and gas works foreman received: "This morning going down to the gas works I found *six* strangers loafing in the house – four young men and two boys . . . I never go down there without finding strangers. Please put a *complete* stop to this practice." To Braidwood, another foreman: "When you have a report to make will you please get some one to copy it at your dictation, and then you sign it. I find myself unable to read some of your words." Capper had to be adjured to stop cutting timber in the Steelworks land as it had already been sold by the estate department. Worsdell also reproved Kean, the head storekeeper: "I have often requested you not to write all over the papers as you have done in this case. If you are short of a few memorandum sheets I can send you some."

How things change but little with the generations is shown by a note of Worsdell in 1873 to foreman Cole: "The following men are to be fined one day's pay for climbing over the fence near the bridge instead of going out the gate [here follows a list of the six], also J. Jones the apprentice who gave in their checks. They may consider themselves very leniently dealt with – the regulation punishment can be dismissal." In the fall of 1979, 106 years later, shops in Crewe Works carried an official warning: "It has come to notice that there is a tendency for staff on both day and night turns to clock on and off the time cards for other individuals. All concerned are warned that this practice must cease forthwith."

Borough status was granted to Crewe in 1877, but by 1880 trouble was arising through the naturally dominant position of the LNWR in the town. The emergence of independent candidates nominated for the town council in the railway interest, and the pressure put by foremen on workers to vote 'independent' or Conservative was fiercely opposed by those of Liberal faith. Friction and strife increased until in 1890 some of the Liberal councillors, after writing to Gladstone, bought a few LNWR shares and attended the annual general meeting. There they moved amendments to the directors' report, which though defeated, resulted soon in political freedom within the works and the retirement of Webb, Whale and other leading officers from active town work. Behind the Liberal 'platform' for political freedom for the workers in town and State was the intention that a Liberal council should control a town half owned and built by the railway, and in which the LNWR would continue as the largest ratepayer without direct representation and which would be expected to continue, and even increase, the numerous public facilities it provided free.

Throughout Webb's time experimental and development activities at the works were continuous. The Old Works handled such things as hydraulic brakes, steel brake blocks, vacuum brake modifications, Westinghouse brake trials, piston-valves, triple-expansion steam circuits, circular slide-valves for locomotives and hydraulic machinery, radial axleboxes, combined injector and clackbox, gauge-glass fittings, train-lighting from steam engine dynamo sets in tenders, automatic condensing equipment for tank engines working in the London district, friction-drive wheels, sight-feed lubricators, and double-exhaust with divided smokebox. The Steelworks developed built-up balanced and unbalanced crank axles of plain and nickel steels, cast-steel connecting rods of I-section, copper alloy and steel side-stays for copper fireboxes, brick-lined fireboxes, water-tube grates, water-bottom fireboxes, intermediate combustion chambers, steel fireboxes of two-piece, circular, figure-8 and normal forms, steel sleepers, and a steel fishplate and joint chair combined in one.

Of all these only the combined injector-clackbox, built-up crank axles, radial axleboxes and circular slide-valves became normal practice, the last-named mainly in hydraulic equipment. Water-tube grates or water-bottom boxes were put in a number of 4-wheel and express engines; intermediate combustion chambers were installed only in 20 compound 2-2-2-2s and one 0-8-0. Piston valves were fitted to various engines for road trials, and to many 5ft 0-6-2T engines as normal practice. The side-stay experiments with steel, and with zinc, tin and aluminium alloys of copper were undertaken around 1900–02 because in Webb's words: "I have charge of 3,000 boilers containing 2½ million stays, and the position is not exactly a bed of roses."

Webb patented more than 75 inventions from 1864 to 1903. Many did not get beyond the drawing board and experimental stage. In his last dozen years the schemes and patent claims were drafted initially in a small locked office off the drawing office by John Scragg, a stumpy, large-nosed untidily-moustached confidential draughtsman who lasted until around 1920. This office was known as the model room, for here full-size models of Stephenson, Allan and Joy motions were set on adjustable cast-iron columns sliding over ground-steel facings; in that room were investigated the theoretical events and merits of other valve motions, including over the years 1899–1903 the Marshall and Younghusband forms, and in Whale's time the Walschaerts gear.

Until the Giffard patents expired in February 1872 injectors were obtained from the English licencee, Sharp Stewart & Co, but by the time of the expiry Webb already had come to an agreement to make at Crewe that firm's patent improved Giffard injector free of royalty for LNWR locomotives, as long as the injectors were stamped 'Robinson & Gresham's patent'. This patent had been taken out in 1864 mainly to eliminate the leakage of the earlier form. From that time all injectors for LNWR engines were made in the Old Works fitting shop.

Beginning with the Greater Britain class in the 1890s Webb incorporated some of the features of the White automatic re-starting and lifting or non-lifting injector, the invention of an ex-Gresham & Craven man, to give more certain action. This had no moving or sliding pieces in the nozzle that could wear or stick, and it was in two parts screwed together. White himself made his injectors and miscellaneous steam fittings for other customers in a small works at Pendleton, Manchester, until well after World War I, while Crewe made everything needed for LNWR injectors. With this development the injector was first retained on the firebox back and had White's own valve for warming the tender water. Later the whole installation was changed; the combined injector-clackbox was given up, the injector was mounted on the back of the ashpan below the footplate, and the joint between the two parts was on a different plane. The clackbox on the firebox back continued to deliver by direct pipe to the centre of the barrel. An early White injector mounted on the firebox back is to be found on the preserved *Columbine* in the National Railway Museum.

Properly presented and unified accounts plus better engine and crew allocations were among the reasons leading to the consolidation of the locomotive divisions in 1857 and 1862. Thereafter Moon continued to expect adequate stores and departmental accounts monthly from Ramsbottom and Webb and their locomotive accountants. As the department grew the accounts became more complicated; departmental wage accounts alone rose from covering 10,600 workers in 1870 to 21,000 in 1900, and all the book entries were finally summated at Crewe, where two or three hundred clerks were employed. Eventually from the works accounts a form of departmental cost accounting was developed. Additional to the monthly statements for the board, which included Crewe production with engine and spares costs, engine mileage, wages, material, and comparisons with the same month of the preceding year, Webb introduced largely for his own purposes of control a system of graphic statistics mainly to show how the cost of coal and other raw materials influenced Crewe works and locomotive-department costs. A figure Webb himself quoted from time to time was the total locomotive-department expenditure as a percentage of LNWR revenue—usually around 11½ percent.

The standard coloured chart came to show variations of 28 items over the 40-odd years from 1860 to 1903, for when compilation of the chart began in the mid-1870s Webb had whatever figures were available from earlier years put in to give the graph a start. This was an early attempt to relate raw materials and works production to the rate of return on investment, a financial yardstick that proved essential in the 20th century for the top-level control of such large undertakings as General Motors. Additional to the chart were monthly statements from the works manager as to repair production in each erecting shop and production per man employed.

Making everything at Crewe reduced the inventory of material and spare parts held in the works against the time they would be needed, and reduced the inventories of certain other departments spread over the LNWR system for which Crewe made parts, so reducing the amount of railway capital locked up in these items, for apart from the steel plant only trifling additions to capital had been needed for the additional manufacturing facilities. This was an aspect to which Webb always gave attention, for he visualised the locomotive department as a unit of the LNWR, to which it had to make a contribution. Rail-rolling and steel-making had arisen from different causes as related in Chapter 3 and Chapter 5, but they were just as closely bound up with the well-being of the parent company.

To give a telling explanation of one section of the works analysis, Webb in the 1890s had a photograph taken of the first 3-cylinder compound 0-8-0 in its finished state, and in front of it stock piles of the materials needed to get it to that condition. These showed that for the

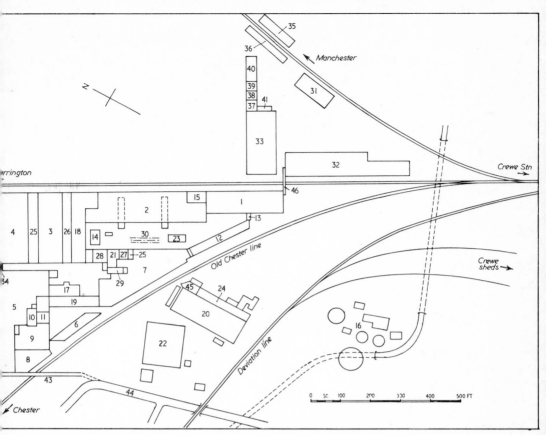

1 No 1 Erecting shop 2 No 2 Erecting shop 3 No 3 Erecting shop 4 No 4 Erecting shop 5 Smithy 6 Forge
7 Fitting shop 8 Forge yard 9 Rolling mill 10 Bolt smithy 11 Boiler house 12 Stores and general offices
13 Clock-tower arch 14 Copper shop 15 Boiler and engine house 16 Gasworks 17 Spring shop 18 Wheel
shop 19 Boiler repair shop 20 Tender shop 21 Stores 22 Iron rail mill 23 Iron stores 24 Stores 25 Frame
shop 26 Tube brazing shop 27 Boiler house 28 Engine house 29 Casehardening furnaces 30 Tyre racks
31 Works entrance 32 Painting shop (locomotives and carriages) 33 Carriage repair shop 34 Carriage repairs
35 General workshop 36 Carriage stores 37 Carriage smithy 38 Carriage turning shop 39 Boiler house
40 Grease works 41 Lamp room 42 Forge Street 43 Footbridge 44 Mill Street 45 Fire engine house
46 Birdswood Footbridge

Fig 26 Layout of Old Works, Old Carriage Repair Works and Grease Plant in 1874

45¾ton (empty) engine 139 tons of material were needed; the
complete breakdown is given in Table 8.

From around 1884 the three sections of the works between them
were, after the receipt of raw materials, making everything needed in
steam locomotives except copper firebox plates, copper bars for side
stays, and tubes of copper, brass and steel; on occasion Crewe even
made the steel for the last-named and sent it to tube makers for
forming. Yet after 1866 neither the Steelworks nor the Old Works was
ever self-contained; there was always much transport of parts between
one and the other. The Old Works continued to make for all engines,
new and repaired, such essential parts as injectors, ejectors, driver's
brake valves, steam-heating cocks and boiler mountings. From the

mid-1880s with the exception of light smith's work and forgings and drop stampings, all the major parts for engines erected at the Old

Table 8   Materials needed to make a 45¾ton (empty)
3-cylinder compound 0-8-0

Material	Weight			
	Tons	Cwt	Qr	lb
Coal	57	10	0	0
Steel scrap	28	2	3	15
Pig iron	24	6	0	7
Wrought-iron scrap	7	6	0	0
Swedish iron	6	9	0	0
Copper ingot	4	19	1	21
Coke	4	12	0	0
Spiegeleisen	2	16	3	17
Cast-iron scrap	1	10	1	15
Limestone		18	1	1
Block tin		4	3	14
Lead			2	27
Tile zinc			2	20
Phosphorous copper			2	14
Ferro-manganese		1	0	20
Red ore		1	0	8
Chrome			1	2
Aluminium				13
Antimony				4
Total	139	0	2	2

Works and Steelworks, such as frames, castings, cylinders and the like, were brought in the rough state from the Steelworks for machining, because until 1903 the main machine shop for the whole plant remained in the Old Works. The intense and complicated transfer of large and small parts was a weak point in Crewe practice that was not eased until 1903 and only rectified in 1927.

By the early 1890s the main fitting-machine shop in the Old Works had over 380 machine tools and employed about 700 hands, but its most irregular shape and even more irregular roof, arrived at by piecemeal additions over 40 years, was congested in the extreme, and in 1893 Bowen Cooke wrote of it as "a perfect maze of pulleys, straps, shafting, revolving wheels and machinery of every description." Some time after the new main office block was built in 1876–77 the fitting shop was extended by putting a series of machine tools and brass-finishing equipment along the ground floor of the original stores and office building, and it was here that brass fittings were made. As related in Chapter 5, that building had been given a third floor in the early 1860s and Webb eventually put an hydraulic lift in the corner against the fitting shop to get parts up and down.

In the Deviation works substantial improvements were made in the second Crewe iron foundry, in the blast through the cupolas, and in the use of moulding machines for thin-wall castings. In the works as a whole a new smelting process was evolved to separate brass and ferrous swarf and borings from the machine tools; new quartering machines were developed for wheel and crank settings, a portable crankpin turner was designed for inside pins that was clamped to the centre portion of the axle, gas-fired furnaces replaced the old slack-fired type in the spring shop, and even such things as grindstone dressing received the personal attention of Webb and Worsdell.

Drop-stamping was initiated in the north-west corner of the Old Works by Webb almost immediately on his accession, and within his first year he was making dome covers by stamping a flat plate under a drop hammer with the plate at red heat; three blows shaped the cover, and two more, with water thrown into the dies, gave it a complete finish. Manhole covers were made in the same way.

Extensions of the buildings at the Steelworks end continued without a break, and in 1874–76 several large new shops began operations. In general these were in accord with the principle of gradual east-west extension in echelon begun by Ramsbottom. Extensions of the steel plant were all in a westward direction from the Bessemer nucleus alongside the Chester main line. The two Siemens converters of 1869 were replaced in February 1876 by four 7-ton open-hearth melting furnaces and a fifth was added in 1881. Two of the 1876 furnaces were on a raised platform; in the other two the casting pit was below floor level. In July 1888 some of the Siemens equipment was replaced by a 20-ton furnace and in 1898 a 30-ton furnace was added; both of these lasted until 1925. The Bessemer plant continued at work and was not given up until the turn of the century, the last blow being on 8 February 1901. After it was dismantled in 1903–04 its site was occupied first by a store for castings, and later by hydraulic accumulators.

While the Bessemer plant was in full bloom in 1878, the well-known engineer F. J. Bramwell during a visit of the Institution of Mechanical Engineers injudiciously poked his umbrella at the open end of one of the cylinders of a blowing engine; material and ribs were sucked in, jammed the engine, twisted a rocking shaft, and cancelled a demonstration due to begin in 20 minutes, and Bramwell doubtless got a hearty damning from Webb.

A complete new steel rail mill was erected beyond the furnaces; the cogging and rolling mills were designed and built at Crewe except for the Hick Hargreaves 1,200hp Corliss-type engine driving the triple-decker rolls. This plant did not begin regular operation until October 1875, after some months of experimental production and adjustments, and by the middle of 1876 production rate had risen to 10,000 tons a year. Change-over from iron to steel rails was described in Chapter 5. This mill produced 30ft steel rails of 75lb/yd section, but from 1887 a 90lb section was adopted as the main-line standard for relaying, though still in 30ft lengths. From 1905 the 95lb BS section was adopted as the LNWR standard, and at the same time an 85lb section was introduced for secondary lines. The Crewe mill produced all of these, along with BS chairs and fishplates.

In 1893 the rail mill equipment was reconstructed to suit a 60ft rail length which became the standard for main-line relaying in April 1894 and was retained until after the end of the LNWR. The first stretch of these long rails was laid at Betley Road, south of Crewe. The greater length necessitated a quicker means of returning the rail to the rolls for the next pass, and this was in the form of an inclined frame with rollers. The alterations needed for the 60ft rails led to the closure of mill and steel plant for some weeks in 1893 while the whole works was on short time.

All rails were of Siemens-Marten steel from 1875, and from 1876 to 1896 production averaged around 20,000 tons a year except in 1893, when as a result of the plant closure and short-time working there was a marked drop. Crewe steel production for all purposes of the LNWR had risen to about 53,000 tons a year by 1884–85, but some products had to pass two or three times through the furnaces, and related to a single pass the production was equivalent to over 80,000 tons, and some 35,000 tons of coal and slack were consumed in the plant each year.

Adjoining the rail mill at its west end was put in 1876–77 a new shop 110ft square for the manufacture of points and crossings. This was equipped with two big 4-tool planers for machining switches. The capacity of this shop was increased in 1880–82, but it was not thereafter enhanced until World War II. Its floor height was some 4ft above normal so that open wagons could be run alongside and permanent way material loaded easily.

Ramsbottom's new boiler shop of 1869–70, originally about 250ft long and 107ft wide, and far to the west of the Bessemer plant but in line with it, was extended westward from time to time by Webb to a total length of 673ft, the last extension being in 1898–99 when new ground to the west of the old Coppenhall Hey lane was taken in. In an alteration in 1890–91 the roof at the then west end of the centre bay was greatly raised in the form of a rivetting tower to enable the 25ft 4in long boiler-firebox structure of the 2-2-2-2 compounds to be rivetted-up while slung vertically. In the later 1960s this tower was removed, but the roof level there is still three or four feet higher than over the remainder of the shop.

One of Webb's earliest progressive installations, around 1872, was Tweddell's hydraulic rivetting machines for boiler-shell and foundation-ring rivetting, and from 1874–75 these were supplemented by others of portable type, just then evolved by Tweddell in conjunction with Fielding & Platt, who made his machines. Webb stated[10] in 1885 that in normal boilers "there was not a single rivet that could not be put in by hydraulic pressure, and hand rivetting had been entirely abandoned", and "the day of drifting and 4½lb flogging hammers had gone."

A few years after the change-over to steel for boiler shells Webb eliminated all firehole rings and brought copper inner and steel outer plates together. A special machine was devised to flange both plates exactly, and another machine with special attachments drilled the rivet holes through both plates together. This was the first drilling of rivet holes in Crewe boilers apart from those in the smokebox angle ring. A later development in large boilers was the flangeing of the outer firebox backplate in similar ogee fashion so that both rivet heads securing it to the wrapper were on outside surfaces. This led to complicated foundation ring sealing, but was desirable so that all rivetting could be done more easily hydraulically, and so that the bigger-waisted inside boxes could be inserted from the back end.

Before the boiler shop had gone over to steel construction for shell, outer firebox, smokebox tubeplate, dome and foundation ring as standard practice in 1874–75, Webb had tried five steel inside boxes in 1872–73, based on part of his patent 3403 of 1869, possibly because to his favour for steel generally was added the American experience of Worsdell, who was for five years on the Pennsylvania Railroad at a time when that system had over 400 steel inner boxes in service. One of these Crewe-built all-steel boilers and an additional inside steel firebox were on show at the Vienna International Exhibition in 1873.

The inner box sides, back plate and front plate were in one piece – that is, a true wrapper. The crown plate was separate and flanged down to make the top seams. The front face of the wrapper had a dished circular hole in the top portion to take a circular firebox tubeplate; the flanges led forward and a copper caulking ring was inserted. Firebox side and roof stays were all of steel. The tubes also were of steel, but as Webb was trying to push home-produced steel for everything, sheets were rolled at Crewe and then formed into tubes by Jas. Russell & Sons at Wednesbury. All these special features were the reasons for failure, not the use of steel itself; though no more of these special boxes were built, there were thereafter always one or two steel boxes of normal form on the LNWR in Webb's time. One of the last Crewe-type 2-4-0Ts (No 3097) sold out of service for £500 in February 1903 had a steel inner firebox and steel tubes when it left.

Boiler shop ingenuity and skill were needed again in 1888–90 with further experimental steel fireboxes, for here Webb was trying to eliminate or substantially reduce the number of side stays at the same time as replacing copper by steel. Some of these boxes were in figure-8 form with two cylindrical portions one above the other, and the top one was of return-flue type. Others were of cubic form with vertical corrugations on the sides and back of the inner box. Both types had D-shaped combustion chambers. A few were applied to Special DX and other engines.

In 1879 the boiler shop constructed a barrel about 11ft long from a single $\frac{7}{16}$in plate of Crewe steel, and this seems to have been not only the first single-ring barrel but also the first English taper barrel apart from one Weston combustion-chamber wagon-top boiler on the Great Eastern Railway, though the taper was only from 4ft 0¼in at the back to 3ft 10⅝in at the front. This was done to make the boiler standard as to front tubeplate, mounting and other details with previous three-ring telescopic barrels.

By the end of Webb's time the boiler shop was employing 1,100 men and boys, and was building and overhauling up to 450 boilers a year in addition to doing much general steel structural work. When the rivetting tower was raised in 1891 it was given two 15-ton electrically-operated overhead cranes, and in the later 1890s five more similar cranes of 10 to 20 tons capacity were put into the remainder of the shop. In the same years electric drive was provided for some of the tools, while many pneumatic portable and semi-portable caulking and rivetting machines were installed.

For many years power at the east end of the shop was given by one of the old wall engines popular in new construction for factories from about 1855 to 1875. They were usually 2-cylinder vertical type attached to a frame in the shop wall and with the crankshaft on top. Another of these engines was in the axle forge and tyre mill and lasted until the end of the LNWR.

The boiler shop and boiler-shop smithy alongside also handled steelwork for signal gantries, footbridges, large and small girder

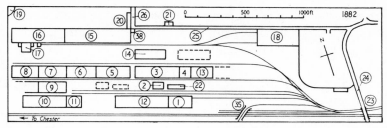

1 Steel plant 2 Boiler house 3 Axle forge 4 Spring mill 5 No 5 Erecting shop 6 No 6 Erecting shop 7 No 7 Erecting shop 8 No 8 Erecting shop 9 Boiler-shop smithy 10 Boiler shop 11 Points and crossings shop 12 Steel rail mill 13 New or iron forge 14 Copper shop 15 Tender shop 16 Iron foundry 17 Rail chair foundry 18 Paint shop 19 Brickworks 20 Workmen's dining room 21 Bessemer Hotel 22 Gas producers 23 Flag Lane Bridge over Old Chester and Deviation Tracks 24 Flag Lane 25 Richard Moon Street 26 Goddard Street 35 Eagle Bridge 38 Workmen's entrance

Fig 27 Layout of shops at Steelworks end, 1882

bridges, and the frames of standard engine sheds; mainly in those shops were fabricated in 1879 the 14 lattice and 28 plate girders, plus flooring plates and angles, spanning seven 32ft gaps for the replacement bridge at Llandulas after the original stone viaduct had been swept away by flood. This replacement structure was designed, and the material produced, put together in sections, and sent off within seven days, though actually 28 days elapsed from the wash-away to the full opening of the new bridge.

Further shops for other products and processes gradually were erected in parallel lines north of the steel-plant/boiler-shop row, the next row being made up of the boiler-shop smithy in 1869–70 (known later as the angle-iron smithy), a flangeing shop, and the plate stores. This row was end-on to the two principal boiler houses and gas-producer groups. This smithy eventually was extended to contain 60 hearths and three steam hammers. It handled, *inter alia*, the rivetting of the drop-stamped steel chairs from the Old Works on to the Webb steel sleepers that were rolled in the main west-end forge. Upwards of 100,000 trough-type steel sleepers, each weighing 100lb, were laid along LNWR main lines between 1880 and 1888. By 1907–08 all had been replaced by wooden sleepers and cast-iron chairs except for a short length outside the Crewe main office block, which remained until LMSR days, as did the adjoining wooden walkway made up of segments from old Mansell carriage wheels, and the wall base made from old stone sleepers from the GJR track of the 1830s. It was just here, also, that a pre-Deviation milepost lasted until the years of World War II.

A third parallel line of shops still further to the north eventually came to consist, from east to west, of the steel foundry, iron (or new) forge (1879), spring mill, axle forge and tyre mill (sometimes known as the steel forge), and the four erecting shops Nos 5 to 8, all 105ft wide and all with two bays. The axle forge was extended from the original forge buildings of 1864. The first west-end spring steel mill (August 1872) was located against the cogging shop of the Bessemer plant, and was moved into the axle-forge row in 1875 to make room for the new steel-rail mill.

As detailed in Chapter 5, erecting shops Nos 5 to 8 were among the first buildings in this row. No 8 as built was the shortest of all, until in 1898–99 it was extended to become the longest, and from that date the overall length of the four shops was 1,142ft. When brought into use all had the Ramsbottom cord-type overhead cranes. Traversers were provided at the west ends of Nos 5 and 7.

In Nos 1 to 4 shops in the Old Works the frames of new and repaired engines were set-up with the help of piano wires along the centre lines, whereas in the newer Nos 5 to 8 shops the frames of all repaired engines were re-erected on the base of lines scribed on the frames. In both works a repair engine was stripped and re-erected throughout by the same charge-hand and his gang, and new engines were erected in similar fashion in the Old Works.

Until 1897 all new engines were erected in No 4 shop at the Old Works but in that year, when an extension of No 8 had been agreed, the first two Jubilee 4-cylinder 4-4-0s Nos 1501–02 were erected in No 8, being followed by the remaining engines of that class, and from 1901 by the 4-cylinder compound 0-8-0s. Construction of smaller new engines, mainly the 5ft 0-6-2Ts, continued on a declining scale in No 4 until 1903, when with the commissioning of yet another Steelworks erecting shop, No 9, all new construction was transferred there, with Nos 4 and 8 reverting to repairs only.

When new engines came to be built at the Steelworks all frames and cylinders were set-up on stands at the east end of No 8 under the supervision of one charge-hand who kept to that work. Erection was with the use of templates and spirit levels, with the centre lines scribed on the frames. Then the frame structure was lifted one stage at a time westward, where at each two fitters and one apprentice performed certain defined operations, to which they were confined. The engine was completed at the west end of the shop and went straight out the west doors. This was the initiation of what 30 years later was developed into the Crewe belt system.

In Nos 3 and 4 shops in the Old Works the handling of new and repaired engines on coming in and on completion was difficult. After the elimination of the east-end traverser at the beginning of the Crewe

Rope-driven hornblock grinding machine for the thrust faces, introduced by Ramsbottom in the early 1860s. The machine here has been brought out on the shop traverser into the light for photographing. It dressed all 12 faces on a DX at one setting   (*NRM, York*)

Below: Bolt-making machine of Ramsbottom's time that operated for many years in the Old Works   (*NRM, York*)

Bottom: One of the 26 Webb rebuilds of the 1870s of Crewe-type LFB 2–4–0s into 2–4–0STs. No 1924 originally was No 310 *Isis* of 1853

No 4 erecting shop looking east, probably in autumn 1873. The left-hand wall is that below Forge Street. Nearest the camera is a Webb-built Newton 2–4–0; in the centre bay is a Webb-built Samson, and beyond it a wheel-and-axle pair from a Problem 2–2–2 on the shop cross-track, under the wrought-iron portion of the crane-run

"A perfect maze of pulleys, straps, shafts and revolving wheels" was Bowen Cooke's description of the Old Works fitting shop in the early 1890s
(*NRM, York*)

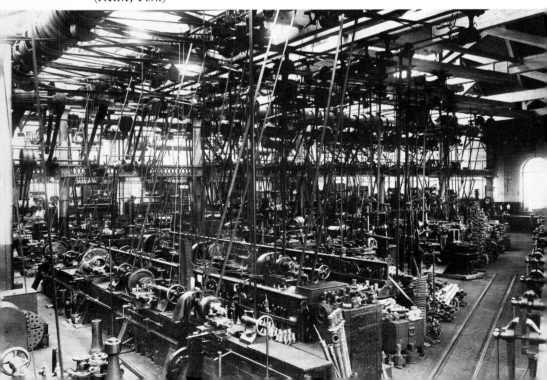

widened and avoiding lines scheme, all engines had to be lifted by crane and swung round at right-angles on to a cross track that ran through both shops. A Greater Britain or John Hick 2-2-2-2 had to be lifted by two cranes and tortuously swung round, and when the first Greater Britain was completed the gap in the arcade had to be widened to clear the swing. Once dropped on the cross track the engine was pulled through No 3 and proceeded straight on and out through the clock-tower arch. Small turntables were provided on the cross track to serve each of the inter-pit tracks in the shops, and small shop wagons could come in from the old Chester-track sidings via a narrow passage between the fitting shop and the smithy.

Erection of a new engine at the Old Works normally took around four weeks from the time the frame plates came forward to the shop, but on occasions of pressure it could be done in 14 days. Erection of a new 0-6-0 coal engine in 25½ working hours in August 1878 was simply a stunt. All the finished parts were laid ready by the pit or, like the boiler, were waiting to be dropped in. This engine was Crewe motion No 2153 and LNWR running No 1140. Normal working shifts were kept; erection began at 6.00am on Monday and was complete by midday on the Wednesday.

Erecting work at Crewe as well as the manufacture and machining of many constituents was done from early days by piece-work. With new equipment, methods, and increased skill of the workmen who were kept largely to one kind of job, piece-rates were cut from time to time to reduce costs or to keep them steady against increase in raw material prices. This led to the disgruntled outburst of a *Crewe Chronicle* correspondent in 1887, the year of Webb's mayoralty of the borough, stigmatising His Worship as "never behind in reducing workmen's wages" – a double thrust, for 'Never Behind' was the Crewe civic motto. The seal of the borough was neither a work of art nor a work of heraldry. Including the motto it depicted, and still does, five forms of transport, five horses, two men, one woman, fourteen words and one date.

By Crewe nomenclature from 1843 onwards erecting shops were not just what the term denoted, for wheel lathes, cylinder borers, planers and slotters were crammed into the narrow arcade between the two bays in several shops. Further, in Crewe terms, 'fitting shops' were really machine shops with fitters' benches and vises along and between the walls, and this applied especially to the main 'fitting' shop in the Old Works, which until 1903 was the main machine shop of the whole establishment. There were no separate real fitters' shops as were found in most locomotive works.

The steel foundry came to lie in the same echelon as Nos 5 to 8. It was not completed until the turn of 1883–84, and only in the latter year were the first wheel centres cast, after Webb had devised a centrifugal casting process with a machine on top of a Brotherhood 3-cylinder capstan engine turning at 40 to 60rpm according to the wheel size. By the summer of 1885 all wheel forges at Crewe were dismantled. This quick changeover in one of the principal features of the works completed the disappearance of the old wheelwright, which had begun a decade earlier when cast-iron wheel centres were introduced en masse for mineral engines. From 1885 all new engine and tender wheel centres were cast of iron or steel, though wrought-iron centres lasted all LNWR time through the practice of re-using old centres in good condition for new or replaced stock.

Despite this large foundry, about 335ft long and with three 10-ton melting furnaces, Webb never felt able to implement the patent he was granted in 1869 while at Bolton for a complete cast-steel frame block with cross-stretchers, hornblocks and all brackets, a proposal not put into effect anywhere until the 1920s with the first American cast-steel locomotive beds.

The iron forge, in its early years called the new forge, had three steam hammers, a quintuple set of rolls for bars and plates, three shearing machines, seven cranes, and a circular saw for hot metal ingots. This saw was originally in the Old Works and was transferred in 1873 just prior to the visit in June of the Shah of Persia, who was affrighted by the combination of noise and sparks when it was operated for his edification. The saw was 7ft diameter and ran at a maximum peripheral speed of 13,000ft per minute. Ramsbottom had it driven by a pair of standard 17in by 24in locomotive cylinders running at 150rpm and driving through step-up gears; when the saw was transferred the drive was replaced by a Brotherhood short-stroke (14in bore by 8in stroke) 3-cylinder single-acting engine coupled direct to the saw spindle.

In the axle (or steel) forge and tyre mill were rolled tyres for the carriage and wagon departments as well as for locomotives and tenders, and before the end of the century these shops were producing over 600 tyres a week. Equipment in this forge eventually included four steam hammers from 2½ to 8 tons, and two hydraulic forging presses, one of 1700 tons (from 1897) and the other of 2000 tons (from 1902). The latter had an early electric turning gear to handle large blooms. The single-throw crank axles of the three-cylinder compounds were bent in similar but smaller presses from 1883 to 1889, from a single 10in steel bar. Some of the punchers and other tools in this shop were driven for years by a diagonal steam engine.

When in 1874 this line of shops was practically complete except for the steel foundry and new forge, Bessemer Street still lay alongside the north wall of the axle forge, and in the large parcel of ground to the north-west acquired in 1864–65 there was only the brickworks. But in that year the first shop in that ground was erected – the tender shop, located some distance up Goddard Street and on the west side. When built, it was the largest single shop constructed at one time; it measured 530ft by 120ft and was in three bays. It came into full use through 1875–76. Like the erecting shops it had many machine tools, but these were all arranged in one bay. After the first two or three years, when there was a rail entry at the east end, vehicles could enter or leave the shop only by a traverser located near mid-length. In the later years of Webb the then new 20-ton steel wagons for locomotive coal traffic were built in this shop.

The next extension was into that portion of the new ground to the east of Goddard Street, and involved the disappearance of Bessemer Street, the Bessemer Vaults, a few houses, and the workmen's dining room put up in 1866. By this means ground was cleared for another row of shops in east-west line from the tender shop. The works entrance then was moved up Goddard Street (which was thus shortened), and outside the new long north wall was laid out Richard Moon Street in which was built (though not by the company) the Bessemer Hotel to take the place of the Vaults.

The first shop on this new eastward line was a paint shop, construction of which was begun in 1876–77, though use of the first portion seems to date from 1878. It was at the eastern end of the company's property to get it as far away as possible from the dirt and smoke of the other shops and the brickworks. It was on a different system of construction, for to suit its purpose it had no side windows, and light was admitted through short northern lights in a saw-tooth roof, while the roof-supporting pillars were of light section as there were no crane loads to carry.

This new shop was about 335ft long and 125ft broad with entrance and exit at the west end only, through wooden doors with semi-circular tops; distinct from all other shops, the extensions to it from 1884 were by the addition of further standard bays on the south side, and the length remained unaltered. Eventually it had a width of 205ft and standing room for nearly one hundred 6-wheel engines and their tenders on 16 tracks.

Just where completed engines were painted in the two decades before this shop was opened is an elusive subject. There was a painters' shop portion in No 2 machine shop in the Old Works from early days, but it held only stores, brushes, and so on. There are 'painting shop' references from 1867, but no drawing available shows where the shop was, nor do surviving plans show any undefined building. There existed at one time also what was known among enthusiasts as the 'Crewe paint shop book' begun in 1851–52 and into which had been put certain earlier dates like that of *Columbine*; more correctly this book was an erecting shop book into which some painting dates had been put. Painting *may* have been done in the erecting shops, or possibly in the coach painting shop to the east of the Warrington line; certainly it was coincident with the disuse of the latter shop and the building of a new carriage establishment away to the west that the new locomotive paint shop was put in hand.

Tender and paint shops were separated by some 1,080ft, and this space was not filled up for some years. In the meantime a new line of two-bay shops was started between the axle forge and tender shop rows. It began with a coppersmiths' shop on what had been the site of the Bessemer Vaults and the old workmen's dining room. A new dining room to which the men brought their own food was built in Goddard Street to the north of the tender shop. Rules were strict that men should use this and not eat their meals in the shops, so food-heating and tea-boiling facilities were provided.

Next to the east from the copper shop was the wheel shop, 281ft long and of the 85ft width standard for this echelon. Among equipment transferred from the Old Works was one lathe that could take the 8ft 9in (with 3in tyres) wheels of *Cornwall*; that lathe must have dated from 1847. In this shop tyres were shrunk onto the centres. Turning and boring mills for centre and tyre machining were installed, and machining done for new solid cranked and straight axles. Until built-up crank axles were introduced the crank throws were cut out of the forging by one of Ramsbottom's nibbling machines, and the rough turning done by the seven-tool lathe (see Chapter 5). For a dozen years or more until 1903 locomotive frame plates were slotted in batches up to ten in this shop. Two 30hp gas engines provided power for most of the shop machines.

Last built of the shops along this short line was the nut-and-bolt shop, commissioned in 1888. It was 184ft long, had a forge at one end and a machine-tool section at the other. This shop also made washers, rivets and nails. Previously, from 1866, it had been on an upper floor over part of the Old Works fitting shop and had been staffed largely by younger apprentices, which gave rise to its colloquial name of 'the nursery'. The new shop continued to employ mainly apprentices, and

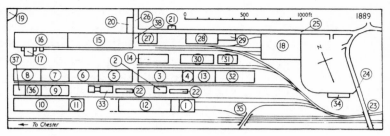

1 Steel plant 2 Boiler house 3 Axle forge 4 Spring mill 5 No 5 Erecting shop 6 No 6 Erecting shop 7 No 7 Erecting shop 8 No 8 Erecting shop 9 Boiler-shop smithy 10 Boiler shop 11 Points and crossings shop 12 Steel rail mill 13 New or iron forge 14 Copper shop 15 Tender shop 16 Iron foundry 17 Rail chair foundry 18 Paint shop 19 Brickworks 20 Workmen's dining room 21 Bessemer Hotel 22 Gas producers 23 Flag Lane Bridge over Old Chester and Deviation Tracks 24 Flag Lane 25 Richard Moon Street 26 Goddard Street 27 Brass foundry 28 Signal shop 29 Signal stores 30 Wheel shop 31 Nut and bolt shop 32 Steel foundry 33 Boiler house 34 Mortar mill 35 Eagle bridge 36 Flangeing shop 37 Plate stores 38 Works entrance

Fig 28 Layout of shops at Steelworks end, 1889

the new boy after a day or two was expected to be able to tap his 60 nuts an hour. No one expected him to keep up that rate throughout a 9½-hour shift, though years ago two celebrated ex-Crewe 'premiums' tried to assure the author that *they* did. When this new shop was equipped it was given many ancient machines from the Old Works, and for many years power was supplied by a gas engine.

To the north of this short line, in the tender paint shop row, came the later transfers from the Old and Deviation Works, such as the brass foundry (1883), the signal shop (1884) and the signal stores. The 'north-west frontier' space along this line, beyond the tender shop, was earmarked for a new iron foundry—the third in Crewe history. The structure of this, 463ft long and 120ft wide in three bays, was completed in 1882, and the equipment installed gradually; full functioning did not come until the autumn though official opening celebrations were in May, as still recorded today by the words cast on one of the crane-run beams: "Success to the New Foundry. Opened by R. Moon, Esq. May 13, 1882". From that time inside cylinders were cast in pairs; in the Old Works and Deviation foundries they had been cast singly and bolted together.

One of Webb's earliest activities had been to change the second foundry's cupolas to work with closed tops and chimneys, and he reckoned to save about 25 percent in the blast by so doing. This method was applied to the new west-end foundry; to this new shop was transferred from the Deviation foundry the special machine for moulding Webb's cast-iron chimney tops, which were only ³⁄₁₆in thick. All the machines in this new foundry were driven by a wall engine at one end, which was supplied with steam from three small locomotive-type boilers.

Along part of the south face of this building was put another smaller foundry confined to the casting of iron rail chairs. About a decade later, against the north-east corner and adjacent to the tender shop, was built a new pattern shop and store to take the place of Deviation buildings gutted by fire. These pattern buildings were of simple construction, with pillars of old rails and corrugated-iron sides and roof with pitch-pine interior lining, but Webb is reported to have been pleased with the economical construction, though probably the patternmakers were not. In the 1870s the old pattern shop had been refitted with American-type working benches having simple arrangements for screwing-up framed work and forcing home tenons. These appliances, introduced by Worsdell from his Altoona experience, were perpetuated in the new shop.

Co-incident with the 1874–84 extensions at the Steelworks end, the southern annexe of the Old Works was remodelled. The iron plate and rail mill was given up and became a rail store. In 1874–75 the old tender shop took up signal manufacture, but after 1884 it was adapted into the large out-station shop, with the smaller buildings to the east becoming the tinsmiths' shop, oil-gas plant, oil stores, and the waste-cloth cleansing plant. In 1900 the works ambulance room and hospital were erected at the north end of Mill Street, facing Oak Street, and were adjacent to the old bath-house dating from 1860.

With the continuous extensions the millwrights' department became correspondingly more important, and the millwrights' shop in the Deviation Works was lengthened in 1882–83 by the absorption of the old iron foundry, and years later by extension over the gutted portion of the pattern shop and store. The shop then came to have a length of over 600ft. Here was centred not only maintenance work and replacement parts for the various power houses, machine tools and drives, but also file cutting, grinding and hardening, the erection and repair of cranes, hydraulic lifts, capstans and turntables, coal hoists, water troughs, pumping sets, and steamship auxiliaries, much of which came to the millwrights via the out-station department. From around 1890 the machining of webs for built-up crank axles was done here, with planing and milling machines taking up to ten webs at a setting. Small millwrights' stores were located in the Old Works and Steelworks, and in the latter was a self-contained small millwrighting section for the steel plant.

In the millwrights' shop was refurbished and re-erected the very old Richard Trevithick high-pressure engine bearing Hazeldine & Co's works number 14 that had been found among a load of scrap bought by the LNWR in 1883. This engine is now in the Science Museum at

South Kensington, but it did not get there until LMSR days, and in the meantime spent long years stored on the inner end of No 1 road of the paint shop.

Adjacent to the main millwrights' shop, against Flag Lane bridge, were the chain-making, chain-testing and materials-testing shops, all supervised by one foreman. They were first organised separately on this site in 1883 when the brass foundry was moved to the Steelworks end. Webb was particular on the subject of materials testing, especially with boiler plates having punched holes. In addition to tensile and bending tests, a strip of $7/16$in boiler plate $2\frac{1}{2}$in wide had to have a $\frac{5}{8}$in punched hole drifted out to 2in without cracking.

With modernised facilities and equipment Webb expected his works managers to cheapen the cost of constituents and whole engines, or at least to keep costs constant against any advance in raw materials prices. This was difficult to do because Ramsbottom's prices at the Old Works had been low, and higher-priced steel had replaced iron, though its use was justified by longer life or higher mileage. For example, wrought-iron straight driving axles of the Problem-class 2-2-2s averaged 74,000 miles, whereas the replacement Bessemer steel axles went 158,000.

The net cost of rebuilding a Crewe-type 2-4-0 into a 2-4-0T and giving it a new iron boiler and side tanks was £575 in 1871; net cost of a heavy overhaul of a Crewe-type LFB 2-4-0 (without tender) was £392 including the cost of a new iron boiler and new 16in by 20in cylinders. General overhaul of a Problem 2-2-2 including a new iron boiler was £300; that of a DX (without tender) in the early 1870s, including a new iron boiler, was £338. In all these figures allowance is made for the scrap value of the old iron boilers, which for a DX or Problem was estimated at £180, of which £80 was from the scrap copper of the inside firebox.

In 1871 a pair of DX cylinders including covers cost £32 3s 4d [£32·17] to produce and finish, of which the castings took £15 1s 5d [£15·07]. A DX crank axle in steel cost £19 10s 4½d [£19·52] for making, machining and fitting, and the finish turning was responsible only for £2 0s 0d of this. Ramsbottom quoted this exact figure to the LYR board 13 years later when advising on the equipment of the new Horwich works; strictly it did not include all items, and when in 1875 another cost analysis was made at Crewe that included such items as the cost of coal in all operations the value came out at £25. The amount of coal used in the various aspects of production was reckoned to be $2\frac{1}{2}$ tons.

At a later stage, through 1883–85, the cost of a new 0-6-2T with 4ft

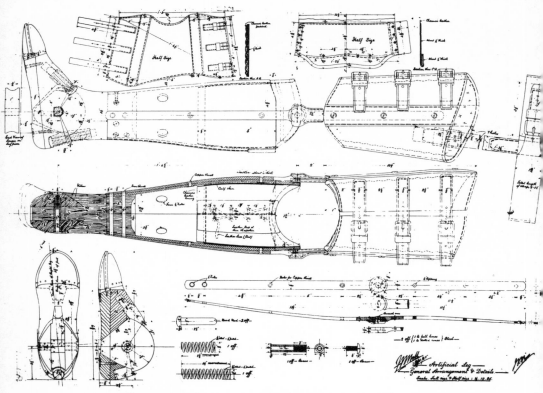

Fig 29 Wooden artificial leg as made at Crewe according to individual needs from the early 1880s

3in cast-iron wheels was reduced to £963 from £1,050 at a time when 20 to 30 of these engines were being built in a year. Around 1883 the cost of a 2-4-2T engine with 4ft 6in wrought-iron wheels dropped from £1,100 when just a few were being turned out to £1,075 apiece when 26 were completed in six months. After two or three hundred had been built, the cost of one 0-6-0 coal engine with 4ft 3in cast-iron wheel centres was said to be only £500. This may well have been so, for design and materials were the simplest, but such a cost could have been achieved only exclusive of tender and without any basic overhead charges attached. In fact, none of the prices quoted above includes overhead charges, which were shown separately as a lump sum in the locomotive-department accounts.

These costs are not to be confused with the 'valuations' made later by the accountant for the capital investment account, or with those made for outside purposes such as rating appeals, in which, for example, an 0-6-0 coal engine and tender were entered at £1,840 and a Special DX at £2,200. By the turn of the century the Problems, still in capital stock and much rebuilt, were valued at £1,950 though nominally 35 to 40 years old.

Overall economy in production cost was paramount with Webb. He was not inclined to sanction the machining or dressing of surfaces needing those processes only for appearance. In 1884 a member of the Iron & Steel Institute wrote of Crewe: "The whole of the work is sound and excellent, but not equal in finish to that turned out in other railway shops, where, perhaps, first cost is not regarded as of so much importance. Mr. Webb has the reputation of being able to build cheaper locomotives than anyone else, and it is, we suppose, impossible to combine first-rate finish and moderate price."

LNWR signal manufacture was established at Crewe in 1874, after a supply agreement with Saxby & Farmer had been terminated the year before, and not long after the Railway Companies Bill of 1871 had included clauses to make compulsory the absolute block system on passenger lines. Though this Bill was defeated by the Parliamentary 'railway lobby', obviously the railways would have to pay more attention to their safety engineering; not until the Regulation of Railways Act 1889 (52 & 53 Vic, cap. 37, 30 August 1889) was the block system made compulsory for lines having passenger traffic.

In the 1870s the LNWR did not have an all-line signal superintendent charged with policy and equipment. Webb's standing with Moon may have been sufficient for his ideas on signal construction to be accepted, and Newman and Edwards, the ostensible telegraph and signals officials, had to work in close collaboration with Crewe. On the resignation of Edwards, C. Dick was appointed in 1877 as Webb's assistant for manufacture and actual installation and repair work, and under him the slotting of signal mechanism made great progress.

With the subsequent development into electro-mechanical methods Webb retained his hold, and Crewe Works made apparatus on the Webb-Thompson system, A. M. Thompson by then having been appointed signal and telegraph superintendent and given a residence at Crewe. The first installation of this type was at Gresty Lane, the junction at Crewe of the Shrewsbury line, and the largest was Crewe North box with 266 levers. The Webb-Thompson apparatus for single-line working also was manufactured at Crewe. By the end of the 19th Century approximately 20,000 signals were maintained by the signal section of the locomotive department.

Signal manufacture at Crewe began in the original tender shop south of the Old Works, when tender-making was transferred to the Steelworks. The large increase in the amount and complexity of signal equipment following the extension of block signalling necessitated a new and more commodious shop, 280ft by 85ft, in the most northerly echelon at the Steelworks, so machining, assembly and repair were transferred there in 1884. From the start, the machinery was driven by a 48hp gas engine. On the upper floor of the adjacent signal stores were made and repaired wooden station name and notice boards, but most of these items were in cast-iron. Signal posts and level-crossing gates were made in the sawmill section of the Deviation works, and in part of the upper floor of the adjacent joiners' shop were made wooden arms and legs (Fig 29).

By the Regulation of Railways Act 1889 automatic continuous brakes were made compulsory for all passenger trains, and all this increased the activity in the erecting shops and in the Old Works fitting shop, largely because of the LNWR brake muddle. From 1886 to 1891 around 700 engines were still fitted to work the Clark–Webb chain brake on the train, and in 1892 all this apparatus was removed. Meanwhile, in 1887–88 over 900 engines were fitted to work the simple vacuum brake on the train, and this apparatus was removed gradually until 1893. From 1888 engines gradually were fitted to work the automatic vacuum brake on the train, and by 1892 around 1,250 were equipped but without similar braking of the engine. Automatic vacuum braking of the engine began in 1891 and by the end of 1893 about a thousand engines had been fitted, all work being done at Crewe.

Under Webb the locomotive department also came to have charge of the electric lighting systems all over the LNWR, the provision of water and coal for all purposes, and the supply and repair of all cranes, weighing machines and hydraulic equipment used by the traffic department. Construction and maintenance connected with all these things was centred at Crewe, working through the outdoor department. There was an outdoor superintendent for all this and for work to do with the locomotive sheds, and he was responsible directly to the locomotive superintendent.

Gas supply continued as another activity. When the Deviation line was built it did not affect the gasworks area except for the gasworks cottages. At that time the annual gas production was over 40 million cu ft and there were 4,800 gas flares in the locomotive works. A fourth and larger gasholder was provided at the same site, but in the early 1870s a large gasholder was built on the north side of the Valley Brook beyond Stewart Street and a pipe line laid from it to serve the growing needs of the west end. Later the whole plant was transferred to this area at the corner of Wistaston Street and Stewart Street, and was on an enlarged scale, but for some years in the 1880s it had the reputation of supplying poor gas. At first most of the new plant's production was for the works, for in 1885 only about one-fifth of the houses in the town had gas points, all these being company-owned houses. Production increased steadily until 1908–09, when the annual production was 273 million cu ft. Manufacture of carburetted water gas began in 1897–98, but after 1909 the production declined. Gas supplied to the town rose to about 50 percent of the total production by the end of Webb's time.

The Crewe town water supply also continued as a responsibility of the locomotive department, with staff located at the main works; the supply was never guaranteed, and throughout LNWR days the town legally was supplied simply with water surplus to works, shed and station requirements, this being one reason why no other major industry was attracted to the town.

In the same area as the new gasworks, carriage cleaning, storage and maintenance shops were begun in the late 1870s south of the main Chester line. Though they did not belong to the locomotive department or form part of Crewe Works, they had a standard-gauge rail connection with the Steelworks area via the Eagle Bridge spanning the Chester tracks. Eagle Bridge was so named, and had a name board, because it was adorned with four cast-iron eagles found among a load of scrap that came into the steel plant. Immediately south of this bridge was another girder bridge spanning most of the carriage yard tracks.

Adjoining the east end of the carriage storage sheds and flanking Bridle Road was a private railway clothing factory that had been built by the railway in 1880 to house John Compton's business on its removal from similar premises in Sandon Street. Away to the west of the carriage repair shops were two cooling ponds for the main power houses in the Steelworks.

Though all carriage works shunting was done by a Special 0-6-0ST in carriage-department stock, for many years from the late Webb period a daily locomotive-department working ran through the carriage area. This was the steel slag trip that ran from the area of the melts and the steel foundry, over Eagle Bridge, down into the carriage yard, on into the gasworks yard, and finally up the tip on the south side of Victoria Avenue, a journey that involved three reversals and finished on an ever longer and steeper grade until by the end of World War II the tip had attained a height of 70ft.

First application of electricity in Crewe was a small-scale experiment at lighting at the station around 1878. In the late 1880s a small electrical sub-department was set up, at first to deal with lighting at the works and in stations and on some of the company's steamships, and then to handle the developing electric power-drives in the shops; an early effort was made to standardise dynamo sizes and make the magnets of Crewe steel. The railway never supplied electricity to Crewe town; that service was undertaken by the municipality, beginning in 1900 with a small plant at the corner of Edleston Road and Electricity Street.

In the early 1890s small electric welders, 2¼hp movable drillers and reamers, and semi-portable tube cutters were introduced into the works. These were odd special tools, and a much more intense application was electric drive to lines of shafting driving fixed machine tools. Also by 1897 well over a dozen electric cranes varying from 4 to 30 tons in lifting capacity were installed, most of them replacing the old Ramsbottom cord type. They had separate motors for each crane movement, but the speed of operation was not quicker than that of the old cranes. At the end of the century the big engine-boiler house between Nos 1 and 2 erecting shops was demolished and a steam-electric power house erected in the yard on the site of the old copper shop. A few years later the Deviation works was also given its own steam-electric power plant.

The electrical section was steadily enlarged, but in 1908 it was taken away from Crewe and the locomotive department and expanded into a full department with a company chief electrical engineer and head-quarters were fixed at Euston. This was done when the first moves were made towards the electrification of the London suburban lines, but all electrical matters connected with Crewe works remained under the locomotive department.

Despite the progress of electric drives, until the 1920s the three sections of Crewe works were based primarily on steam power, arranged in groups as the works extended, amounting in 1903 to 64 stationary steam engines of individual outputs up to 1,200hp, and supplied by 63 separate boilers, which also supplied the numerous steam and drop hammers, shop-heating systems and other equipment. As far as machine tool drives were concerned the direct belt or geared drives from the old stationary steam engines to lines of shafting were replaced by steam engines driving dynamos that supplied current to group motors driving lines of shafting, or to individual motors for the largest tools. The day of grid supply had yet to come.

Each boiler group had its own chimney, and Crewe was not a smokeless town, though Webb claimed in 1884: "At present all our steel-making and heating furnaces are on the gas principle . . . The result of working on the gas principle is that we are enabled to live in comparative comfort in the town." Years later many Crewe

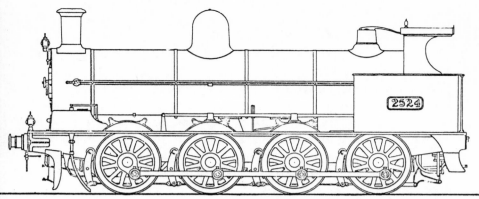

Fig 30 The first 8-coupled engine built at Crewe (1892); simple expansion with two
19½in by 24in inside cylinders and 4ft 5½in wheels; weight 49 tons

inhabitants scarcely agreed with the last part of the statement, particularly when a south-west wind was blowing smoke from the 36 chimneys in the Steelworks.

The works layout included two hydraulic mains for equipment in the Steelworks, one at 2,000lb/sq in pressure for the largest flangeing and other presses, and the second at 400lb/sq in. The pumping engine for each was formed of two of the standard 17in by 24in locomotive cylinders and valve motions. In the Deviation Works was a 100lb/sq in water main for fire services round the saw mill, joiners' shop and timber yard, put in after the fire in the pattern shop, but other mains ran through the works, as did a sewage system that led eventually to the main outfall serving both town and works.

In 1874 the long-standing works fire brigade was reorganised by Webb with strict and comprehensive regulations. On a call-out, the superintendent got 4s 0d [20p] for the first hour and 1s 6d [7½p] an hour thereafter; the captain was paid 3s 0d [15p] and then 1s 3d [7p], and the firemen 2s 0d [10p] and 1s 0d [5p]. On occasion this fire force dealt with outside fires, such as that at Moseley's farm near Gresty in 1872, when the Sun Fire Insurance Company was invoiced £2 7s 6d [£2·37½] for the services of 15 men, and in 1873 when £11 15s 1d [£11·75] was debited against the Sun for attending a fire at Mr Heath's haystack. By the end of the 19th Century the house of every member of the brigade was in one-way electrical communication with the works fire station. Additionally, three prolonged blasts from the works hooters gave warning to all concerned – and to all in the town not concerned.

Ramsbottom retained his offices in the Old Works in the original building alongside the clock tower. Webb occupied these until 1876, when to get a more central position and to ease the terrible congestion in the offices, the major portion of the still-existing main office block was built facing the old Chester line and the east end of the Deviation Works, with an inconspicuous public entrance at the north end of Chester bridge and a 'works' entrance off the old Chester tracks. The rear of this building blocked up the south end of the three short *cul-de-sac* Dorfold, Bentley and Tollitt Streets running off Delamere Street.

Webb is said to have had an internal telephone in his room with connection to one or two clerks and leading officers from 1879, and in the mid-1880s a primitive telephone system was installed throughout the office block. By 1897 there was a comprehensive network linking the offices with all the main shops east and west, this eliminating many messenger boys and men. By that time all the clocks in the office block were electric, with a master regulator that transmitted an electric impulse every half-minute. There was another clock system in the shops, and at the end of the century the 74 clocks there were being maintained under contract by J. B. Joyce & Co of Shrewsbury at 5 shillings [25p] per clock each year. From 1888 Remington typewriters were in use in the locomotive department ofices.

Additions in 1900–01 increased the office accommodation; the 525ft ivy-covered curved frontage facing the old Chester tracks is well-known as the background of many LNWR and LMSR official photographs. For years there was a narrow raised bed of grass and shrubs between office and tracks, and a further line of shrubs and trees on the south side of the tracks hid the adjacent Deviation shops from the ground-floor windows. To the west of and somewhat back from the main office block, and long ante-dating it, were Chester Place, from the early 1860s the official residence of the locomotive superintendent, Deva Villa for the works manager, and West Bank, Windycote and The Grove for other leading officials. Trees and shrubs hid these houses from the tracks and the Deviation shops.

On the ground floor of the office block were the rooms of the loco-motive superintendent and his chief clerk, the works manager, the two running superintendents and the outdoor superintendent. On the first floor were the locomotive accountant's and works accountant's offices, the stores office, and a laboratory with a photographic room. The drawing office on the ground floor was 200ft by 30ft. Webb's organisation of it, which lasted the remainder of LNWR days, was under the chief draughtsman in three sections: locomotive, general engineering, and buildings and structures. In Webb's later years and in those of Whale and Cooke, the chief was J. N. Jackson, and the respective section leaders T. E. Sackfield, C. E. Jones and A. Martin, of whom the last-named was considered as senior in service and deputised for Jackson. From time to time the drawing office was used

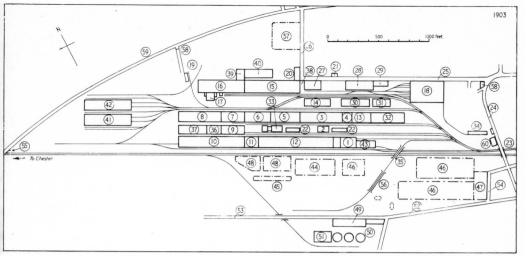

1 Steel plant 2 Boiler house 3 Axle forge 4 Spring mill 5 No 5 Erecting shop 6 No 6 Erecting shop 7 No 7 Erecting shop 8 No 8 Erecting shop 9 Boiler-shop smithy 10 Boiler shop 11 Points and crossings shop 12 Steel rail mill 13 New or iron forge 14 Copper shop 15 Tender shop 16 Iron foundry 17 Rail chair foundry 18 Paint shop 19 Brickworks 20 Workmen's dining room 21 Bessemer Hotel 22 Gas producers 23 Flag Lane Bridge over Old Chester and Deviation Tracks 24 Flag Lane 25 Richard Moon Street 26 Goddard Street 27 Brass foundry 28 Signal shop 29 Signal stores 30 Wheel shop 31 Nut and bolt shop 32 Steel foundry 33 Boiler house 34 Mortar mill 35 Eagle Bridge 36 Flangeing shop 37 Plate stores 38 Works entrance 39 Pattern shop 40 Pattern store 41 No 9 Erecting shop 42 Main machine shop 43 Steel plant extension 44 Carriage repair shop 45 Carriage washing plant 46 Carriage storage sheds 47 Railway clothing factory 48 Cooling ponds 49 Gasworks retort house 50 Gas holders 51 Gas purifier house 52 Wistaston Road 53 Victoria Avenue 54 Bridle Road 55 Merrill's Bridge 56 Bridge over carriage yard 57 Football field 58 Crewe technical college 59 West Street 60 Large water tower

Fig 31 Layout of shops at Steelworks end, December 1903

as a dining room when the works was being visited by engineering institutions or similar parties, and could seat up to 300.

The general English coal strike and the ensuing lack of work in 1893–94 already recorded had a considerable deleterious effect on Crewe and the LNWR. Train services had to be cut, and there was insufficient fuel and incoming materials to keep the works going at anything like full capacity. Steel production was only one-quarter of the normal, and from the summer of 1893 to January 1894, after some reduction in work force, the whole works was reduced to four days a week operation, then five days until June 1894, when the full 54-hour week was resumed. This was the reason why erection of eight of the ten Greater Britain engines was not resumed for a year after the first two were running, why production of the first three-cylinder compound 0-8-0 was delayed a year after the single simple-expansion 0-8-0 went into service, and why the LNWR dividend went down from 7 to 5⅜ percent.

Resumption of full work came only a week or two before the works annual holiday, which by then was usually the first or second week in July instead of the Whitsun week common up to 1892. The break always left the town under half-populated and relatively silent, for the background hum of the works and noise of the yard were absent, and none of the numerous short blasts denoting approach of starting time and going-home time was to be heard in the six groups from 5.30am to 5.30pm.

It was a sign of those hard times, too, that the railway battalion of the Cheshire Volunteers had to do its week's training camp in the works holiday; the companies were marshalled in the Market Square to go off to the special train. These volunteers, the 2nd Cheshire Royal Engineer (Railway) Volunteer Corps, was brought into being on 1 April 1887 largely as a result of Webb's efforts. It comprised six companies made up of men from the locomotive department and adjacent carriage shops. George Whale commanded No 1 company, of men in the running department; No 3 company was mainly office staff captained at first by W. Norman, then chief draughtsman, with J. N. Jackson a sergeant in it. No 5 company, of works men, was captained by H. D. Earl, with W. Warneford as first lieutenant, both then being works assistants. The corps was inspected by the old Duke of Cambridge, C-in-C of the British Army, when he opened Queen's Park in July 1888. Of the 760 men, 245 were classed as regular reserves of the Royal Engineers and were liable to be called up in times of emergency. The first active service was in the Boer War, with a company under the command of Major Schofield. The whole corps was disbanded in 1912 on War Office instructions resulting from the formation of the new Territorial Army.

An unusual Crewe event around the turn of the century was a works holiday without loss of pay in June 1900 to mark the completion of what was claimed to be the 4,000th new steam locomotive to be built at Crewe. This was the compound 4-4-0 *La France*, which was sent to the Paris Exhibition in charge of a French-speaking 'premium'. The works was closed at midday on the Friday and re-opened on Monday.

Last of the important improvements and enlargements to Crewe works in Webb's time were the new drop-stamping equipment in the Old Works, the lengthening of the boiler shop and No 8 erecting shop, the elimination of the old Bessemer plant, and the building away on new ground to the far west of No 9 erecting shop and a large fitting-machine shop alongside. This brought the published works area up to 136 acres, including 46 acres roofed, and the west-end layout to that shown in Fig 31.

The nucleus of the new drop-stamping plant began in 1899 when Webb adopted the Brett system with a battery of two 7-cwt stamping hammers and one 5-cwt roughing-out hammer. These were applied first to the manufacture of small signal parts, and then extended to

Top: Steelworks wheel shop in the early 1890s with a built-up single-throw crank axle in the lathe; balance weights not yet attached   (*Courtesy J. P. Richards*)
Below left: Half of a White injector being repaired in the Steelworks fitting-machine shop
Below right: An old shaper of pre-GJR vintage that worked in Crewe shops for many years
Bottom: Deviation Works power station with five 125hp and one 100hp engine-generator sets, 1906   (*NRM, York*)

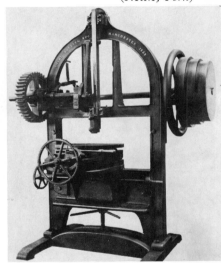

Above: The main office block, built 1876, from the west in 1882 before any creepers had grown up the wall; old Chester track in centre; Deviation works behind trees on the right (*NRM, York*)

Below: A view from the clock tower of the Old Works, looking south 1869–70. Grey building to left is the old carriage repair shop; lines on right lead to Crewe engine sheds; Manchester line bears off to left behind signal box (*Brian Radford collection*)

brake-rod ends, levers and handles, and later to other details. By the end of Webb's time there were 14 drop hammers in the Old Works, varying from 7cwt to 1½ tons.

No 9 erecting shop was brought into use early in 1903 more especially to build and repair the larger eight-wheel passenger and goods engines. It brought the effective repair-pit capacity of the whole works up to over 300 engines at a time, and from its inception all new engines were built there. This shop was 463ft by 110ft, and it had wooden roof beams and light steel-rod roof trusses as distinct from the wholly wooden roof frames of the older shops except the 1898 extensions.

The shop had two three-road bays with machine tools in the arcade between the bays, and initially was provided with four 40-ton electric cranes and one small one of four tons' lift. The roof was fully-glazed and the shop was heated by hot-water pipes beneath gratings in the wood-block floor. Lighting was by electric arc lamps, and the machine tools had group electric drive. This was in the forefront of practice, but the proportions of the shop were not, and the cramped space between the pits showed Webb still had a bent for economy in things static as well as mobile. As in No 8, new locomotive frames were lined-up and erected on stands at one end of the shop under only two erectors, and the assembly was then transferred above a pit for erection.

As No 9 was approaching completion it was realised that the transport of an ever-growing number of small and large parts from the Old Works fitting shop was becoming too onerous, and sanction was given for the construction at an estimated cost of £12,000 of a new fitting-machine shop alongside No 9. This was commissioned late in 1903, and had the Crewe characteristic that it was really a main machine shop and not a fitting shop. Another Crewe feature was that not all the machine tools were new; some were *very* old. The building was the same length as No 9 and 83ft wide. The real innovation was electric drive for all machine tools. Between this shop and No 9 was an open space with a siding.

By the time of Webb's retirement in May 1903 the LNWR had a stock of 3,100 engines including duplicate stock, valued at about £5¼ million. In his time he had been responsible for about 3,000 new locomotives and for about 45,000 locomotive general repairs and rebuilds, and for the doubling of works capacity and the size of the locomotive department; he had impressed his personality on the whole LNWR to an extent greater than any general manager since Mark Huish.

7
The 'Running' Era, 1903–20

Webb's retirement, though long foreshadowed, brought a situation to which the LNWR board had not forethought a constructive solution. Webb himself had not been able to guide matters in his last few years to give a smooth transition. As far as Crewe and the mechanical engineering side were concerned, the works manager stood second in rank, and H. D. Earl had been a competent chief for almost 15 years, handling equally well periods of intense productivity, short-time working, steel mill rearrangements, ever larger engines, and new shop construction, and he was earning a salary 30 percent greater than that of any previous manager. Nevertheless Harrison and Turnbull, the LNWR general manager and operating superintendent respectively, were anxious that the chief mechanical engineer should report to the general manager, and to eliminate Crewe elements that had been close to Webb. The indifferent express passenger train performance from the Jubilees and the first few Alfreds over the years 1901–02 had given them a handle with Lord Stalbridge, who had succeeded Moon as chairman in 1891.

From their point of view the long-standing seniority of George Whale as a running superintendent made him a possible candidate for the top position, and this would obviate any difficulty in asking him to serve under his younger brother-in-law Earl. Whale was the antithesis of Webb in almost every respect, and he had always been willing to 'meet' the operating department in accident enquiries, engine shortages and failures; with his philosophic temperament he was *persona gratissima* with the higher management. At that time there was no thought of separating 'running' from mechanical engineering. Whale therefore was made chief of the whole locomotive department, Earl being promoted out of the way to be wagon superintendent at Earlestown, a position that made him independent of Whale but brought him only a 16 percent increase in salary.

As works manager Whale was given A. R. Trevithick, who had been assistant manager of the locomotive works only from the beginning of

1900, his first works experience since his Crewe apprenticeship, for he had been some 20 years in the running department, finishing up as district locomotive superintendent at Carlisle before returning to Crewe. Additionally, J. Homfray, who had succeeded Trevithick at Carlisle, was brought to Crewe as assistant locomotive works manager. Thus the 'running' side took over the higher direction and management of the locomotive department and of Crewe Works.

Though the LNWR directors were well aware that Whale was 60 years of age when they made him chief, and so could have only a brief tenure of office, they took no steps to ensure he brought forward a successor or to prevent a repetition of anything like the 1903 situation; in fact they permitted Whale straight away to re-divide the running department, with two 'equal' superintendents responsible direct to him as chief mechanical engineer without the intervention of an all-line superintendent (see Chapter 2). When Whale went in 1909 after scarcely six years as head, Trevithick and most of the department expected Trevithick to succeed. This even got into print, but the board preferred Bowen Cooke, the Southern Division running superintendent, and an uncomfortable transition period followed with Cooke as chief and Trevithick as works manager until in 1910 an opportunity arose for the latter to be promoted to Earlestown.

Top direction of the department thus was not only given to a sectional chief of a sub-department, who jumped two big steps at once, but remained in hands inexperienced in production and repair, and in the handling of thousands of men forming a congested and closely-knit group as distinct from thousands spread evenly over a large area. Cooke made a good job of his new position as far as personality was concerned, but he had had no works experience since the end of his Crewe pupilage in 1880. Neither in his term of office nor in Whale's was any major progressive step taken in Crewe practice or equipment, though there was a revolution in locomotive size and practice in the 17 years from 1903 to 1920, and a revolution in labour relations after World War I. Thus at the end of Cooke's life Crewe Works tended to be out of control in regard to organisation, performance and personnel.

The whole Crewe *milieu* was much changed by the 1914–19 war. In the thick of that war Warneford, who had succeeded Trevithick as works manager in 1910, was sent to Earlestown as wagon superintendent, and this led to the recall from France in 1916 of H. P. M. Beames, an old Crewe premium pupil of Webb's, who was made works manager. Beames had occupied various positions in the works since 1901, but never with any large degree of responsibility. In 1914 he had been Cooke's personal assistant.

Cooke died in 1920. With the accession of Beames to the chief mechanical engineer's position in November of that year the 'running era' ended, and the LNWR locomotive department came under a man to whom Crewe works was the major interest in life; like Cooke, Beames was unable to grasp the large-scale needs and inaugurate complete remedial measures in the midst of a disturbed period and when reporting to a board worried by the general economic situation and by the approach of the Railways Act (1921). Thus Crewe Works passed in 1923 to its new owner, the LMSR, just past the nadir of its effectiveness in its first one hundred years. That it was just past the nadir was due to the amalgamation of the LNWR and LYR as from 1 January 1922, which brought George Hughes of the latter system to the senior mechanical engineering position in which, while supporting the measures that Beames was initiating, he at once tried to bring some improvement in those Crewe methods and practices that had become obsolete, and he had in view at least one major reorganisation.

In 1903 Whale had come too late in life to the top position. He was no longer willing or able to extend himself all-out in activities which hitherto he had known only at second-hand, yet which needed just at that time a strong chief of unremitting energy and a forward overall outlook that could cope with the changing trends in transport, mechanical engineering and labour. At the works the close continuous control was eased, statistical and graphic checks were given up, though 'running' charts were elaborated to show performance in mileage, repairs, consumption and so on compared with the engines of other companies, all based on annual reports and Board of Trade returns.

Whale was unable to appreciate the features that led Webb to watch closely the investment charges, returns on investments, purchases of raw materials, and stocks in hand of materials and parts that permitted evaluation of the efficiency of the works, and the contribution made by the locomotive department to the prosperity of the whole company. Interest in these things lapsed, and no continued progress in the efficacy of the works or of the whole department as a unit of the railway was made in the further life of the LNWR.

The new policy at Crewe, quite clearly, was the smooth and easy running of headquarters and various sub-departments, and complete simplicity allied to cheapness in first cost of all new locomotives, the latter taken to such a degree that the first large 4-4-2T had a rigid trailing axle to save the small extra expense of a radial axlebox. Whale felt all these things could be well arranged by his five principal indoor and outdoor assistants without constant check by him. He was rarely about the works, possibly because of the energy shown by Trevithick. His infrequent appearances in the drawing office could have arisen from sheer lack of interest in design as such; Jackson, Sackfield and leading draughtsmen had a much easier time. He relaxed his hold on 'running', and left much to his two principal assistants. When he did inject himself into that side it was not always with the happiest results, and he made errors into which he would not have fallen during his previous 25 years. Webb's tight grip on every phase of the whole department was loosened, and gradually a laxity in higher echelons was discernible, though not in the ranks, for discipline below foreman level was maintained up to World War I.

Whale's inexperience in the direction and management of a whole department, plus encouragement from Trevithick, Harrison and Turnbull to finish with Webb and all his compounds, led him to acquiesce in the scrapping of many engines under 16 years old, and of many others of 1860–87 vintage, at a rate faster than new ones of equal total traffic capacity were built. Withdrawal and construction were not planned in unison, and as a result the LNWR was markedly short of main-line motive power in 1904–05; at times in the summer of 1904 train operation was chaotic from this cause. This imbalance also led to greater piles of scrap in the steelworks yard, and possibly from this dates the great untidiness of the south and south-east sections of the Steelworks yard that was so prominent a feature in the last few years of the LNWR and early years of the LMSR.

Yet in his first five months as chief, before Trevithick's desire to eliminate the 3-cylinder compounds had taken effect, Whale it was who confirmed the order for the last 20 of the 30 4-cylinder compound 'Bill Bailey' 4-6-0s, and he did so when only six or seven of the first batch were at work with indifferent results, and after the order had been placed on Crewe for the first five of the large 2-cylinder simple Precursor 4-4-0s. There must have been serious regrets a few months later at this unfortunate decision, but instead of cancelling the order work was soft-pedalled on the 4-6-0s to such an extent that the last four or five did not leave the works until January/March 1905.

The wholesale withdrawal of Webb 3-cylinder compounds and Ramsbottom Problems and their scrapping in the Crewe shops began in December 1903. For some months thereafter Trevithick walked from time to time along the lines of engines awaiting repair space and chalked 'A.R.T.' on each 3-cylinder compound he saw, to denote it was to be withdrawn. Four-cylinder compounds could hardly be so marked, as new ones of two of the three classes were still coming out of

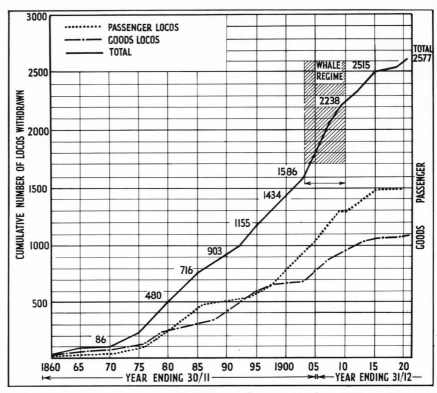

Fig 32 Rate of scrapping steam locomotives at Crewe works from 1860 to 1920

No 9 shop, while the last few of the Alfreds had only appeared in August and were running in shop grey paint until the end of 1903. How the locomotive withdrawal rate went up over the years 1904–09 is well shown by the steepening of the line in Fig 32, an illustration interesting also in showing the rate at which Webb got rid of worn-out or obsolete stock. Only through the war years 1915–18 did the LNWR locomotive withdrawal rate have to be eased (no engines at all were withdrawn in 1917), and Fig 32 indicates that a sizeable portion of the pit lengths at the Old Works must have been occupied in scrapping through much of Whale's time. The cumulative average age of locomotives withdrawn increased steadily from 17½ years in 1861 to 19 in 1871, 26 in 1901, 28 in 1911, and 28½ in 1921, the 16 to 17 years of many of the compounds withdrawn 1904–08 being balanced by the 40 to 45 years of the Problems.

Whale at once had the benefit of Webb's No 9 erecting shop with adjoining machine shop, which had raised the actual repair capacity of the works to well over 300 engines at a time, and gave further pits for the new construction of large Precursor 4-4-0 and Experiment 4-6-0 types. Nevertheless, under Whale, the number of engines standing outside awaiting repair increased at first. Six months after his accession there was an average of 300–305 engines on the pits, plus up to 160 outside awaiting shop space; yet at the same time (November 1903) when the only new engines under construction were the first five Precursors, the balance of 4-cylinder compound 0-8-0s from Webb's last orders, and the 20 compound 4-6-0s ordered under Whale himself, the board was told that short-time had been introduced into the factory owing to lack of work, possibly because despite the urgent need of effective power Whale lacked confidence in his first design, and was not yet sure how he would tackle the whole motive-power situation. This was the first of several lay-offs or short-time workings over the next eight years. A five-day working week was introduced in November 1903 and cut to four days in the December for 1500 workers, and this lasted for some time.

Though full employment on the standard 54-hour week was normal around 1906–08 there was much short time before and after that until 1910–11; that the locomotive side of the works was now too big and was inefficient for the work to be done was scarcely appreciated. There remain no records of any proposals for reorganisation of plant and methods to give shorter repair times or a more compact factory with a smaller number of workers who would not be subjected to repeated short-time and sackings; on the contrary, there were desires for further erecting-shop floor area.

Through the summer of 1904 when every possible engine was needed in traffic, 340 to 350 engines were under repair or in the paint shop at Crewe plus another 130 standing outside, equal to nearly 16 percent of LNWR motive power. By the summer of 1905 the numbers were down to 320–325 and 90. Some 50 new Precursors were then in service and the first five Experiments were almost complete, but for a full three years the whole works and locomotive department were off balance. This was an aspect of the working of a great railway that was glossed-over by the haulage performance and time-keeping of the Precursors over the Southern Division which gave Whale a deserved reputation in that direction, and illogically made railway enthusiasts assume all was well in every other section. Though much more powerful than the engines withdrawn the new 4-4-0s and 4-6-0s did not eliminate piloting north of Preston because the combination of train loads and speeds was still increasing, and the Experiments were not outstanding. By the end of Whale's six years neither Precursors nor Experiments were large in relation to English practice nor adequate to LNWR needs.

In the six years from the end of 1903 to the end of 1909 Crewe No 9 shop turned out 130 Precursors, 105 Experiments, 170 5ft 4-6-0 goods, 50 Precursor 4-4-2Ts and a small number of Webb compounds. Additional work at Crewe included the rebuilding from 1904 of many 3-cylinder and 4-cylinder compound 0-8-0s into 2-cylinder simples, some with larger boilers; the rebuilding from late 1904 of a few 4-cylinder compound 0-8-0s into 2-8-0s; the rebuilding of 45 Webb 0-6-0 coal engines into 0-6-0STs; and the provision of four sets of valve motion in place of two on many Alfred the Great 4-cylinder compound 4-4-0s. The last-named work has always been credited to Whale, but as the first conversion was completed by the end of July 1903 it is probable that the alteration was initiated by Webb before he finally left in the second half of May. The work done at Crewe during the four most intensive years of Whale's regime is summarised in Table 9.

In 1906 a design was drawn up for a 2-cylinder simple 2-8-0 using Experiment cylinders and boiler, and 5ft 3in wheels; though some arrangement and detail drawings were made the needs were met in the end by the conversion to simple expansion of more compound 0-8-0s, and no new eight-coupled engines were completed in Whale's years. For mixed traffic was built the 'Experiment goods' 4-6-0 class.

Table 9   Activities at Crewe Works in Whale's time

Year	1904	1905	1906	1907
Locomotives built	70	75	90	90
Locomotives rebuilt	116	72	50	75
Locomotives cut-up	108	107	113	129
Locomotives sold	1	1	—	—
Locomotives given heavy repairs	1323	1320	1565	1438
Locomotives painted	309	381	388	457
Tenders rebuilt	—	—	—	—
New tenders built	61	75	74	93
Tenders repaired	972	910	1010	903
Crank axles manufactured	92	163	141	112
New boilers built	168	138	153	171
Boilers repaired	314	392	399	434
Average staff employed[1]	7642	7736	7766	7723

[1] Including steel plant and gasworks

Straight away Whale gave up wooden-framed tenders for new construction and changed over to steel, which much altered tender shop procedure and eliminated the tender rebuilding that was a feature of wooden-frame years. Nevertheless, some wooden-framed tenders

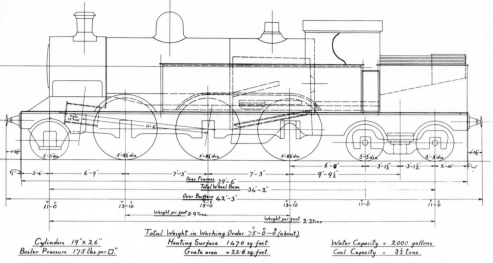

Cylinders 19"×26"   Heating Surface 1470 sq.feet   Water Capacity = 2.000 gallons
Boiler Pressure 175 lbs per □"   Grate area = 22·6 sq.feet   Coal Capacity = 3½ tons

Fig 33 Diagram of proposed 2-6-4T of 1909; replaced for actual construction by the Bowen Cooke 4-6-2T

lasted well into LMSR times. The standard tender size was changed to 3,000 gallons and six tons of coal from the 2,500 gallons and five tons of Webb's largest size. Throughout his time, however, Whale retained wooden brake blocks for tender wheels, but a detail change he did make was to change lever operation of water pick-up to screw action. Also with the Alfred conversions he introduced the well-known LNWR cab with rear supporting pillars for the roof.

A big new stores building in the southern annexe was the only shop extension during Whale's time. It was about 170ft long and 48ft wide and had three floors, the uppermost of which was occupied mainly by samples rooms wherein were displayed standards of articles not then made by the company, such as gas pipes and unions, upholstery, paints, varnishes, clothing material and the like. This building was partly on the site of the old iron rail mill and was opened in 1906. Alongside it was the large out-station shop that had grown up on the original tender shop site. The southern annexe also had another alteration, for after a fire in June 1905 had destroyed the sponge-cloth cleaning house and oil stores the remains were demolished, and the plants transferred alongside the oil and grease works in the angle between the Warrington and Manchester lines. This latter area was still connected with the Old Works by a light footbridge over the northern main line, which had been lengthened when the 'Crewe widened lines' were opened, and which was known as Birdswood bridge. It dated from the 1860s.

In Whale's time and onwards there was also a second footbridge over the old Chester tracks in the Old Works area. It led from the end of the out-station shop to the junction of the fitting shop and the old office block. The other, dating from 1862 and known often as 'the iron bridge', was further west, and provided a public right of way from Mill Street to Forge Street. Between this second bridge and Chester bridge were tracks that held briefly engines coming from the Steelworks end to the weighbridge, on which were examined and adjusted all new and repaired engines before they were passed on to the sheds. Stabled on a short stub partly under Chester bridge was a fire engine and the chief mechanical engineer's coupé, hauled in its time by Old Trevithick singles, by Triplex, and by *Cornwall*.

By 1909 the LNWR engine stock had been reduced five percent below the 1903 total, but there was no corresponding change in the Crewe works force, though in Whale's time measures were taken gradually to get rid of the older workmen, first those over 70 and then those above 65. This did not apply to foremen, and at least two septuagenarians lasted into Cooke's time. Despite the increasing proportion of powerful 2-cylinder simple-expansion locomotives Whale was not able to reduce the number of engine failures per train-mile or per engine in service over the figures for the last four years of Webb. He did however ensure that he had an equal number of locomotives in actual service daily despite the reduction in total stock, but heavy-repair costs per engine in stock rose by 11½ percent between 1903 and 1908.

Though by 1909 Whale's engines were barely keeping pace with train weights and speeds, Cooke was not willing immediately to depart from the small-engine policy, and got the necessary increase in capacity temporarily by superheated versions of the Precursor and Experiment designs in the shape of the George V 4-4-0s and Prince of Wales 4-6-0s. Main-line freight was given a 2-cylinder 0-8-0 developed from the large-boiler conversions of the Webb compounds and at first non-superheated, and 60 of these were ordered under six lot numbers before the first George V and 4-6-2T classes. The first superheated 0-8-0s came in January 1912.

The first really big engine of the LNWR, the Claughton 4-cylinder simple 4-6-0 of 1913, marked the incapacity of Cooke, Jackson and Sackfield as designers able to move with the times into higher powers. Vital lessons from the GWR *Polar Star*'s running from Crewe North shed in August 1910 were unabsorbed, particularly in boiler, valves and valve motion, possibly because contrary to what is generally supposed it was the GWR that initiated the exchange. Despite the small 5ft 2in diameter of the boiler barrel and moderate working pressure of 175lb/sq in, the locomotive weight and axle loads were right up to the maxima acceptable to the chief engineer. Walschaerts motion was the only Crewe innovation in them except for the size. Day by day performance was too variable for them to be called successful, and they were expensive to run and maintain. Cooke himself realised that there were major defects, and was known to say that when the post-war rush of work was over he would take them in hand.

An unusual feature of LNWR locomotive practice from 1903 was the spliced main frame, put first on the Precursors and used on all new 8-wheel, 10-wheel and 12-wheel Whale and Cooke engines thereafter. The big 4-4-2T and 4-6-2T engines had frame splicing at both ends. This arrangement, though linked to the 'running' era, seems to have arisen through a Homer's nod on the part of Webb and Earl. Until 1903 most frame machining was done for years in the wheel shop and frames up to 32½ft length were slotted there, but the frame slotters in the new main machine shop appear to have been so designed and located that they could take only 28ft, and no subsequent replacement or move of these slotters was made to rectify this, possibly because the spliced frame proved so convenient to repair after collisions. The last 20 Webb compound 4-6-0s of 1903–05, however, had their frames slotted in the wheel shop.

General unrest of railway workers and many symptoms of wider unrest throughout the country in 1911 affected Crewe works to some extent and the rest of the locomotive department more, but works production was affected most by the general moulders' strike of that year, which brought out the men in the iron and steel foundries for some time. As far as Crewe was concerned the unrest might well have intensified had not 1912–13 been busy years with full employment, and from then onwards the war kept the unrest just under the boil until 1919.

By the time of the Royal visit to the works in April 1913 the establishment was still just on the plateau of acceptable performance, and few could see how rapid was to be the overall decline due to the circumstances of a European war. Just at that time was effected the last shop enlargement under LNWR ownership; in the second half of 1913 No 9 erecting shop was extended some 300ft westward and the adjacent machine shop by about 200ft. Both shops then butted on to West Street and had curved ends, so that the length of No 9 became 800ft along the north wall and 880ft along the south wall. At the same time the space between the two shops, which had carried a dead-end siding, was roofed to form an arcade housing machine tools.

Within a matter of months these extensions justified themselves by the increased capacity for war production. As regards locomotive repairs, though partly justified by the numerous longer locomotives, the extensions showed that Ramsbottom/Webb shop methods were to remain undisturbed, and that no attempt was to be made to expedite engine-repair time over the pits.

Arrangements in the Steelworks then were much as they were when Webb left. The melting furnaces were still fired by 58 Wilson hand-fired gas-producers which served also other furnaces and reheaters via an underground flue system. The rail mill and its 1200hp Corliss-type engine were just as they had been since the 1893–94 re-arrangement. Nos 6 and 8 erecting shops concentrated on the overhaul of 0-8-0s, Webb and Whale small-wheel 4-6-0s, Jubilee and Alfred 4-4-0s, while a large number of 0-6-0STs were handled in No 5. No 7 was still apportioned largely to boiler mounting and test work. Nos 6 and 8 had been given two 40-ton electric overhead cranes apiece early in the century, whereas cranes in Nos 5 and 7 were not above 25 tons capacity. The traversers through the west ends of Nos 5 and 7 were now electrically operated. No 9 handled all general repairs to Precursor, George V, Experiment, Prince of Wales and Cooke 4-6-2T classes, to Claughtons also from the end of 1913, and did all new construction.

The commissioning of No 9 in 1903 had led to appreciable track re-arrangements in the west end of the works area, particularly for the stabling of engines outside awaiting shop space, and for getting completed engines over from the far west end to the paint shop. Engines coming in for repair had first to be separated from their tenders on the tracks parallel to Nos 5–8, the tenders taken off to the tender shop and the dead engines brought over to the new waiting tracks alongside the south wall of No 9.

Signal equipment manufacture was continued at the Steelworks, but after the retirement in 1912 of Webb's collaborator, A. M. Thompson, the department was reorganised. J. T. Roberts, who had been a premium and pupil of Webb's 1885–90 and from 1891 an assistant to Thompson, became signal assistant to the chief civil engineer, and the chief mechanical engineer then acted simply as a contractor with no say in design. Roberts had a separate small signal drawing office at Crewe; the permanent-way assistant to the chief engineer also had a small Crewe drawing office and his own staff in the stores department.

In the Old Works, No 1 erecting shop took in for repairs only small 4-wheel and 6-wheel tank engines, but much of its floor space was occupied with boiler mountings and small-engine scrapping; No 2 repaired small non-compound 6-wheelers and scrapped others. It still had a traverser at mid-length to get boilers and small engines in and out without disturbing too much of the westernmost pit length. No 3 was devoted chiefly to repairs on 6-wheel passenger engines, but some of the floor area was occupied by machine tools; No 4, with two 25-ton electric cranes in each bay, repaired 6-wheel passenger engines.

With the general electrification of the Old Works initiated by Webb and finished under Whale, that factory came to have a power station of its own, made up of three Lancashire boilers fed with fuel by underfeed stokers, and five Bellis & Morcom 240hp compound engines, attached dynamos supplying 650V dc. This plant was got into the area between the main fitting shop, No 2 erecting shop and the valve motion shop, and the Old Works then attained the maximum congestion in its whole history. When this power plant was commissioned the old steam boiler and engine plant between Nos 1 and 2 erecting shops was dismantled, and space being absorbed by No 2 shop. (Fig. 34, p 146).

On the declaration of war on 4 August 1914 the railways automatically came under the control of the Railway Executive Committee, but not until the November was formed the relevant Railway War Manufacturers' sub-committee of chief mechanical engineers, convened to decide what war equipment could be made in the railway works and how it should be apportioned. Cooke was active at this stage, and the first contracts he obtained were for axletrees, wheel naves, stop plates and elevating arcs for gun carriages, much of which work was done in the millwrights' shop. In 1915 some Crewe millwrights were sent temporarily to Birmingham to instal machinery in a new works for machine-gun manufacture.

In 1915 two armoured trains, each containing two gun vehicles and two infantry vans, were made up at Crewe for home service on lines along the East Coast, but as propelling power the War Office provided for each train an armoured GNR 0-6-2T with an extra tender attached, this group being placed in the centre of the train. The locomotive could be handled from the footplate or from either end, while one of the vans had coal and water reserves for the engine. The infantry vans were converted at Crewe from GWR 40-ton coal wagons; the gun vehicles were made up from Caledonian 30-ton bogie flats on which Crewe put special gun trucks. Train lighting was by acetylene, with a generator in each van.

Gradually Crewe took up manufacture of drop-forged paravane brackets and cases for various shells up to 6in. The steel plant provided the metal for the latter both for Crewe and for certain other factories, though against the consumption of 6in shells in France the production was not large, reaching a total of 100,000 only in 1918. Crewe's long experience in the making of wooden artificial limbs was also drawn upon; manufacture of more modern light-weight arms and legs was undertaken.

Graze fuses, experiments with which were begun at Woolwich in March 1915, formed some of the most important work, and after development the Crewe production rose from 150 per week to 3,000 and 4,000 a week, the total production being over quarter of a million. A portion of the stores department was equipped to handle this work, assisted by machining in the shop next to No 9. It was in the production of these fuses that fine-limit gauge work first came to Crewe. The gauges were stored, checked and maintained in the tool room. After experience with them in other armament work, some efforts were made to adapt them to locomotive-part manufacture, but without enthusiasm, and the works generally was content to retain the standards attained under Webb. In after years Beames claimed this was the beginning of the finer-limit working that came to Crewe in LMSR years, but on overall view it was the influence of the LYR in 1922 that formed the embryo of the much later LMSR limits-and-fits system.

Copper caps and bands for shells cases led to the installation of a new 130-ton hydraulic press operating at a water pressure of 2000lb/sq in, and this eventually produced 700 caps a day for shells up to 8in. Full advantage was taken of the drop-stamping plant in the Old Works to produce limber hooks and trunnion brackets for 6in howitzers, and latter supplanting previous cast-steel brackets that gave too high a failure rate. Eventually a new 4-ton drop hammer battery with boiler, reheating furnaces and cranes was put in specially to manufacture these brackets, but it did not begin production until early in 1918. It was installed at Ministry of Munitions expense at a cost of over £15,000, but in July 1919 was bought by the LNWR for £12,000, then was diverted to producing major valve gear parts and other locomotive components. The whole drop-hammer establishment was increased to 22 hammers in eight batteries, and the output in 1917 was 1,450 tons contrasted with the 400 tons in Webb's last year.

Crewe also supplied much machinery for the ROD locomotive repair shops at Audricq, Berguette and Borre in France, including hydraulic pumps, boilers, cranes, wheel drops, levelling blocks and case-hardening furnaces. The biggest cranes were two of overhead travelling type of 45 tons lifting capacity and 58ft span, and the lifting and travelling speeds were considerably higher than Crewe-crane averages. Special lifting tackle also was made for the easy loading on ships of the 111 LNWR engines (85 Webb 0-6-0 coal engines and 26 of the 0-8-0s) sent to France and Egypt. Heavy repairs were given at Crewe in 1916 to three engines just sold to the War Department by the Dublin & South Eastern Railway, which originally were LNWR Webb 2-4-2Ts, and in 1918 to two Belgian steam locomotives, 0-6-0s Nos 2929 and 3970 of 'Caledonian' type.

Shortage of petrol led in 1917 to the establishment of a small plant for making 'motor spirit' as a fuel for some of the company's vehicles and plant, and a total of 26,000 gallons was made up to March 1920, when an extension was made to give up to 1,000 gallons a week.

Perhaps the most publicised of Crewe's World War I productions was the so-called 'Crewe tractor', a standard Ford Model T chassis of the time to which flanged steel wheels were fitted to suit it to the railway system behind the lines in France. In his book *Deeds of a Great Railway* G. R. S. Darroch, a Crewe assistant works manager (and the only recorded Old Etonian premium and pupil) gave credit for the inception of this tractor to Cooke's daughter, Faith, and wrote that the idea came to her while talking to a young officer in Paris during the war. A likelier version is that the idea occurred to an ex-Crewe premium, Reggie Terrell, then serving in France with the Grenadier Guards. He put the idea to a friend in the right department at the War Office and suggested that he got in touch with Crewe to see what could be done.

One of the lesser-known activities of the Steelworks through the years 1916–18 was the supply of steel rails to other English railways when their normal steel suppliers could promise only long delivery times; but the Crewe supply, though to BS sections and specifications, was in the LNWR standard 60ft length, and in this fashion longer rails came first to two or three other lines, including the Great Western. By the end of the war the steel plant was rolling 1,600 to 1,800 tons of rails a month despite the steel demands for other purposes.

Many men left Crewe to enlist in the first few months of the war, and others went off with the Royal Engineer (Railway) companies of Territorials. In 1915 women were employed in the works for the first time, and the number grew steadily until 1918. Dilution of male labour increased after opposition from the trade unions. These two factors plus the general war conditions and increased militancy of the unions brought a distinct decline in the long-standing works discipline and morale.

Around 1916 the complete repainting of repaired engines in the paint shop was limited to around six at a time, all lining was abandoned, and touch-up painting in the erecting shops was the rule. Full painting and lining was not resumed until the end of 1921. Naming of passenger engines also ceased through the same period. Engine repair work, though not always to pre-war standards, was kept going by overtime above the 54-hour week. Through 1917–18 usually there were 330 to 370 engines under repair or in the paint shop plus 75 to 90 outside awaiting pit space. This decline, plus deteriorating standards of driving, firing, maintenance and poor quality coal, led to more numerous failures in service, around 130 a month in 1917 and 160 a month towards the end of 1918.

From the beginning of 1915 to the early months of 1919 Crewe completed 180 new locomotives, of which 70 were 0-8-0s, 40 were Claughtons, and 30 were Prince of Wales class. This average of only 45 a year was a measure of the upset caused in Crewe routine by armament work; it emphasises the lack of War Office and Ministry of Munitions planning and Cooke's willingness to take on almost anything.

Increasing war traffic, the reduced capacity of the works for locomotive repair and new construction, and the loan of 111 'war engines', led to departures from long-standing LNWR and Crewe tenets. In 1916 the first outside order for new locomotives for 44 years was placed – 20 Prince of Wales 4-6-0s with the North British Locomotive Co. Half were built at Hyde Park and half at Queen's Park. The tenders were provided by Crewe, and the engine number plates bore 'Crewe Works'. This was the only wartime outside order for new engines, though a proposal to order 20 0-8-0s from Beyer Peacock was publicised. The poor labour and materials situation through 1919–21 led to another contract being placed in 1919, this time with Beardmore, for no fewer than 90 Prince of Wales 4-6-0s which were delivered 1920–21; only 60 of these had Clyde-built tenders. Both these and the NBL Princes were given Crewe lot numbers and Crewe motion numbers.

Though Cooke's lamented death did not occur until October 1920, Crewe activities from 11 November 1918 onwards belong to another vital and troublesome period lasting until the formation of the LMSR rather than to 'the running era', and this is dealt with in the succeeding chapter.

Steelworks end from the south at Gainsborough Road, 1909. To left on skyline is the raised riveting tower of the boiler shop; then, going right, the wooden cooling towers near the ponds, the carriage works (with the short dark chimney) and behind it the line of the boiler-house water tank, the rail mill and the melts with a large group of chimneys, and the steel foundry (with higher roof)

(NRM, York)

The Steelworks end from the tower of the RC Church in Delamere Street, during the works holiday in 1895. To the left is Eagle Bridge and the carriage shops. The group of four chimneys is at the melts, and behind it on the skyline is Beeston Hill. Between the two tallest chimneys is the riveting tower of the boiler shop. The saw-tooth roof to the right is the paint shop; behind that are the signal shop, tender shop, iron foundry, and the circular-kiln brickworks with central chimney

Above: An old Bury 0–4–0 off the Cromford & High Peak line rebuilt to 0–4–0T in the 1870s to shunt in Crewe works. Photograph taken 1879

Below: One of the four early conversions of Crewe-type 2–4–0s to 2–4–0T crane locomotives; No 519 at work on the Llandulas viaduct demolition after the wash-away in 1879 (*Brian Radford collection*)

Bottom: No 2 erecting shop in the early 1890s showing under repair 0–6–0ST, Special DX, and the square-tanked condensing 0–6–0T No 50, later named *Liverpool* and re-numbered 3021. Note central arcade with machine tools (*NRM, York*)

8
Years of Transition, 1919–22

From going all-out with 10,000 workers and much overtime, Crewe Works went into an immediate flat spin on 11 November 1918, but this lasted only a few weeks, for in accordance with Government wartime promises to the trade unions a 47-hour week at the works and 48 hours for the running staff began on 1 January 1919. The 47-hour (nominal) week was made up of 8.00am to 5.00pm on Monday, Wednesday, Thursday and Friday, 8.00am to 6.00pm Tuesday, 8.00am to 12 noon on Saturday with midday breaks; from April 1919 the steel melting furnacemen went on to three 8-hour shifts. Though the shorter hours were known some months in advance, no detailed study for a smooth changeover had been initiated at Crewe, and the almost stop-gap solutions were complicated by dismissals of wartime labour and the re-engagement of old Crewe men back from the Forces. These matters were not fully settled when there was a general railway strike 26 September to 5 October, followed by a general moulders' strike that disrupted the iron, chair and steel foundries, and led to much of the works being set on short time from October 1919 to the end of February 1920. The shops through that period were closed from 5.30pm Thursday to 8.00am Monday, while all night-shift work was stopped. A minor result was that a few new engines left the works without their cast-iron number plates. By the Spring of 1920 little progress had been made in overtaking the backlog of repairs that had accumulated through the war years.

At the end of 1918 the Railway Executive Committee suggested that the railways should have locomotives repaired by private firms to try and ease the growing deterioration of motive power. The LNWR approached Armstrong Whitworth, as the established locomotive builders could not promise quick repair by reason of substantial orders for new engines. Tentatively AW agreed in January 1919 to take up to six engines at a time into Openshaw works, and in April a contract was sanctioned for 240 engines to be given heavy repairs over 18 months at the rate of four per week after delivery began, confined to Whale and Cooke 4-4-0s and 4-6-0s.

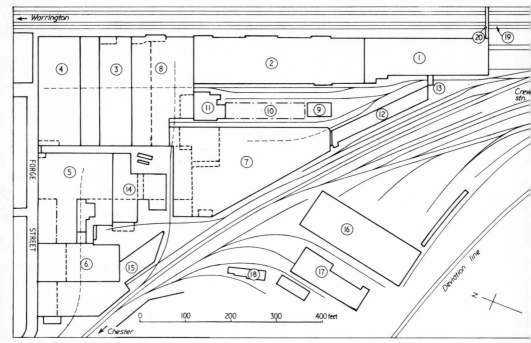

1 No 1 Erecting shop 2 No 2 Erecting shop 3 No 3 Erecting shop 4 No 4 Erecting shop 5 Smithy 6 Forge
7 Fitting shop 8 Motion shop 9 Iron stores 10 Gantry crane 11 Power house 12 Stores 13 Clock tower arch
14 Casehardening shop 15 Smithy stores 16 Out-station shop 17 Stores building of 1906 18 Stores
19 Warrington line tracks 20 Birdswood bridge

Fig 34 Layout of Old Works around 1920, at the time of maximum congestion

This outside work, plus the 90 new Beardmore-built 4-6-0s mentioned in the preceding chapter, led to a class of man with which Crewe, because of its self-sufficiency in materials and products, was largely unfamiliar – the outside inspector, and ex-premiums and others from the works and drawing office had to be trained rapidly to undertake the duties. There was a certain wryness about all this, for one of Cooke's successes through the war years had been the way he managed to keep hordes of War Office and Ministry inspectors out of the works.

Another new feature for Crewe arising from shortage of effective motive power was the purchase from the Ministry of Munitions in 1919 of 30 of the ROD 2-8-0s at around £10,000 apiece, and the hire of many more. At one time as many as 150 (purchased and hired) were operating on the LNWR and were allocated to Crewe for general repairs. These engines brought a new problem, for being a Great Central Railway design every part of engine and tender was of a type and specification completely unknown to the works, so much so that a separate single order for one cast-iron sandbox was placed with NBL as being cheaper and quicker than making one at Crewe. Also, for the first time, the works had to deal with the repair of Westinghouse air brakes.

Another critical situation arose from the backlog in boiler repairs. All 111 engines sent overseas had been given boilers in first-class order, and the replacements had not all been brought back to satisfactory condition. Estimates made in January 1919 showed that 248 new boilers would be needed that year, including 70 for the 1920 locomotive-building programme. Maximum capacity in 1914 had been four new boilers a working week, but with the 47-hour week and arrears of repairs production could hardly reach 200 in the year despite the large use of No 5 erecting shop for boiler work. The diversion of No 5 was made during the war because its cranes no longer were suitable for handling anything but small 6-wheel engines, for which there was ample repair capacity at the Old Works, yet this shop had no compressed-air supply for pneumatic tools until 1919!

Another obsolete feature of the boiler department was that every new and repaired boiler was fired-up individually for its steam test at great expense in fuel and labour; not until 1920 was a permanent locomotive boiler allocated to supply steam to all boilers coming up for test, which could sometimes number two and three in a working day.

During the war some boilermakers had left for, or been drafted to, Merseyside for work on marine boilers, and the post-war shortage of such labour was accentuated by lack of housing accommodation in the town. To ease this, board sanction was given in the autumn of 1919 for a new small estate of 69 ex-army huts near Victoria Park. Private tenders were deemed excessive, and the locomotive department had to do the job with some little help from the estate department, and to lay in all gas, water and electricity mains. Known as Park Place, the estate was completed in 1920. It was acceptable at the time as a supposed temporary (15-year) measure, but it lasted longer; in 1956 a Cheshire journal described it as "the worst blot on the town–a shanty town."

To ease the immediate boiler situation NBL was given an order in 1919 for 70 new boilers for 0-8-0 engines (new and converted from compounds) at a total price of £186,608, and construction was spread over all three NBL works in 1920. Ten boilers for new Claughtons (including that for No 1914 *Patriot*) were built by Vickers at Barrow in 1920 and some for Renown 4-4-0s were supplied by Nasmyth Wilson. Beardmore also gave repairs at Dalmuir to many LNWR boilers, and it was one of these, on Webb 4-cylinder compound 0-8-0 No 134, that exploded at Buxton on 11 November 1921 due to wrong safety-valve seat angles and incorrect valve-wing tolerances.

Quite apart from the backlog of repairs, by the end of 1919 the work allocated to the shops compared with that at the end of Webb's time represented an increase of 18 percent in the number of engines, 14 percent in the number of valve motions, 21 percent in the number of cylinders and connecting-rods, and 40 percent in wheels, axles and axleboxes. To meet this, the increase in covered shop area since 1904 was only some five percent, and the acquisition of new plant and more progressive measures was insufficient; in fact, the methods, organisation and discipline were inferior when balanced against the need. This, with the board's financial indecision, was reflected also in a number of orders, principally for 0-8-2Ts, being cancelled after Crewe E-numbers had been allotted, a feature almost unknown at Crewe after the mid-1850s.

As a fruit of the abdication of strict control by 'the running men', supplemented by war conditions and the ensuing labour changes, two chaotic procedures had grown up and came to their apogee in 1919–20. First, leading foremen went along the reception roads at the west end and selected from what had come in on a general mileage or time base the engines they thought should be shopped at once. Invariably the boilershop foreman favoured engines different from those selected by the erecting shop foreman, and the wheel shop foreman's ideas were different again.

A second equally disturbing procedure in several erecting shops that a boiler needing only light repair was often dealt with by the boilermakers while still in place, or was lifted off and repaired alongside the pit. Either method was a source of inconvenience to the erectors. A chargehand erector still had five engines at a time to look after, with a small gang on each, and it was not unknown for one or two of his gangs to be unable to work on their engines for some hours owing to the activities of the boiler men. Again, a small spare boiler float had not been maintained for classes carrying a large number of engines.

These were some of the reasons why in 1920–21 large engines were on works for 60 days for general repairs, but with gradual easing of these factors the repair performance improved. Through 1921 some 415–420 engines were under repair at one time or were in the paint shop, and another 55 to 75 lay outside awaiting pit space; anything up to 25 percent of all LNWR motive power was out of action at a time in shops or at sheds.

Neither Cooke nor Beames was able to evolve a scheme for a works re-organisation based on a substantial cut in the time taken to repair each engine. Only piecemeal measures grounded on more pit capacity and a larger work force were applied for and sactioned, but the sanction was sometimes countermanded. In 1914 brief proposals for yet another erecting shop had been made, and early in 1920 Beames began to press for this shop, and authority was granted in the September, a month before Cooke died, for a new shop alongside No 9. Authorisation was reluctant, for the estimated cost of the structure and equipment was £162,500, or five times the sum that would have been sufficient in 1914.

R. A. Riddles was put in charge of this work in November 1920, but the walls were only some seven feet high when the board stopped the work in view of the economic position of the company and the upset caused by the forthcoming Bill for railway grouping, then in its initial stages. Perhaps this was fortunate, for the plans were on the old, old Crewe principle of two bays with pits too closely spread, between the bays an arcade crammed with machine tools, and with brick walls taking the crane loads. Use of such a shop would hardly have reduced the repair time per engine. The partly completed walls remained a feature of the west end for some four years.

Various small measures were undertaken by Cooke and Beames through 1919–21. The tool shop was improved, for up to the end of the war it could not maintain the self-centering chucks on modern machines. The west-end wheel shop capacity was slightly increased. Lighting at the Steelworks was improved by a new system fed by a 1000kW turbo-generator set that supplanted the old arc lamps and numerous small generating sets. Much of the shafting in the Old Works was overloaded by long hours and bigger machines; ball bearings were installed for the main lengths to try and eliminate the long week-end hours of millwrights' maintenance. The layout of the Old Works, then not far off the end of its life as a locomotive-repair factory, was then as shown in Fig 26.

Before Cooke's death authorisation was given for an improvement in the steel melting plant, to include two mechanically-charged re-heating furnaces at a cost above £20,000, plus six more gas producers. The latter were installed, but financial sanction for the furnaces was cancelled, and nothing more was done for steel-making during LNWR days except that from August 1922 Crewe gave up its own steel specifications and went over to BS. In 1922 designing was begun for a complete new steel plant. Another and even more effective project due to Beames also was delayed; this was the closure of the three works power stations in favour of obtaining current from outside. The work was put in hand during 1921–22, but not until early LMSR days did the scheme come into full operation, power then being taken through two substations from the North Wales Power Supply Co and its associate the Mersey Power Supply Co. Only one new locomotive design appeared in the time of Beames; this was the 0-8-4T, but the first was out-shopped only after the LMSR took over.

Crewe clung on too long in those days to obsolete practices and tools, particularly in view of war-time advances in production engineering. When Hughes became chief mechanical engineer on the amalgamation of the LNWR and LYR in January 1922 he found that Crewe's standards of accuracy, measurement and production techniques were not equal to those in force at Horwich works of the LYR. He was said to be appalled to recognise machines on which he had worked in his 'premium' days in the 1880s and which even then had not been regarded as new. Further, Horwich engine-repair times were markedly below those at Crewe, and the bases for bringing in engines for repair were different.

Hughes made attempts to have Crewe practices improved, and arranged for frequent reciprocal interchange visits of supervisory

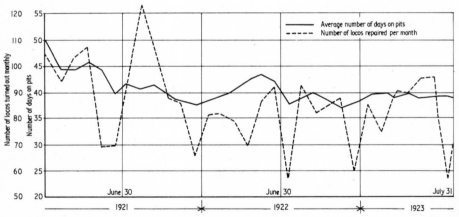

Fig 35 Repair position at Crewe in the years immediately preceding the formation of the LMSR

personnel between Horwich and Crewe; when he tried to bring Crewe to the Horwich method of thoroughly examining engines two months before their statutory repair visits, and making a report on the major work needed, he met with opposition from Beames, who claimed it would cost £3,000 a year for no purpose.

The pre-Grouping fusion of the LNWR and LYR in January 1922, which in itself followed the appointment of Arthur Watson as general manager of both railways in January 1921, led to the consolidation of the locomotive, carriage and wagon departments under one head, the chief mechanical engineer; running was taken away from the locomotive department and put under the operating division. Further, erection and maintenance of many of the structures belonging to the locomotive department were transferred to the civil engineer, and so was intensified the disintegration of the long-standing numerous activities of the LNWR locomotive side at Crewe.

It was the separation of mechanical engineering from running that made so lamentable the resistance of Beames to the efforts of Hughes to put LNWR engine-shopping methods on a more effective base; some progress *was* made in 1922, and it led at the time of the Grouping to the marriage of this new idea to a small existing Crewe feature, and an issue of the union was the LMSR works reorganisation scheme of 1925–27.

In Cooke's time simple progress boards came into use in two or three shops, and were operated by the shop clerks under the foremen's direction. Big wartime expansion of progress systems was reflected at Crewe only to the extent that these boards, with new additions, and the attendant clerks, were brought together in February 1920, housed in a 24ft by 8ft wooden hut against the sawmill in the Deviation area and became part of the works manager's office organisation. Until 1922 this hut was simply a recording office and the personnel had no executive authority, but later they formed the nucleus of the progress department, without which the modernisation of 1925–27 could not have been mooted or authorised.

The brief year of Hughes in charge of mechanical engineering opened the eyes of younger officials to the obsolesence at Crewe, and a wider and more progressive outlook was engendered except at the top. Also that year itself gave Hughes and a few seniors time to accustom themselves to the problems of management and direction of much larger conglomerate railway systems than those to which they had been attached. In this fashion the questions that had so disturbed Crewe over the years 1846–57 were now to be repeated on an immeasurably greater scale.

9
LMSR Ownership, 1923–47

When the LMSR took over Crewe works on 1 January 1923 the chaotic procedures described in the preceding chapter had been terminated, and along with rather greater control and discipline had helped a reduction in repair time from 50 days on the pits in 1920 to 39 days early in 1923, (see Fig 35). Much of the Old Works smithy production had been transferred to the west end; the efforts of Hughes to manufacture to greater accuracy were bearing fruit and micrometers had appeared in the works; insistence that engines should be examined at the sheds before shopping, and a schedule made of the main work to be done was despite the distaste of Beames, making headway.

The gradual build-up of a progress system of repairs based on the new scheme for shopping engines was given to R. A. Riddles, who was largely free because of the stoppage of work on the new erecting shop and the transfer of 'structures' to the civil engineer. A small staff absorbing the sawmill-hut men, was established in another hut near the north-west gate, and soon it began to progress major items of work through the shops, for unless this was done the bottleneck would simply be transferred. This new department was given executive authority. By 1924 it was informing all shops what engines would come in and when, the work to be done by each shop, and the date by which each shop had to supply its quota, but the system could be effective only as far as permitted by the existing Crewe equipment, layout, and morale of staff and workers. All of these were insufficient for a railway the size of the LMSR with a policy of closing smaller works and handling all repairs at four major plants. Nevertheless by the autumn of 1924 the average time on the pits for a heavy repair was down to about 32 days, though the time the engine was in the Crewe Works areas was still above 40 days.

In 1922 Hughes had proposed to concentrate all Crewe operations at the west end; such closure of the Old Works was sacrilege to the Crewe tradition, but had the LNWR continued that closure would have been pushed through. With the formation of the LMSR,

The steel rail mill in 1895 after being remodelled to produce 60ft rails. The cogger is on the right and the triple decker rolls to the left. Electric arc lighting already installed in part of the shop (*NRM, York*)

Webb's last erecting shop, No 9, completed in 1903, showing a batch of Precursor tanks under construction in 1906. Hot air came up through the floor grilles. The roof framing was lighter and had more glazing than earlier shops (*NRM, York*)

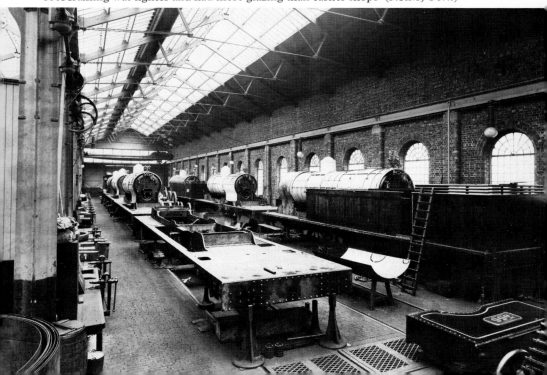

The Webb family in the early 1870s. F. W. is at the back on the left and his eldest brother on the right. Front row from left to right: F. W.'s sister, his younger brother Walter G., his father, his elder brother Arthur (later the canon), and his mother

(NRM, York)

Webb (against the window) as a young works manager, with his foremen in 1864, when the works was employing nearly 3,000 men. Back row: J. Roberts (assistant in No 1 shop), J. Bland (Joiners), T. Bebbington (Bricklayers), J. Croft (Buildings), P. Redfern (Bessemer plant, not yet in production). Centre row: E. Stott (Iron rail mill), Hymers (Iron foundry). Beazley (Painters), G. Ollier (Labourers), J. Bebbington (Smithy), G. Bailey (Wheel shop). Front row: Antrobus (Copper shop), Price (Gasworks), H. Hawkins (Fitting shop), W. Williams (Tender shop), Geo. Dingley (Nos 3 and 4 shops), A. Hunter (No 1 shop), J. Allison (Forge and Smithy; later steel plant manager), G. Pottie (Millwrights), W. Ellis (Boiler shop), R. Hawley (No 2 shop). "Ollier" is mis-spelt as "Hollier" in the photograph.

(NRM, York)

Above: Employees with 50 years' service in 1911, with Sir Gilbert Claughton, LNWR chairman (centre), Bowen Cooke (third from right), Warneford, works manager (second from right), Homfray, assistant works manager (extreme right). Second from the left is Henry Cooper, chief boiler shop foreman, who joined the service in 1852.

Left: Chester Place, the company's house for the locomotive superintendent, built in the early 1860s, and which housed in succession Ramsbottom, Webb, Whale, Cooke and Beames (*NRM, York*)

Bottom: Richard Moon (Sir Richard Moon, *Bart*, from 1887), LNWR chairman 1861–91, with his wife, sons and daughters, and Webb (second from right at back), in the grounds of Chester Place, *circa* 1886

GWR 4-cylinder 4–6–0 No 4005 *Polar Star* at Crewe North shed during its fortnight of trial running on the LNWR in 1910. Midge Bridge in the background

Below: Prospero, the Experiment 4–6–0 converted 1915 to a 4-cylinder simple with only two piston valves and two sets of valve motion on Dendy Marshall's system. In Crewe works yard

Bottom: The boiler from the Ditton smash Jumbo 2–4–0 in 1912 after being brought back to Crewe works. The only boiler known to have broken its back in a derailment. After being dragged sideways along the track for a hundred yards the rivets over the top half of the throatplate sheared on striking bridge abutments

however, Crewe matters had to be considered against a wider background. Hughes talked things over with the deputy chief mechanical engineer, Sir Henry Fowler, and after the latter had inspected Crewe he wrote to Hughes on 1 June 1923: "I fully appreciate the object you have in view of shutting down shops that are so old as those near the station . . . But I would refer to the crowded state which exists in certain of the shops at the Steelworks where the work is to be concentrated . . . No 9 erecting shop is so congested that I feel sure work cannot possibly be carried out on the best lines. The mistake seems to have been made of trying to get more pits in, with a central arch, than the width of the shop will allow."

Hughes did not at once bring the locomotive works re-organisation up to board level, because he felt the progress system should be developed further, and because a new steel plant had high priority. For the latter a more comprehensive scheme than that of 1919 was put forward, and board sanction was given on 29 November 1923 for the replacement of the whole steel-making plant at an estimated cost of £206,466 "to concentrate the company's manufacture of steel at Crewe." This qualifying phrase was to cover the closure of the ex-LYR steel plant at Horwich, which had a capacity of 12,000 tons of ingots a year.

At this date the Crewe steel plant still consisted of the three old 30-ton and seven 20-ton hand-charged Siemens-Marten open-hearth furnaces. They, and the three 10-ton furnaces in this steel foundry, were fired by 64 Wilson gas producers. Maximum production of ingots was around 72,000 tons a year, and 340 men and boys were normally employed in the melting furnaces with an additional 30 tending the gas producers.

The new plant, erected on part of the old site but in new buildings, was given two 40/45-ton acid open-hearth furnaces and two 60/70-ton basic open-hearth furnaces of about 84,000 tons annual potential. Furnace charging was done by a number of Wellman 3-ton revolving machines, and the furnaces were fired by six large Morgan gas producers needing only 21 men for full operation and brought into commission successively between January and September 1925.

The furnaces were commissioned gradually, the two 45-ton units in January–March 1926 and the two 70-ton plants in September 1926 and July 1927. Drying-out of the first 45-ton furnace began at the New Year of 1926, but an explosion occurred on 16 February; the gas was put on again on 22 February and the first tap was on 5 March. Drying of the first of the big furnaces began on 15 March, but owing to the general strike the fire was not put in until 30 September and the first tap was on 1 November. Misfortune also attended the second 70-ton furnace, for drying commenced on 15 October, but soon after the fire had to be put out and the first tap was delayed until 21 July 1927.

Outside the plant the tracks of the open stack yard were served by two overhead electric cranes each with a 5-ton lifting magnet. Inside the plant a short length of the 18in-gauge tramway was laid. Distinct from the methods of Webb, the whole design, demolition and construction were given to an outside contractor, the Wellman–Smith–Owen Corporation, for whom the gas producers were put in by International Combustion Co.

After some years of successful operation came the major financial slump of 1929–31. The English steel industry was hard hit, and in 1931 the leading ironmasters (at least one of whom was on the LMSR board) approached Sir Josiah Stamp, then LMSR chairman and president, and offered to supply all the steel needed by the company at 10 percent less than current prices for a period of ten years. Stamp agreed to this offer, partly on the larger issue of Brtish industrial and economic well-being in a difficult world situation, a factor that Stamp, as an internationally-known statistician and economist, could hardly ignore; another influence was that a major renewal of the rail mill was due, and this would involve fresh capital expenditure above £120,000, a factor known to the ironmasters. Finally, several non-LNWR elements on the LMSR that had Stamp's ear were opposed to Crewe producing everything that it needed.

The company announced officially that it could no longer make its own steel economically, but Stamp had made no close investigation of Crewe steel costs, which including delivery were lower than those offered by industry. The rail mill, not referred to in the announcement, was a critical factor; £120,000 investment at that time was a more serious matter than it would have been if included in the 1925–27 reorganisation costs of around £750,000. Thus the last heat of steel began on 23 September 1932 and the steel plant was shut down on 30 September, along with the rail mill, and over 400 men lost their jobs. Shortly afterwards the brickworks were closed.

Neither plant nor buildings at the steel-making section were dismantled, and they continued to stand almost derelict. Following a Ministry of Supply decision in June 1940 the furnaces and melting plant were refurbished, the two acid furnaces were converted to basic, new ladles and carriages were obtained, the whole department was 'blacked-out', and the plant was restarted in March 1941 to cope with war requirements. Unsuitable scrap quite different from the heavy 'railway' scrap of pre-1932 years caused some difficulties in operation, while incoming light bulky scrap, arriving most irregularly, often had to be taken over Eagle Bridge and dumped temporarily in the eastern part of the old carriage area. The whole carriage plant itself had been disused since 1932, when of course there had been another pay-off.

Monthly output of ingots was 3,000 tons in 1941-42 and 4,000 to 5,000 tons through 1943-45, and the plant was run to meet the needs of the Ministry of Supply. In 1946 the steel-making department was finally closed and the equipment removed, though the buildings remain to this day. Total steel production from 1864 to 1945 was around 3,300,000 tons, of which 1,391,805 tons were rails rolled between 1875 and the last rolling on 30 September 1932. In the space vacated from 1946 cutting-up of condemned steam locomotives was done for some years, but when the BR mass withdrawal of steam power began condemned engines were sold to scrap merchants.

A corollary of the closure of the steel plant in 1932 was that less work was required from the main works forge, and much of its major equipment also was removed; of the steam hammers only that of eight tons and one of 50cwt were retained, which worked on blooms obtained from outside. After war began they and the forge heat-treatment plant were fully employed, the latter being in 168 hours-a-week operation for long periods.

Extra to both steel plant and locomotive works reorganisation was a thorough remodelling in 1925 of the gasworks. This was sufficient until 1938, when around 256 million cu ft a year were being made. In 1939 the establishment of the Rolls Royce engine works at the west end of the town, and the new dwellings associated with it, brought a big new demand, and this was increased further with the extra war load from that plant and the railway works. Therefore in 1941 the carbonising plant was increased by three arches, and by 1944 over 500 million cu ft a year were being generated, of which about 30 percent was taken by the railway works, 20 percent by Rolls Royce, and 50 percent by public and civic consumption. Two of the smaller gas-holders commissioned in 1886 were replaced in 1941 by two modern spirally-guided holders, and another charging-discharging machine for the retorts with other ancillaries were added to the plant in 1942.

Ideas as to the desirable locomotive works re-organisation advanced with the development of shopping principles and scheduled work flow for repaired engines, but as the matter came up to higher managerial levels an outside opinion was desired. R. W. Reid, the LMSR carriage and wagon superintendent, an ex-Derby man, visited the works, and on 25 August 1924 reported to H. G. Burgess, the LMSR general manager: "It is quite evident the works need overhauling to be

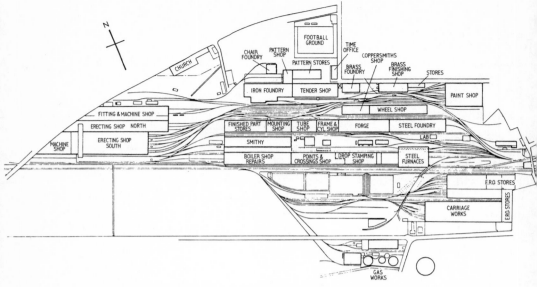

Fig 36 Layout at the Steelworks end after the 1925–27 reorganisation

efficient. The general layout is bad, chiefly on account of the geographical difficulty, and the shops and yards are untidy, and tons of scrap could be picked up and disposed of with advantage. I think your best mechanical engineer should be resident at Crewe, and it will take five years, at least, to put things straight there . . . I do not think the design of the present erecting shops is good. The pits are too close together, the centre aisle is crammed with benches and machines, and it is difficult to get material to and from the engines under repair, particularly with the dreadfully slow cranes they have. All Crewe cranes seem to be very slow – 11ft/min travel and 2ft/min hoist instead of 300ft and 50ft respectively . . . I think the Crewe habit of making everything themselves needs looking into."

This report, though resented in certain Crewe circles as detrimental and as 'Midland interference', accorded well with the quiet efforts of Hughes and his staff to ensure higher authority would feel from all sources that money would have to be found for a comprehensive works re-organisation. Plans for this had been developed gradually through 1923–24; the progress department had come to advise advanced measures for imposing programmed control on all works operations and cutting down substantially the time an engine was in for heavy repairs, and fortunately Beames gradually began to develop keener interest.

On 26 February 1925 the rolling stock committee of the board sanctioned the works re-organisation scheme submitted by Hughes at an estimated cost of £427,151. This scheme was approved by the 'old board' of the LMSR, the one prior to the appointment of Sir Josiah Stamp as president of the executive from 1 January 1926. It was Stamp who most appreciated the benefits and who, in his later drive to get greater economies in the locomotive and running departments, was impressed by the detailed costs and statistics available for Crewe repairs and the individually-costed Western Division locomotive performance when he could find adequate or authentic costs for little else. By the time the re-organisation and re-equipment were complete in 1928 the cost of the re-organisation had risen to £750,000.

As sanctioned, the scheme had three major aims: (1) the re-organisation of the whole Steelworks end to get much shorter repair times by a tightly-programmed work flow in the erecting shop and in the various shops feeding work to the erectors; (2) a big cut in the shunting and transfer movements within the works area; and (3) the rebuilding of the four erecting shops and the valve motion shop in the Old Works into a new boiler department that would build all new boilers for all divisions of the LMSR. The drop-stamping shop and the smithy in the Old Works were to be retained, while the signal work was to be moved to the old fitting shop from the west end.

Apart from one large erecting shop there was little actual new building, but many alterations were made inside other buildings of 1866–1903 construction and of 1843 buildings in the Old Works to suit them for other purposes. To get better siding space and more convenient transfer routes at the vital far west end, the southern end of the brickyard was given up and the high ground excavated; the brick kiln itself continued to function for some years and produced the bricks for the new erecting shop. The trackless-vehicle internal transport, begun in 1919, was developed fully as the general inter-shop system over concrete runways for all except the heaviest parts such as boilers and wheel-and-axle sets, and the 18in-gauge tramway was taken up except in the new steel plant. An electrically-operated transporter to take 1½-ton loads was put in between the finished parts store and the erecting-machine shop block. The Deviation shops continued almost unaltered, with the testing department, millwrights and joiners, and the sawmill. The southern annexe to the Old Works was now limited to locomotive and general stores.

Right in the midst of the conversion came the general strike of 1926 that more-or-less closed the works and then upset every activity connected with it for months; only a portion of the conversion work could continue while the works was empty and so ease one of the most complicated aspects of the whole scheme – the maintenance of normal

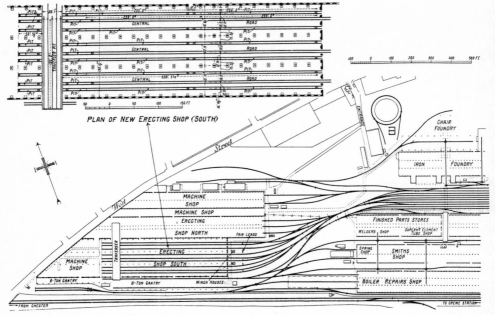

Fig 37 Layout of the new (1927) erecting shop south and the track rearrangements at the far west end to suit it

repair output during the alterations. That any conversion work at all could be done was due to the 200–250 non-railway casual labourers who had been engaged to do the structural work and remove the tools. Before conversion was complete the shops were given additional load through the alteration to oil-firing of many engines, mainly Claughtons and Princes, to counter the effects of the continuing coal strike, and shortly after came the removal of all that equipment.

The new layout at the Steelworks end is shown by Fig 36, and the re-arrangement can be seen by comparing that illustration with Fig 31 in Chapter 6. Work was begun in 1925 and by mid-1927 two-thirds of the new erecting shop was in full function. This shop was on the site of the partly-erected No 10 shop of Beames, but it did not take that number, and from 1928 was known as erecting shop south. It handled all repairs and new construction and the older erecting shops were converted to other purposes. Thus about 13,500sq yd of erecting shop floor area under one roof replaced 30,000sq yd under eight widely-separated roofs, neglecting No 7 – the greatest single advance ever made in Crewe shop practice.

The new shop had three bays 642ft long by 63ft wide, and each bay had two pits and a central track, so there was far more room than in Nos 1 to 9. The structural framework was built-up as one unit of steel, the brick walls taking no part of the working loads. Within 60ft of the west end was a 100-ton traverser that was carried on into the south bay of No 9 shop, giving a traverser run of nearly 300ft. All engines for

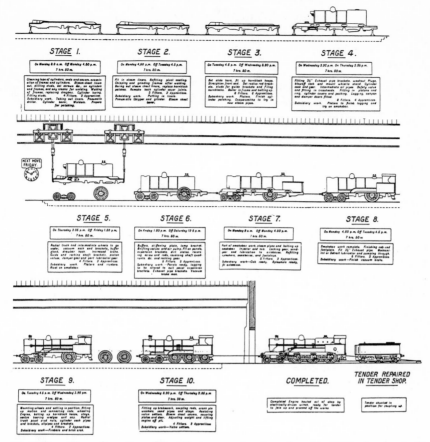

Fig 38 Operation of one line of the belt system when introduced in 1927, showing both Prince of Wales and Claughton 4-6-0s on one line

repair were brought in on this traverser, to the west of which were nine 50ft pits corresponding with the six pit tracks and three centre roads of the main part of the shop. These pits were mainly for engine cleaning and stripping, and the space between them and the curved end wall butting on to West Street was occupied by a machine shop laid out in the same three bays, but with a height to eaves of 27ft 7in contrasted with the 37ft 5in of the erecting shop proper.

Each bay of the main shop had two 50-ton four-motor overhead electric cranes which were great improvements in Crewe practice, for travel speed was up to 20ft/min, cross-travel up to 80ft/min, and the auxiliary hoist up to 20ft/min; the main hoist was limited to 6ft/min. Additionally each bay had three 10-ton cranes at a lower level.

An engine coming in on the traverser was placed on one of the two adjacent stripping pits in each line (see Fig 38) where it remained for two days. Stripping then being complete, the frame *ensemble* was lifted forward to one of the four repair stages, numbers 1 to 4, where it remained for four days; four gangs moved from one to the other of

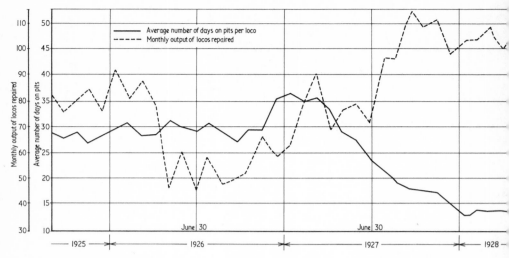

Fig 39 Reduction in repair time and increase in number of monthly repairs by the belt system in the year or two after its introduction

these four stages, doing their own particular work on each engine. On the seventh day repaired bogies and one other wheel pair (or two wheel pairs for a 6-wheel or 0-8-0 engine) were brought to stage 5 and the frame-and-boiler assembly from one of the four preceding stages was lowered on to them. The succeeding positions, stages 6 to 10, were connected by a steel cable pulled by an electric winch outside the shop at the east end. The work on each stage was so planned that every 7 hours 50 minutes of working time the men ceased operation for 10 minutes, during which time the winch pulled the whole line of five engines forward one stage, and the men at each stage then resumed work on the next engine. This it was that gave rise to the name of 'the belt system.'

Each 'belt' produced a completely repaired locomotive every working day, and an engine passed through the shop in 12 working days. On its last move, to the outside of the shop at the east end, the engine was coupled to a repaired tender which had been shunted into position after repair on a modified belt system in the tender shop, in which five of the seven tender-frame stages were connected by a cable to a winch, which effected a forward movement approximately every three hours. Tender tanks were repaired in five stages, with crane transfer. The graphic effect on repairs of this system is shown in Fig 39.

Usually one line in erecting shop south was occupied in new construction; another of the pit lines had only eight stages to suit small

Chester Bridge from the east, with general office block above to right. Decorated for the Royal visit, April 1913. Standard 0–4–0ST No 3001 with the two works cabs specially cleaned and upholstered. CME's coupé standing on stub below the bridge   (*NRM, York*)

Below: Prince of Wales class 4–6–0 of 1921 build in Crewe yard for scrapping, April 1935; brickyard chimney in background to right

Bottom: Ernest Craig, MP, addressing a meeting of 2,000 men in the boiler yard arcade (now the paint shop) on 28 July 1915, to stress the need for greater armament production. Warneford is the left-hand figure on the platform

Above: Last parade of the Crewe Volunteers (Railway Engineers) in 1912 on the break-up following the formation of the Territorial Army. The parade is in the carriage yard, with the yard viaduct to the left and Eagle Bridge on its right.

Below: Mechanics Institute library in the early years of the 20th Century. All the rooms were lit by electricity from the early 1890s *(NRM, York)*

Bottom: F. W. Webb in 1900 with a group of Whitworth Scholars and Exhibitioners who gained their awards between 1872 and 1900 while employed at Crewe. The well-known Crewe designer T. E. Sackfield is fourth from the left in the front row; George Ravenscroft, for many years Beyer Peacock's steel foundry manager, is in the centre of the back row (with bow tie) *(NRM, York)*

engines, which passed through the shop in ten working days in place of twelve. For some time at the beginning one pit line was run on a group system, with gangs working on numerically small classes not scheduled for perpetuation. As an average in the early years, 50 men and 29 apprentices worked on each line – fixed stages and belt – but by the mid-1930s the number had increased. As an example, a 3-cylinder Royal Scot 4-6-0 heavy repair required in erecting shop south 230 man-hours in stripping and 770 man-hours in re-assembly, with 27 fitters and 15 apprentices engaged for various times in the former operation, and 90 fitters and 43 apprentices down the ten stages in the latter work.

The new plant started on the 246 Prince of Wales 4-6-0s to gain experience, but soon two or three classes could be handled on any belt at one time, largely because repairs to boiler, cab, splashers, bogies, axleboxes, wheel sets, motion and so on were strictly controlled as to time in the various shops, and adequate transport facilities, often to definite schedules, were provided for transfer from and to the erecting shop. Nevertheless, a float of at least two spare sets of wheels, two pairs of cylinders, four sets of axles, and six percent of boilers was needed for each numerically-large class.

The first engine off the belts was ready on 5 May 1927, and in the ensuing twelve months 850 engines were given heavy repairs. With all six lines in operation the average capacity came to be regarded as 30 to 35 heavy repairs a week plus up to 100 new engines a year. Within three or four years full-belt operation was found to be rather too inflexible, and soon after Beames was transferred to Derby as deputy chief mechanical engineer the cable was disconnected except for the final haulage of the completed engine into the yard, and all other movements were made by cranes. After this, locomotives of up to five different classes could be handled on any one line at a time. Nevertheless the name of 'the belt' was retained by the erectors for many years. About the same time the transporter between the erecting-machine shop block and the finished parts stores ceased to function, and all inter-shop transport was confined to rubber-tyred trucks, though the gantries of the transporter were not dismantled until BR times. The tender shop belt also was replaced by crane lifts in the early 1930s.

As the years went by erecting shop south proved capable of dealing with much bigger engines like the Stanier Pacifics, for such sizes had been visualised in 1925–27 through the earlier proposals of Hughes and Fowler for large 4-6-2s and 2-8-2s; even 2-6-0+0-6-2 Garratts were repaired in later years, while at the other end of the scale were the Clee Hill Sentinel shunter and the Leek & Manifold 2-6-4T, which were

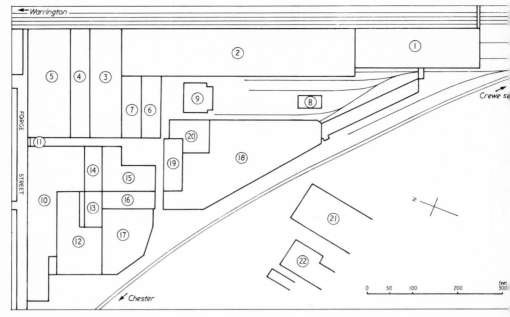

1 Plate stores 2 Boiler flangeing and machine shop 3 Boiler mounting and assembly shop 4 Boiler roof bar shop 5 Boiler finishing shop 6 Boiler stay shop 7 Brass and finishing shop 8 Stores 9 Disused building of the old power house 10 Smithy 11 Works entrance 12 Drop-hammer shop 13 Boilers 14 Tube shop 15 Spring shop and copper store 16 Die-sinking shop 17 Iron stores 18 Signal shop 19 Galvanising shop 20 Tin shop 21 Stores 22 Stores

Fig 40 Old Works re-organised in 1925–28 to build all new boilers needed by the LMSR, and to do the signal work and make a few small products

handled away in a corner. A difference between repairs and new construction for some years was that the latter had the front of the engine to the east whereas repair engines on the belt always had the cab to the east.

In 1922–23 around 3,200 engines were allocated to Crewe for repairs, and as many as 460 to 470 could be found at one time in the eight erecting shops (that is excluding No 7), in the paint shop, and outside awaiting repair space or a berth on the weighing machine, equivalent to 14½ percent of the total stock. By 1928, with erecting shop south in full function, 3,800 engines were allocated, but engines in the works area averaged only 260, or seven percent of stock, and this gain of 200 engines in traffic was one of the principal economies of the re-organisation.

Erectors came off piecework, and at first were given a 33 percent increase on basic pay rates. Once the belt system was in full operation a reduction of staff was warranted, and the men retained then got an increase to 40 percent, stepped-up after certain devices and procedures were introduced to 45 percent and finally to 50 percent, by which time the number of men in the shop had decreased by 20 percent.

Of the Steelworks old erecting shops No 5 became the heavy

machine shop, dealing with frames, cylinders, footplates and other massive parts, and wherein complete structures of side plates, cylinders and cross-stretchers were erected. No 6 became the tube shop in which by concentration and the use of new handling processes, tube cleaning and repair times were cut down by several hundred per cent. No 7 remained as the boiler-mounting and tubing shop, and also carried out boiler steam and water tests. The northern bay of No 8 was converted entirely on Horwich principles into a finished parts store; the southern bay was turned into a welding shop, in which one of the most important jobs was the repair of superheater elements.

The southern bay of No 9 was changed to handle light boiler repairs; the rest of that shop repaired tanks, cabs and splashers on a progressive system. The arcade was combined with the adjacent fitting-machine shop of 1903 to form the principal machine shop of the whole establishment, and this was given a conglomeration of all the best machine tools from Old Works and Steelworks and was provided with 120 new ones.

Finer machining limits throughout all engines came with the 1925–27 re-organisation, accompanied by an extended use of drilling and frame jigs to give interchangeable parts and engine chassis. In the machine shop five stepped sizes were adopted for worn motion parts and pins, piston valves and liners, piston rods, brake gear and other parts; greater use was made of grinding in finishing-off fine-limit parts.

After the closure of the steel melting department the foundry equipment was modernised in 1934–35 with four Sesci rotary furnaces, and these were fired by a pulverised coal ball-mill plant which, though effective, was a great dirt producer. Heavy repairs to boilers were concentrated in the old Ramsbottom-Webb boiler shop, which also continued with general plate work for the outdoor department and scrapped condemned boilers. Repaired boilers went to a stacking ground north of the main machine shop.

Concentration in the old boiler shop of heavy repairs was practicable only in conjunction with the more far-reaching decision that all new boilers for the LMSR should be built at Crewe in the converted Old Works (see Fig 40). This scheme was economic because it did away with the need to instal new and larger equipment at Derby, Horwich and St Rollox to cope with rapidly-increasing boiler sizes, and eventually a peak of 360 new boilers in a year was attained, with the stay shop turning out annually nearly 300,000 side stays and 5,000 firebox roof stays.

In the new boiler department plates and other materials came in at

Table 10 Crewe works performance over the years 1935–43

Year	1935	1936	1937	1938	1939	1940	1941	1942	Jan–June 1943
Western Division locomotives allocated to Crewe for repair	2705	2678	2674	2508	2642	2638	2570	2549	2538
General repairs	382	424	566	485	538	620	515	513	227
Service repairs	951	1031	915	759	859	1088	904	1076	597
Other repairs	387	360	437	316	270	350	427	372	202
Total classified repairs	1720	1815	1918	1560	1667	2058	1846	1961	1026
Average output of classified repairs over 50 working weeks	34·4	36·3	38·36	31·2	33·34	41·16	36·96	39·22	39·46
Additional non-classified repairs	–	–	–	432	272	262	191	157	100
New locomotives built	74	64	43	46	33	5	14	18	38[1]
New boilers built	581	581	770	663	258	122	95	87	198[1]
Boilers repaired					389	622	618	698	c 560[1]
Boiler mileage between heavy repairs	83,731	89,199	98,736	108,056	111,650	109,903	105,347	107,175	106,686
Average number of weekdays in shop, heavy repairs	17·88	16·02	19·08	19·80	18·00	16·76	20·49	15·33	15·20
Average mileage: general repair to service repair	–	–	–	57,945	65,393	57,719	50,770	56,255	54,620
Average mileage: service repair to general repair	–	–	–	44,533	45,306	50,769	42,508	45,268	44,248
Average mileage between general repairs	114,368	125,460	136,304	136,730	134,463	137,329	139,738	151,333	152,946
Average percentage of stock in Crewe for repair	8·5	8·0	6·2	6·4	6·84	3·98	3·9	5·4	4·8

[1] For full year

the south end of the old No 1 erecting shop and came out of the old Nos 3 and 4 shops as completed boilers, the work being done on the strictly-controlled progressive-flow lines adopted at the west end. Flangeing and most machine work were done in the old No 2 shop, rivetting and boiler shell assembly in Nos 3 and 4, and shop roofs were altered at two points to enable rivetting towers to be put in so that large barrel-firebox assemblies could be slung vertically on the hydraulic rivetters. In these shops were built, *inter alia*, all the Stanier and many BR taper boilers, the steel inside fireboxes for ten Class 5s, and the ten Crosti boilers for the BR 2-10-0s Nos 92020–29, while plate flangeing jobs were done for other LMSR works.

The policy pushed by Stamp and E. J. H. Lemon from 1930 of working the traffic with far fewer locomotives was helped by Crewe's substantial reduction of repair times, but it could make real headway only when a considerable number of first-class engines was in service. Though average daily mileage per engine increased steadily from 1930 it was not until after the mid-1930s, when many Stanier engines with excellent axleboxes and good frame structures were in traffic, that the whole repair position could be once again advanced. This was done by giving piston and valve examinations every 40,000 miles or so; wheel, axlebox and light repairs were done every 70,000 miles or more; and heavy repairs, including boiler overhaul, were given every 150,000 miles or more, the mileages varying according to the class of locomotive. Both types of repair were done in the Crewe erecting shop, so that the works came back to the practice of Ramsbottom in handling many intermediate repairs, but these were now done on progressive lines.

As chief mechanical engineer of the LMSR from the beginning of 1932, Stanier came to have a decided influence on Crewe shop practice and morale because of his great personal interest in machine tools and works practices. Through his insistence a much finer precision and quality of finish were introduced, especially for axleboxes and axle journals, which were so machined and finished that no scraping or fitting were required – or allowed. This, combined with the new design of axlebox, so reduced the number of hot boxes that by 1940 axlebox performance was no longer a consideration in about 1,300 of the larger locomotives.

The 3,800 Western Division engines allocated to Crewe for repairs in 1928 had been reduced to 2,700 by the end of 1935, and the number of locomotives owned by the LMSR had fallen from 10,316 in 363 classes in 1923 to 8,000 in 200 classes. The number allocated to Crewe for repair was reduced still further in succeeding years, but from 1938 the work done was affected by endeavours to get as many engines as possible into first-class order before the obvious coming war broke out. That two or three hundred engines were not in the best repair in 1938 was due to substantial budget cuts in two years after 1930, enforced from the president's office at Euston purely for financial book-keeping reasons. These cuts had greatly affected the even work flow at Crewe, and subsequent considerable additional work was needed to bring things back to even keel.

Table 10 shows in broad outline the work done at Crewe over the years 1935-43 and the corresponding mileages between repairs. The peak was reached in 1940 with 2,058 classified repairs plus 272 others; some of these others were bomb damage cases. From around 1930, as the tight work control matured, the work force as a whole could be reduced, and from 1932 until the beginning of World War II the number of men employed never reached 7,000, but the standard of discipline was probably higher than at any time since 1903. From the 1929-31 slump until the spring of 1939 the works operated largely on short time against the basic 47-hour week. This was arranged in an unusual way with three shifts through the 24 hours (06.00 to 14.00, 14.00 to 22.00, and 22.00 to 06.00) with five shifts a week in each. Men on the 14.00 to 22.00 shift received 'night pay' from 18.00 onwards; this meant that men on the day shift (06.00 to 14.00) earned less than those on the other two shifts, so they were allowed to work also for four hours on Saturdays.

Crewe's war effort through 1939-46 was quite different from that of 1914-18, principally because armaments formed an appreciable proportion of total work only until the middle of 1942, but also because as early as 1934 under Stanier and Sir Harold Hartley a survey had been made for the Committee of Imperial Defence of all LMSR machine tools in relation to war and armament capacity. Even at the peak of government orders only 22-23 percent of the staff were engaged on that work, and over the years 1943-45 only five percent were on armaments. In the summer of 1942 when locomotives were raised to a higher order of priority by the government, production of armaments at Crewe virtually ceased; all efforts were concentrated on keeping engines in good repair with a big percentage always at work, and in doing certain other locomotive work such as modifications to Stanier-type and American 2-8-0s to fit them for service overseas and in Britain. Contrasted with World War I, all armament and locomotive work had to be carried out under strict blackout and ARP control, along with the constant threat of, and some actual, bombing. For the fire-fighting service the westernmost of the two cooling ponds by the carriage works was allocated as a 1¼-million gallon reservoir.

At first numerous different manufactures led to disruption of the main work of locomotive repairs. The principal early product was the light Covenanter tank, design of which was initiated at Euston and Derby in 1938 after an earlier design of a 30-ton model had been negatived. Of the three works concerned, Crewe built 161 of these tanks (with turrets from Derby), and in 1942 carried out important modifications to 150 Covenanters in nine weeks, these being brought to Crewe in special trains of wartime flats. This latter work led to tool-room strengthening in order also to undertake tool-making for other tank constructors (English Electric and Leyland), and by the acquisition of new grinders, lathes and milling machines, supplementing the two special Pratt & Whitney jig borers put in during 1938 and 1940. At this time all the machines in the tool room were given individual drive. Many spare parts for tanks, including Rackham clutches, final-drive mechanisms, turrets, turret rings and tank hulls for other models were built.

Much government use was made of the drop-stamping plant, then larger and more modern than in 1914–18; over a million drop stampings were turned out, of which some 30,000 were for other railways. An extension of two 3-ton batteries was needed at a cost of £40,000, and the 45-ton foundation block for each of these was cast in Crewe iron foundry; the moulding and transport were complicated matters. To these were added a 4-ton set from the Old Works, the driving mechanism of which was made electric on the transfer, and the whole was put into the vacant east end of the old rail mill.

The steel foundry produced over 70,000 castings for government work and 5,000 for other railways. Many of the government castings were thinner and smaller than railway types and required new staff and procedures, but by 1943 the foundry was back to 100 percent railway production for locomotives and wagons.

Further Crewe production included 130,000 copper shell bands, 97,000 chemical-shell container forgings, 4,000 gun-carriage axles, 56,000 malleable-iron track links for caterpillars made in the iron foundry, in which a new Morgan tilting furnace was installed, and miscellaneous other equipment including 100 radio-location turntables and, in the Old Works boiler shop, Bailey bridges.

Assistance in the production of locomotive parts had to be given to the other Group railways, principally to those building LMSR Stanier type 2-8-0s to government order, and also to private locomotive builders in order to accelerate their new locomotive construction rate. In addition to the castings and drop stampings 740 heavy forgings and

5,800 flanged plates were supplied, as well as 700 connecting- and coupling-rods and brake cross-beams for Vulcan Foundry and Beyer Peacock.

Signal and telegraph work increased because of the number of new junctions and sidings for armament works, munition dumps and military camps, and to make good war damage to LMSR equipment. For the same reasons trackwork manufacture increased, and it was at this time the old points-and-crossings shop was extended into the still vacant west end of the old rail mill and half the intervening wall was knocked down.

The works grid power supply dating from 1923, but with some modifications from the 1925–27 re-organisation, was provided with reserve transformer capacity and alternative distribution routes in 1939–40 to reduce vulnerability in air raids, and an additional 6000 kVA 33/0.6kV transformer was installed in the Steelworks substation.

The progress office instituted in the 1920s was still functioning when war began, but by then was a routine control and ordering department rather than an authority initiating new measures. Government orders necessitated a much wider range of planning and work control. At first this was done almost piecemeal, with the major work crowded in a small office; control of the piecework system was done elsewhere, and the special jig-and-tool draughtsmen were housed in the locomotive drawing office. The locomotive progress and stock order office was in yet another location. After R. C. Bond took over control of the works on the departure of F. A. Lemon all these sections were brought together at the east end of the Deviation works in November 1941.

After a few months the work of this office changed much by the cessation of government contracts and the concentration on locomotive work, but a result was that outside locomotive-constituent contracts could be undertaken efficiently and on the ordered flow lines of LMSR locomotive repairs, for the office staff handled not only planning but also estimating, delivery times, machine loading, and, in particular, control of the loading of different sections of the works. Close personal liaison could be maintained with all sections housed together.

Especially in regard to locomotive repairs the orders-in-advance for spare parts had to be kept up meticulously, by the resident storekeeper placing orders on the shops. There might be up to 10,000 separate orders on the books at one time, placed at rates up to 1,000 a week. During the time government work was in hand total orders in progress reached 13,000 on occasion. Operations on this scale were facilitated by the complete revision of stores and stocks procedures initiated in the 1925–27 re-organisation and developed further during the 1930s, but also they required strict allocation of machine capacity, often weeks ahead.

Another development due to Bond was routine all-in telephone conferences on the lines of the daily operating department conferences that had been established on the LMSR years before the war. Instead of a weekly meeting of the chief mechanical engineers and motive power department divisional assistants to determine the engines to be sent to the shops, a twice-weekly telephone conference with all divisions connected was begun. This was controlled by the shopping bureau, which re-allocated any surplus stopped engines to other workshops which had some capacity still available, and ensured that no engines with any further 'life' between repairs were taken from traffic while others were already stopped waiting for shops. Weekly advices were circulated to all works recording details of any spare capacity. By the same means repaired engines could be re-allocated to a different division to that from which they had come, if a shortage occurred.

The long-established flow-progress system and the large proportion of total motive power made up of comparatively few highly-standardised classes, added to the close shop control and latterly the telephone-conference control, enabled Crewe to take three engines a week from the Central Division through 1940–41, and through 1941–43 nearly 200 engines normally allocated to St Rollox were repaired at Crewe.

One difficulty often experienced with the belt system from its inception in 1927 had been the time taken to repair cracked frames, especially in early days with the Prince and Claughton 4-6-0s; by the time of the World War II a proportion of the pit length was always occupied with frame repairs. Though spare cylinders and boilers had been accepted as necessary, it was not until Bond's time that spare frames were authorised, with a spare set each for the Stanier Class 5, the ex-LNWR G class 0-8-0, and the ex-Midland Class 4F 0-6-0, with the benefit that these engines could pass through the erecting shop in the normal eight to ten days, whereas cracked frames might need 12 to 14 days for proper repair. In addition, the heavy machine shop was extended by taking in part of the old forge to help in the preparation and assembly of frame structures.

Scrapping limits for various parts were revised early in the war when much government work was in hand, in order to give some increase in life before renewal. For example, large axles in general were allowed to wear 0.75in below original journal diameter contrasted with 0.5in pre-war. The same principle was applied to

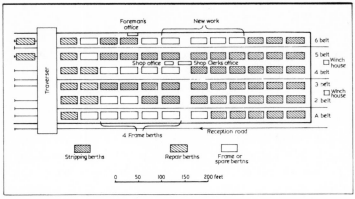

Fig 41 Arrangement and purpose of berths and pits in erecting shop south in the last years of the LMSR and the early years of British Railways

tyres, piston rods, valve spindles and the like, but in all cases the *contra* side for the works was the provision of further sizes in brasses, bushes and glands.

Finer limits of work in new and repaired engines had been brought to Crewe first from Horwich in 1922, and were developed at the 1925–27 re-organisation as noted already. During the war the fine limits needed for armament work again brought the question into sharper focus, and from 1943 under Bond and his successor, Rankin, the whole LMSR limits-and-fits policy was steadily developed and was ready for application in all LMSR works by the end of 1947, though actually put into force with the formation of British Railways.

Additional to the new machine tools, drop-stamping plant and other measures outlined above, several changes were made during the final decade of Crewe under the LMSR. A further 50-ton crane was put into the north bay of erecting shop south; engines coming in for repair had the brick arches removed and the smokeboxes cleaned out on a pit well inside the west-end entrance instead of a long way off at the Old Works entrance, and this saved up to a day in the time the engine was on works. A greatly increased number of wagons came into the works area and re-opened steel plant in the war years, and special measures had to be taken to clear them quickly, especially as scrap, pig, fuel and so on did not come in regular flow. Much progress was made in the welding of copper fireboxes in repairing cracks, renewing part plates, and building-up wasted areas, and cast-iron replaced cast-steel for the wheel centres of some of the smaller engines. War-time shortage of material led to more intensive salvage and re-use of material, and Crewe reckoned that 8,820 tons of material were reclaimed in three years, of which 8,375 tons were re-used within the works.

After the outbreak of war great endeavours were made to convert to solid fuel or creosote mixtures various oil-burning installations for flangeing presses in the Old Works, for the smithies, and for brass foundry. Efforts to save coal and electricity resulted in a 10 percent cut in energy per man-hour. Oxygen consumption was economised in various ways, but to improve supply rail transport with a service of special wagons running between Bromborough and Crewe was begun in place of the pre-war road transport. A swarf briquetting plant was introduced and dealt with about 16 tons a week of cast-iron turnings which were fed in briquette form to the foundry cupolas. Chip-crushing machines were put in to deal with 2,000 tons a year of bushy steel turnings. A whitemetalling plant was installed in the far south-west corner of the erecting shop with a conveyor system to distribute the work, and this was alongside the axlebox bay.

When World War II ended Crewe relatively was in a much better state than in November 1918. The labour force in the war years had never exceeded 7,500 compared with 6,500 in 1939 and 10,000 in 1918, while the proportion of women was about 14 percent. For some four years most of the men had worked alternate fortnights on day and night shifts, with over-time to 8.00pm as normal on day shift, and with work on alternate Sundays. This gave successive weekly hours of 59, 70, 66 and 55. Women workers did not exceed 60-hour a week and had one day off in seven to keep within the Factory Act.

After the end of the war in 1946, though ex-LNWR engines had largely disappeared, the first, or south, belt of the erecting shop was still reserved for those types, mainly Princes, George V, Webb coal engines, 18in 0-6-0s and 5ft 6in 2-4-2Ts. These had four frame berths to deal with the extensive frame repairs, and with the diminishing numbers in these classes one stripping berth and five assembly stages were enough. The shop capacity as a whole was allocated generally as shown in Table 11, from which it will be appreciated that only the old ex-LNWR types retained the original 7 hours 50 minutes between belt shifts. Three of the other lines had reduced times, and one a longer time. No 6 line, on which four of the five assembly stages were normally engaged in new construction, was shifted at 14¾ working-hour intervals. Only two of the pits west of the traverser were then used for stripping; the others handled bogie repairs and wheel cleaning and examination. These arrangements lasted until the end of the LMSR and into BR days, and are illustrated in Fig 41.

Table 11 Allocation of belts and berths, Erecting Shop South, Crewe, 1946

Belt	No of Berths		Time on each berth or stage (working hours)	Total time locomotive in shop (working hours)	Classes of locomotive repaired
	Stripping	Assembly			
A	1	5	7hr 50min	47hr	General repairs, small engines, ex-LNWR 0-6-0 coal, 18in 0-6-0; 5ft 6in passenger tank, George V, Prince of Wales, etc.
2	2	8	5hr 32min	55hr 20min	Service repairs; Royal Scot, 3-cylinder 4-6-0, Class 5 4-6-0.
B	2	10	5hr 32imn	66hr 24min	General repairs; Royal Scot, 3-cylinder 4-6-0, Class 5 4-6-0.
4	1	6	8hr 35min	60hr 5min	Service and casual repairs; large and small locomotives.
5	2	10	5hr 32min	66hr 24min	Service and casual repairs; large and small locomotives.
New work					
6	2	5	14hr 45min		Service and general repairs 4-6-2s; casual repairs all classes

Table 12 Allocation of belts and berths, Erecting Shop South, Crewe, 1953

Belt	No of Berths		Time on each berth or stage (working hours)	Total time locomotive in shop (working hours)	Classes of locomotive repaired	No of repairs per week
	Stripping	Assembly				
A	1	5	7hr 50min	44hr	All repairs; small and medium classes	6·0
2	2	8	10hr 5min	51hr 40min	All repairs; all classes except 4-6-2s and Garratts	8·5
B	2	10	5hr 10min	62hr	All repairs; all classes except Class 8 4-6-2s and Garratts	8·5
4	1	6	8hr 0min	56hr	All repairs; all classes except Class 8 4-6-2s and Garratts	5·5
5	2	10	5hr 10min	62hr	All repairs; all classes except Class 8 4-6-2s and Garratts	8·5
6	2	5	14hr 40min	102hr 40min	All repairs; Class 8 4-6-2s and Garratts	3·0
					Total	40

Spare berths in shop used for casual repairs, accommodating spare frames, and giving extra heavy frame repairs

10
Nationalised Works

When Crewe works passed over to British Railways (BR) on 1 January 1948 its allocation for general repairs was made up of over 2,500 steam locomotives, including 49 Pacifics, 262 three-cylinder 4-6-0s, 536 Class 5 4-6-0s, 535 Class 8 2-8-0s, 218 ex-LMSR 0-6-0s, 218 Class 4 2-6-4Ts, and over 550 ex-LMSR and ex-LNWR engines of ten to a dozen classes. New construction under way included one Pacific (No 6257), about 50 Class 5 4-6-0s, some with variations such as roller-bearing axleboxes, Caprotti motion and double exhaust, and a variety of Ivatt small 2-6-0s and 2-6-2Ts.

On BR a heavy repair was defined as when an engine had to be reboilered or the boiler taken out of the frames for general repairs, and any two of the following: (a) new tyres fitted to four or more wheels, (b) fitting new cylinders, (c) fitting new axle or axles in engine and tender, (d) re-tubing, (e) turning-up wheels and re-fitting boxes, or motion and brake work stripped and overhauled, (f) boiler repaired in frame with not less than 50 stays renewed; the two items in (e) would not of themselves constitute two separate items for a 'heavy'. On this basis, erecting shop south in 1952 gave 966 heavy repairs, 625 intermediates, and built 41 new engines. With this amount of repair work and 40 to 50 new engines a year, about 10 percent of total man-hours throughout the works were absorbed in new construction, 75 percent in repairs, and 15 percent in work for the outdoor and other departments. These percentages included the work on the 581 boilers repaired and the Old Works construction of 109 new ones.

A defect not remedied in BR days was the length of time that a steam locomotive was at Crewe for heavy repairs. In the pre-modernisation years of BR, steam engines were got through the erecting shop in one to two-and-a-half weeks according to the size, most of them in five to nine working days, but the average time a locomotive was in the Crewe Works area was still above 20 days, and this was longer than in 1938–39, though few engines went to the paint shop after repair.

In the erecting shop the movement times were altered a little from those given in Table 11 (Chapter 9), for a five-day week was in force contrasted with wartime hours, while by the end of 1953 most of the old LNWR types other than the 0-8-0s had gone and the new BR types were coming in for repair. This reduced the number of classes handled from the 25 of 1948–50, but countering difficulties were that steel and other materials were still not coming in so regularly in 1953 as in war and pre-war years. The times in 1953, when BR standard types were beginning to come in, are shown in Table 12.

Erecting shop south had been improved in later LMSR years by the installation of more portable equipment. This was found to be necessary to maintain closely-scheduled repair and movement times, and cylinder and piston-valve boring machines, Hi-cycle tools and grinders and several multi-operated ac welding units were acquired. More design use was made of welding, and the new type of BR main frame centred above the axleboxes and springs depended much on welding, as did frame repairs, and for new work a large size of rotating jig was installed in the heavy machine shop.

Frame repair problems continued, and a number of positions over the pits were reserved for this work and for holding spare frame sets in readiness for transfer. In particular, LMSR Pacific cylinders were working loose and fracturing, with bad consequential effects on the frames. To reduce the time in the shops a spare set of front-end plates was made that could be welded in after a defective front end section had been burned through, but the full repair still occupied three weeks. Therefore a complete assembled front end of two frame-plate sections with inside cylinders, smokebox saddle and motion plate was held spare and put in as needed, the withdrawn assembly being reconditioned and then held as the spare. The burning-off, exchanging and welding-up operations remarkably took only nine hours.

Before the end of steam construction frame making was much improved by the acquisition of a Monopol flame-cutting machine in which the profile was cut automatically on the base of an accurate drawing reduced to 1/100 scale, the photo negative of which was placed in the optical control head of the machine and guided the movements of the cutters. Other details in the handling of steam repairs improved after nationalisation included a hot-water cleansing plant on one of the reception roads with high-pressure nozzles applied before the engine went on to the shop traverser, and which at times took 400 to 500lb of dirt off a big engine; argon and nitrogen arc welding techniques for copper inside firebox repairs and part renewals were developed; plastics were introduced in pattern-making in place of wood; machine moulding was increased in the iron foundry; a new seven-table locomotive weighing machine was acquired in 1955; a steel welding shop was begun in the old points-and-crossings shop.

In the main west end forge were produced all heavy forgings needed for new steam locomotives built at Crewe, Derby and Horwich, and up to 70 tons of work a week were heat-treated in new equipment put into the forge. The smithy (the old boiler-yard smithy) was given a 75-ton mechanical press and a mechanical forging machine; springs also were made in this shop from 1954 on a new progressive system that led to a capacity of a thousand new springs a year and 20,000 handled for repairs by the late 1950s. Steel castings for all locomotives built and repaired at any BR works were made in the Crewe foundry, the only BR steel foundry, and output was up to 60 tons a week. This shop was given two 3½ ton Birlec-Efco electric-arc furnaces.

The paint shop of 1877–80 was little used for its original purpose, and it became more a general and signal store, but for some years of BR one road still held a few old engines for preservation, including *Lion, Cornwall, Hardwicke,* and the Midland compound. Scrapping of old engines still continued in those years in 'the melts', and among notable engines cut-up there in 1951 was the former-NER counter-pressure braked test-train 4-6-0 locomotive No 1699.

On 22 September 1953 R. A. Riddles laid the foundation stone of a new apprentices training school on the cleared site of the old carriage repair shops to the west of Eagle Bridge. The school was opened officially on 23 September 1955 by Sir Brian Robertson; present on this occasion were two previous works superintendents – F. A. Lemon and R. C. Bond – and the then works chief I. C. Forsyth. This school was part of an LMSR plan initiated in 1940 and put in charge of Edgar Larkin; the first practical result was the Derby school opened in 1947. The Crewe school continues to take up to 100 apprentices a year on a strictly-controlled progressive course. Since 1966–67 its work has been supplemented by adult training courses of four weeks on diesel and electric subjects, and the school has also been used for public evening classes. During the late 1950s the ground south of the school and near the cooling ponds was further cleared to permit the building of the Crewe electric locomotive service depot and electric control room, opened in 1960.

First of the new BR standard steam locomotives, *Britannia* itself, was built at Crewe and was steamed out of the works on 2 January 1951. The other 54 engines of the class also were built at Crewe, as were the ten Clan Pacifics, No 71000 *Duke of Gloucester,* a few 2-6-2Ts, and 198 of the Class 9 2-10-0s. BR standard steam engines built at Crewe numbered 289 out of a total of 999, but did not include a single 4-6-0. One of the small 2-6-2Ts of Ivatt type, No 41270, was hailed in September 1950 as the 7000th steam locomotive to be built at the works. The last of the 2-10-0s, No 92250, was the last steam locomotive to be built at Crewe, and was reckoned as the 7331st, but was more likely 7357th; it left the paint shop on 16 December 1958. At that time the sponge-cloth cleaning plant was still handling over five million cloths a year and cleaning 45 tons of cotton waste, and had a staff of six.

In 1957–58 new plant and equipment was installed and new arrangements made to cope with three main objects: first, the continued repair of steam locomotives, though on an ever-decreasing scale; second, the building and subsequent repair of diesel-electric locomotives with engine, transmission and control equipment bought outside; third, the overhaul of single-phase electric locomotives and the eventual new construction of such machines. The first new diesels were completed in 1958, and by 1959 the number of steam heavy repairs at 20 a week was down to half the number produced during the war years, while up to six new diesel shunters and four new diesel line-service locomotives were being completed every month. The shunters were handled in eight progressive steps down one line of the erecting shop.

At this time several shops were re-sited, and the yard layout at the far west end was again altered, first in order to accommodate a large double-floor finished parts store to the north of the main machine shop, which could hold over 40,000 components, and second, to get in a big traverser with a run of 500ft to the east of the erecting shop block, to enable new and repaired locomotives of any kind to be fed out of or into the erecting shop and any of the shops east of the traverser, including the new diesel test plant then being planned. This traverser is 16ft broad, 90ft long, runs on eleven rails, has a control cabin at each end, and can take an aggregate load of 200 tons. When commissioned in the early 1960s the test plant comprised four outdoor berths and two small test houses with two flanking sound barriers 20ft high.

In 1958 one line of the erecting shop was relieved of its single remaining winch-hauled stage, and over the next year or two the others were removed gradually as diesel construction and repair spread and steam locomotive repairs decreased; the progressive system in the ancillary shops was modified as diesel locomotive parts replaced steam constituents. From 1959, with new steam construction at an end, boiler repairs were transferred to the Old Works, which had no further new boilers to build; smokeboxes, ashpans and structural steelwork

Top left: Cornwall by the Old Works fitting shop, showing footbridge over old Chester tracks

Top right: 2–4–0 *Stewart* about to be cut-up in the yards after being involved in the Lichfield accident

Centre left: No 9 shop with new 0–8–0s under erection

Centre right: Two of the 18in-gauge Ramsbottom tram engines at work in "the melts"

Lower left: Rail motor engine No 9 in for repair

Lower right: Cooke 4–6–2T awaiting repair after slight collision; walls of partly finished erecting shop No 10 behind

Bottom: Hazeldine & Co's Trevithick stationary engine of *circa* 1814 refurbished and stored in the Crewe paint shop

All photographs on this page by the late D. H. Stuart, 1920–22

Left: Two of the standard 2ft 6in "cut-down" shunters between the signal stores and the paint shop

Below: A corner of "the melts" after the 1925 modernisation

Bottom: Lifting a 6oft rail ingot out of the furnace in the then new steel plant, 1927

also were moved to those shops. The last steam heavy repair was to Britannia Pacific No 70013 *Oliver Cromwell*, despatched on 2 February 1967, so there was a long transition stage in the erecting shop while diesel construction, diesel repairs, straight electric repairs and steam repairs were being done on adjacent lines. The departure of No 70013 was marked by a brief ceremony organised by the then

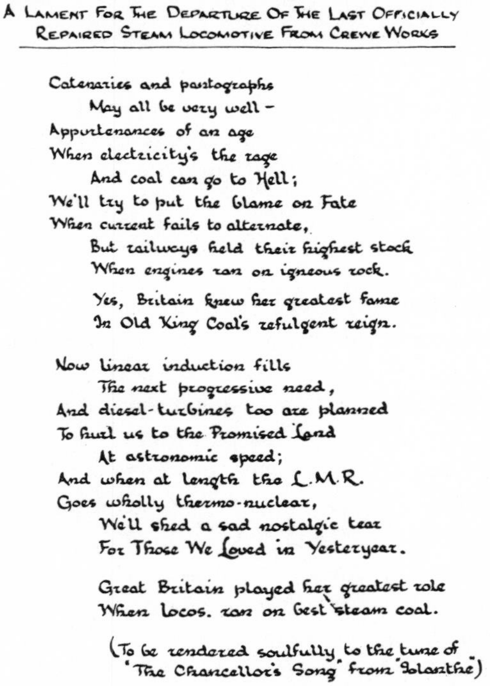

A LAMENT FOR THE DEPARTURE OF THE LAST OFFICIALLY
REPAIRED STEAM LOCOMOTIVE FROM CREWE WORKS

Catenaries and pantographs
   May all be very well –
Appurtenances of an age
When electricity's the rage
   And coal can go to Hell;
We'll try to put the blame on Fate
When current fails to alternate,
      But railways held their highest stock
      When engines ran on igneous rock.

      Yes, Britain knew her greatest fame
      In Old King Coal's refulgent reign.

Now linear induction fills
   The next progressive need,
And diesel-turbines too are planned
To hurl us to the Promised Land
   At astronomic speed;
And when at length the L.M.R.
Goes wholly thermo-nuclear,
   We'll shed a sad nostalgic tear
   For Those We Loved in Yesteryear.

   Great Britain played her greatest role
   When locos. ran on best steam coal.

   (To be rendered soulfully to the tune of
    'The Chancellor's Song' from Iolanthe)

Fig 42
"Or, ravished with the whistling of a name See *Cromwell* damned to everlasting fame." *Pope.* Poem on the despatch of the last steam repair at Crewe works, Britannia Pacific No 70013, 2 February 1967

works manager, J. J. C. Barker-Wyatt, which incidentally gave rise to the last of the Crewe poems, and also marked the end of about 125,000 steam locomotive repairs since 1843.

Under the Railway Executive the various locomotive works of BR were controlled directly by the mechanical engineering headquarters at Marylebone, and the major efforts made in the early 1950s to get all shops operating on the same general principles did not affect Crewe practices, which conformed to the desired standards and were indeed the model. When the 1953 Transport Act abolished the Railway Executive and gave direct management of the railways to the British Transport Commission the workshops were put under the immediate control of the separate Regions in which they were located. Central policy and oversight were weakened, and works managers had greater freedom without any definite enforcement of a single policy. What guidance there was came through the Regional general managers and their relation with headquarters.

Nine years later the 1962 Transport Act abolished the BTC in its turn, and Dr Beeching set up a separate board for each activity. One result was that in 1962 the various works were combined into a Workshops Division separate from the central mechanical organisation. They ceased to be so closely identified with the day-by-day operation of BR, and just at a time when repair policy needed the fullest integration because of mounting troubles with large diesels.

Under these repeated high-level fluctuations a steady managerial policy in regard to production and repairs was impossible, and Crewe had its share of loose control. Nor did matters improve *ipso facto* when under the powers of the Transport Act 1968 the Workshops Division was translated in 1970 into British Rail Engineering Ltd (BREL), which could quote for and accept any outside work if surplus capacity could be used.

Nevertheless, under the Beeching plan and the formation of the Workshops Division a large amount of money was made available for modern equipment and re-organisation. From this source a sum of £2,106,000 was allocated in 1964 for a further major modification of the whole of the Steelworks end at Crewe to increase productivity per man employed in locomotive repairs and other products, and to provide for the building and repair of diesel and electric locomotives. The programme involved the closure of the Old Works more than 40 years after the first proposals, and the abandonment of the Deviation shops and grease works. The works as it is today results from this scheme, and with general policy continued largely unaltered through a decade has led to firm management control with acceptable discipline and performance.

From the last-mentioned financial provision came a further re-siting of shops. Maintenance and millwrighting were transferred from the Deviation area to the old iron foundry of 1882, chain making and general testing going to the smithy/fabrication area; progress was made with the fuel pump and injector plant in the main machine shop, also with component-cleaning facilities; cleaning and testing equipment was put into the electrical repair shop; outstanding new machine tools were acquired. Also a new boiler house was erected to provide all works needs, and was composed of four oil-fired John Thompson boilers of 30,000lb capacity each, and which needed only two men per shift, or six through the 24 hours to look after them.

The numerous new remote-controlled or automatically-operated machine tools bought from 1964 began with a Burgomaster six-station numerically-controlled driller with punched-tape control, followed in

1965 by turret lathes with plugboard and segmental controls, and then by much wider applications of tape-controlled milling machines and others, taking advantage of each new computer development, for diesel and electric components are more suited to these methods than the old steam locomotive repair parts. Crewe today is a thoroughly modern locomotive factory.

Under this major programme a second traverser was put into the west end of the erecting shop to give easier handling of large diesel-electrics, which at 69ft 6in overall were much longer than the 4-6-2 and 2-10-0 steam types without their tenders. The old erecting shop traverser of 1927 remained, but its tracks are blocked off at the south end and it is now used mainly for the transport of bogies, power units and major spares to and from the adjacent machine shop. The pits between the two traversers are used for stripping and initial cleaning of incoming locomotives. The southernmost road to which the outside 200-ton traverser feeds is the reception track for the erecting shop, and this is laid to a mixed gauge of 4ft 8½in and one metre, because in 1970 after BREL had acquired the works there was a project for repairing many diesel locomotives from abroad, but this fell through.

The early stages of the re-organisation initiated by the Workshops Division coincided with the approaching withdrawal of the last steam locomotives and a big increase in the number of 50-cycle electric loco-motives. New diesel locomotive construction was nearing its end for some years at least, and though repairs to electric locomotives were undertaken from 1962, not until 1972 was new construction of such machines begun. Since that time new locomotive construction has been a smaller proportion of total work than hitherto, though countered by the building of advanced forms of HST train power cars and bogies.

What the changeover from steam to diesel and electric traction has meant to the works can be shown succinctly by Table 13, which gives the state at the end of 1967 when the last steam repair was long past and BR had only a handful of run-down steam locomotives in service. In the composition of staff Crewe is seen to have followed the two-generation trend in all other major industries of a greater proportion of non-productive payees.

Table 13   Shop staff in 1967 when all steam work was ended

Shop	No of Men
Erecting shop	517
Unclassified repairs shop	171
Diesel test centre	125
Main machine shop	650
Heavy machine shop	59
Power-unit repairs	207
Traction-motor repairs	132
Auxiliary-motor repairs	105
Generator repairs	36
Paint shop	88
Wheel shop	91
Plates, fabrication, welding	389
Copper shop	116
Tin shop	38
Bogie repairs (erecting shop)	107
Bogie repairs (tender shop)	180
Steel foundry	155
Signal shop	48
Stores dept.	140
Millwrights and joiners	329
Boiler house	6
Apprentices and juniors	539
Miscellaneous	339
Supervisory (workshops)	332
Salaried staff	439
Management	39
Total	5377

All shops worked day and night shift except diesel test centre (3 shifts), boiler house (3 shifts), and tin shop and signal shop (day shifts only)

The first diesel shunter to be built at Crewe was No 3419 in 1958, and the first new line-service diesel, No 5032 of 1160hp, was driven away from No 14 road of the paint shop by the mayor of Crewe in June 1959. From the first shunter to the line-service diesel No D1111 of Class 47 in 1972, a total of 476 diesel-electric locomotives was produced. Additionally, to give a work spread, 44 large C-C diesel-hydraulic locomotives of the Western class were built, and more quickly and cheaply than those constructed at Swindon, a result paralleled in steam days, for the prices of Crewe-built Class 9 2-10-0s were 10 to 15 percent below Swindon prices. Indications in early 1981 were that diesel construction was being resumed on a limited scale.

The 1960s did not form a smooth decade for Crewe works, because in the midst of new activities and the initiation of the new Workshops

Division, both of which needed time to settle down, 700 large diesel locomotives had to be brought in succession into Crewe, their engines removed, sent to the maker's works at Barrow for re-balancing, and then put back into the locomotives when returned. This caused much upset in normal repairs and production. When this work was more or less complete, and when the scheduled number of classified repairs was just being attained, there came a period around 1967 when about a third of the erecting shop floor space was occupied by 1250 passenger coaches being altered from steam to electric heating and given new bogies, and then by many large bogie hopper cars being fitted with continuous brakes.

Normally, incoming Brush diesel locomotives were cleaned, lifted and stripped in the two stages between the two shop traversers and the first one in the main part of the shop, and then were moved eastward along the length of the shop through one double light-assembly stage, one double heavy-assembly stage, and one double final-assembly stage, occupying a total of 118 working hours. The south bay of the shop was laid out for general repairs to Brush 2750hp Co-Co locomotives and English Electric 2000hp 1-Co-Co-1 locomotives, and the north bay was developed on a progressive stage system to give classified repairs to straight electrics.

In 1964, soon after the Workshops Division took over, Crewe effected 312 classified and 177 unclassified steam repairs, 98 classified and 250 unclassified diesel repairs, and 34 classified and 19 unclassified electric locomotive repairs; in that year a hundred new Brush-type diesel locomotives were completed. In the twelve months following the last steam repair the figures were 365 classified and 457 unclassified diesel repairs plus 145 classified and 27 unclassified straight electric locomotive repairs. The diesel unclassified totals give an indication of the chaotic state of BR diesel traction in the 1960s. At that time many of the unclassified repairs were done in what is now the electric repair shop, day and night shifts being worked. The sides, ends and roof of this shop were entirely reconstructed and heightened, and new cranes and crane-runs put in. In the last-mentioned year (1967) nine new electro-diesel locomotives were built, but new construction included 34 English Electric type bogies for Class 1 locomotives and 486 B4/B5 bogies for passenger stock. With these totals the erecting shop staff numbered over 500, of whom more than 400 were skilled workers.

All locomotive activities at the Old Works ceased in 1965, and by the end of 1966 the signal work, stores department, and the tinsmiths and galvanising sections were transferred to the west end. From 1967 the

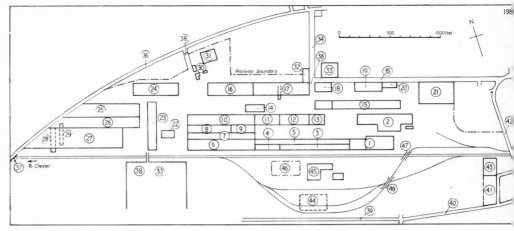

1 Disused steel melting plant (used for stores) 2 Steel foundry 3 Chain shop and smithy 4 Sheet-metal shop 5 Welding and plate shop 6 Fabrication shop 7 Paint shop 8 Electric erecting shop 9 Spring shop 10 Electric equipment shop 11 Copper shop 12 Heavy machine shop 13 Steam-generating shop (diesel heating boilers) 14 Asbestos cleaning shop 15 Wheel shop 16 Maintenance and millwrights' shop 17 Bogie repair shop 18 Signal shop 19 Brass foundry 20 Stores 21 Old paint shop, now used as general stores 22 Diesel test bank 23 Large traverser 24 Main stores building 25 Main machine shop 26 Diesel power-unit repairs 27 Diesel and electric locomotive erecting and repair shop 28 Traverser 29 Old traverser 30 Medical centre 31 Works manager's and administrative offices 32 Workers' dining room and club house 33 Works car parks 34 Goddard Street 35 Richard Moon Street 36 West Street 37 Merrill's Bridge 38 Works entrances 39 Victoria Avenue 40 Wistaston Road 41 Bridle Road 42 Flag Lane 43 ERO offices 44 Electric locomotive running depot 45 Apprentice training school 46 Cooling pond 47 Eagle Bridge 48 Old carriage works girder bridge

Fig 43 Layout of the BREL Crewe locomotive works, 1980

buildings in the original triangle of ground lay derelict. In 1969–70 there was a proposal to use the old No 1 erecting shop and the clock tower as a transport museum, but this outside project lapsed, and the buildings were gradually demolished, the clock tower being one of the last to go, around 1976. Work in the Deviation shops ceased in 1967.

Today the Crewe shops are confined to the west end and are laid out as shown in Fig 43. The newest building, to the north of the present electric erecting shop and dated 1979, handles asbestos removal and cleaning. The old steel melts of 1925 remain disused apart from stores. In the conversion of the older shops to fresh purposes from 1957 the space between the Ramsbottom-Webb boiler shop and the old boiler-yard smithy, originally open and carrying two yard tracks, was converted to a long narrow paint shop, but it had been roofed early in the century, as had the similar space between the old plate stores and the old No 8 erecting shop. The latter is now the electric erecting shop and has been given steel girder crane runs and other structural improvements. The whole breadth of this block of shops is now divided from north to south into the electric erecting, electric generator and motor, paint and fabrication shops. In 1979 the last-named shop went back briefly to boiler making, for in it was built the single-flue boiler for the replica of Hackworth's *Sans Pareil*, for the 150th anniversary of the Liverpool & Manchester Railway.

The old steel rail mill and points-and-crossings shop now house the welding and plate shop, the sheet metal shop, the chain shop and the smithy. The main machine shop and diesel power-unit repairs are concentrated in Webb's last two shops of 1902–03, which are now run as a single shop. The tender shop of 1874 handles bogie construction and repairs; the iron foundry of 1882 does general plant maintenance and millwrighting; the present brass-finishing shop is the signal shop of 1884 and the signal section occupies the brass foundry of the early 1880s, the fourth site since signal manufacture began at Crewe in 1874. The wheel shop was extended many years ago to cover the gap between it and the old copper shop, which was the largest copper shop owned by BR but is now a cubicle shop; otherwise the wheel shop occupies its original site of one hundred years ago plus the space of the nut-and-bolt shop of 1888. The present medical centre is on part of the old brickyard; the works manager's and administration office block built in 1976 is close by, above the foundations of the old circular brick kiln. In line with not uncommon financial practices of today, this last block is not owned by BREL. Until this block was completed the management and administration remained in the old general offices.

BREL works ground area is now 94 acres within the limits shown in Fig 43, of which about 81 acres are north of the Chester main line and west of Flag Lane; the covered area is 32 acres. South of the Chester line and included in the above areas are the apprentice training school and the southern car park of the works. The car park itself is on the site of the Park Place huts of 1919. Works entrances are from the southern car park, from Goddard Street, and from West Street near St Barnabas church. Further west, by Merrill's Bridge, the old Webb Orphanage is now a BR staff training college.

Early in 1981 around 350 line-service diesel-electric and 140 straight-electric classified overhauls were given annually, plus any out-of-course repairs, and there was new construction of HST power cars and bogies. In 1981 a batch of 38 freight diesels of Class 56 was put in hand, while orders for APT power cars and bogies were expected. Additionally, steel castings for all BR purposes, signalling equipment, and miscellaneous engineering articles are made for the railway and for outside customers. Normal weekly working hours are 40, and the work force is still around 4,000 including office and administrative staffs. Compared with one hundred years ago the total man-hours a week are around 150,000 against with 325,000 in 1880.

11
Works Transport

Because of the relative locations of the three works and their size, the rail transport system of the whole establishment in LNWR days eventually was in three broad systems. First was the inter-shop 18in gauge tramway inaugurated in Ramsbottom's time. Second was a segregated standard gauge layout in the melting department of the steel plant. Third was the general standard gauge system with connections to the main line, and which dealt with all incoming traffic in material, fuel and dead engines, outgoing empties and repaired engines, general yard shunting at the Steelworks, and the transfer traffic between Old Works and Steelworks along the old Chester tracks. With the LMSR works re-organisation of 1925–27 the tramway disappeared except in the steel plant and at the east end of the Deviation Works; much movement hitherto undertaken by rail was taken over by rubber-tyred vehicles operating over concrete runways.

Tramway System
The tramway layouts with flat-bottom rails in the Old and Deviation Works had no inter-connection on the same gauge, nor were they similarly connected with the larger system at the Steelworks, and it is doubtful if the system at the Deviation plant was ever loco-worked, for practically all of it was in the timber area and joiners shop. A total of about five miles of track had been laid in the three works before 1914. Traffic was handled by seven small locomotives that bore names but no numbers, which though all built at Crewe were not given Crewe motion numbers or normal Crewe A or E lot numbers. They were always given their general repairs in the millwrights shop, and that shop also had a special tool for machining the 5ft tramway turntables, of which there were very many throughout the works. A list of the tram engines is given in Table 14.

Table 14   List of Crewe Works tramway engines

Name	Date built	Date scrapped
Steam:		
Tiny	5/1862	1929
Pet	6/1865	Preserved
Nipper	1/1867	10/1929
Topsy	1/1867	10/1929
Midge	11/1870	10/1929
Dickie	5/1875	10/1929
Billy	7/1876	1/1931
Diesel:		
Crewe[1]	12/1930	1957

[1] Originally numbered 5519; renumbered ZM9

From the board authorisation of 17 October 1861 the first few hundred yards of track and the first locomotive, *Tiny*, were in operation by May 1862. During the construction, and before a specific name was allotted, the engine was referred to in the shops as 'the dwarf locomotive'. The first extension of the system and more intensive use began with the opening of the steel plant and the re-organisation of the Old Works in 1865–67. This led to the construction of a second locomotive, *Pet*, in 1865 specially for the steel plant, to two more in 1867, and to a fifth, at a cost of £250, in 1870. In 1867 the tender shop, rail mill and one or two auxiliary shops were still in the southern annexe, and though no available works plans prior to that date show the tramway system at all, there may have been from an early stage one line of tramway crossing the old Chester line to that area. Certainly there was one by 1874, and it ran through the original stores shop.

Not until 1878 did the first externally visible adjunct of the tramway appear. This was the long light suspension bridge of 220ft main span leading from the north end of Crewe passenger station over the new Chester tracks into the works area near the clock tower, known as Midge bridge, and occasionally as the Spider. At the northern or works end the bridge abutments and the 18in gauge track over the bridge came later to be spanned by Crewe North signal box. After World War I this bridge was little used by the tram engines, but continued in use for pedestrians and from around 1920 for rubber-tyred trackless vehicles until it was demolished in 1939. Long before that the deck had been used also to support electric cables, including one that connected the small power house in Crewe station to give a small supply to the Old Works during holiday periods to save keeping the larger works plant going. Some of the northern abutment arches still remain.

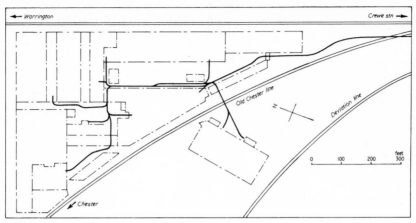

Fig 44 Layout of the 18in-gauge tramway in the Old Works at the end of Webb's time, in 1903

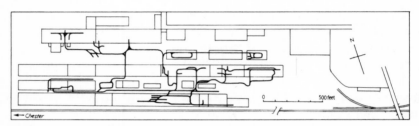

Fig 45 Layout of the 18in-gauge tramway at the Steelworks in 1913–14

Figs 44 and 45 show the layout to which the tramway had developed at the Old Works and Steelworks by 1914. Many of the curves were little better than right-angled bends, and were as much as the 36in locomotive wheelbase could manage, even though top permissible speed was only 4mph. In the steel plant itself some ingots were hauled from the stack to the furnaces and other odd jobs done. The tramway was not taken into any of the erecting shops or into the boiler and paint shops, and there were only two short stubs into the tender shop. In the locomotive sections of the works, stores, tools, rough and finished parts and materials were taken into numerous shops on short four-wheel flat trucks of 2ft 6in wheelbase, with frame, horns and floor in one iron casting. Trains of bins holding swarf and waste ferrous material were taken from the machines to the furnaces or for loading into standard-gauge springless yard wagons. Maximum trailing load of any tramway train was 14 to 15 tons.

The self-contained tramway system at the Deviation Works remained until the shops were evacuated by the railway in BR days. It had remarkable features, for not all of it was on the ground. A steep slope and iron bridge (still in existence) carried tracks to the upper floor of the old joiners shop. Trucks came down by gravity often in mad descent, round the sharp curve at the bottom, and on along the straight, where they could sometimes be stopped by the primitive wooden sprag carried to try and provide some braking, but just as often were stopped by a steel door behind the boiler house.

First of the tramway locomotives was a 4-wheeler of the crudest outside appearance, and apart from odd details the design was perpetuated for the next four engines, all built under Ramsbottom. However primitive, every one lasted in serviceable condition until 1927, and on the mass withdrawal *Pet* was retrieved and is now preserved in Wales. Ramsbottom's five tram engines were built up on inside frames and had two inside 4¼in by 6in cylinders and Stephenson valve motion. The boiler was cylindrical from end to end, and into it was inserted eccentrically a cylindrical furnace 17¼in diameter by 2ft 6in long, from which 37 small-bore tubes ran forward to a tubeplate. This barrel was surmounted at the front by a dome 12¾in diameter by 3ft high, on top of which was a safety-valve. The 6in diameter chimney went up to a height of 10ft above rail level. Frame length was 7ft 5in.

Not until some years after Webb had taken charge did the expansion at the Steelworks end necessitate two further steam engines, which were the last built for the 18in gauge system. These were *Billy*, completed in 1875, and *Dickie*, dated 1876. They were two of the most remarkable steam locomotives ever built for any gauge. Each had a cylindrical furnace, a hexagonal combustion chamber crossed by several water tubes, a triple exhaust blast from the two outside cylinders, a cylindrical dome through which passed three chimneys, circular rotating slide valves driven by gears, spiral key-and-gear reverse, and double-end drive. With the hexagonal combustion chamber all water tubes were of the same length and could be expanded evenly. As built, the two were not the same, for *Billy* originally had a Brotherhood vertical engine between the frames, but it was soon converted to the outside horizontal locomotive-type cylinders and conventional drive as applied to *Dickie* from the beginning.

Melting-Furnace System

The steel furnace 4ft 8½in gauge system extended only over a few hundred yards and was operated by a handful of locomotives cut down in height from the small 0-4-0WTs usually known as the 2ft 6in shunters from the nominal size of the disc wheels. These engines, with double-end driving controls, were taken from a batch of ten built in 1880–82; the other engines of the batch were used at Liverpool docks. From 1886 they were considered as duplicate stock and bore Nos 3010–19, of which Nos 3013–15 and 3019 were at Crewe for many years. By the end of the LNWR only six were duplicate stock and the four at Crewe were departmental stock; only the six duplicates received LMSR numbers. The last two Crewe-based engines were withdrawn in 1940–42, but one of them was in existence at a scrap yard for several more years; they had been used scantily after 1930–31.

The furnace engines were cut down in height to 8ft 9in as against 10ft 10½in in the dock engines, but No 3014 had a chimney going up to 9ft 6in; they did not have the canopy of the dock engines but a heat shield plate was put along one side of each footplate, at diagonally opposite corners. However, at least one canopied engine, No 3017, spent some time at Crewe but not in the steel-melting area. All had a cylindrical boiler with a small-diameter inset smokebox, while inner and outer fireboxes were of oval shape extending below the bottom of the barrel; the upper part of the inner box was prolonged into a combustion chamber which had a single tapered cross water tube. Most of the class at one time or another burned oil fuel, but at other periods were fired with coal or anthracite, and all had Webb's water-tube grate bars. Boiler pressure was 140lb/sq in and laden weight was about 15 tons. Cylinders were 9in by 12in, the 2ft 8in wheels were spread over a base of 5ft 6in, the coupling rods were of open section, and length over buffers was 19ft.

Standard-Gauge Shunting

The general 4ft 8½in gauge system, including the old Chester tracks that provided the inter-works route, eventually totalled over 20 track miles exclusive of the tracks and sidings to the south of the new Chester line that served the carriage establishment.

In Trevithick's time one or two ancient engines were in use over the few tracks at the Old Works. In the Ramsbottom-Webb days one or two machines past service on the line were converted to saddle tanks for yard work, including two Bury four-wheelers that were known as A and B in the 1870s. In 1866 one of the Crewe-type 2-4-0s (No 273) was converted to a 2-4-0T crane engine that had steam lifting gear and hand slewing. Another (No 951) was altered in 1868 and two (Nos 519 and 131) were converted by Webb in 1873. Three were normally about the Crewe works yards, but were expected to go out on break-downs when they could be useful; one was engaged at the Llandulas viaduct replacement in 1879. No 951 was sent to Wolverton.

From around 1872 the Steelworks shunting came to be handled more and more by the standard 0-4-0ST engines with 14in by 20in cylinders introduced by Ramsbottom in 1863 to shunt at any location on the LNWR that could take the 8ft 3in wheelbase and 22¾ tons weight. These engines were built intermittently by Ramsbottom and Webb over a period of 30 years; for a long period a dozen of them were normally employed in the Crewe works yards and received their maintenance at Crewe North shed. They were the first Crewe-built engines to have cast-iron wheel centres and the first to have steel boilers.

Table 15   Crewe Works yard shunting turns, 1909–20

Duty	Locomotive No	Locomotive type	Year built
No 1 Cab engine	3001	14in by 20in	1870
No 2 Cab engine	3009	14in by 20in	1872
Shunting iron foundry and brick-yard area	3007	14in by 20in	1863
Shunting 30-ton furnace	3084	14in by 20in	1872
Shunting 30-ton furnace	3087	14in by 20in	1872
Shunting gasworks and cinder tip	3101	14in by 20in	1865
Shunting wheel shop, paint shop, signal shop and lifting	3246	14in crane	1892
Shunting boiler shop, No 9 shop, main machine shop, west bank	3247	14in crane	1892
Shunting out-station shop and Steelworks	3248	14in crane	1893
Lifting at steel plant; lifting castings and moulds	3249	14in crane	1894
Locomotive stores, fitting shop, lifting	3251	14in crane	1894
Spare crane engine for emergencies	3252	14in crane	1894
Shunting at junction; taking coal to carriage shops	3323	0-6-0ST Special Tank	1878
Shunting 20-ton furnaces, night and day shifts	3013	2ft 6in shunter	1880
Shunting 20-ton furnaces, night and day shifts	3014	2ft 6in shunter	1880
Shunting 20-ton furnaces, night and day shifts	3015	2ft 6in shunter	1882
Shunting 20-ton furnaces, night and day shifts	3019	2ft 6in shunter	1882
Chief Mechanical Engineer's coupé, *Cornwall*	3020	8ft 6in single	1847/58

In 1865 the last two engines Nos 1445–46, of a batch of ten were coupled back-to-back and worked as a twin unit by one crew. Brief trials were made in the works yards, but the real purpose was to try and handle trains up and down through the Lime Street tunnel at Liverpool. These experiments could not have been successful, for rope haulage through the tunnel continued until 1870. Ramsbottom suggested that such a combination with one of the units fitted with horizontal toothed wheels to grip a centre rail might be the solution for the Mont Cenis Railway, then much in the public eye.

The boiler was of Napier type having a single cylindrical flue 2ft 6in dia, from which ran forward 91 tubes of 1¾in outside diameter. Ramsbottom's engines had normal grate bars; those built by Webb mainly had water-tube bars. Grate area was 11sq ft, heating surface 353sq ft, and boiler pressure 120lb/sq in. The 4ft 3in ten-spoke cast-iron wheels were centred in the frame length of 18ft 11in. Ramsbottom's 23 engines were cabless when built; Webb's engines had primitive cabs consisting of two weatherboards and a roof plate, but in later years the cab side panels of some engines were heightened to give more coal space. Many of these engines retained to their ends in LMSR days the old form of lift-up smokebox door.

A supplementary class of standard-gauge power was formed of eight 0-4-2ST crane engines, three of which were built in 1892–93 and five in 1894–95. They were based on the standard 14in shunter but with crane and extra axle added, and weighed around 33 tons in working order. Two were always to be found at Wolverton and the other six were in the Crewe yard area. Lifting capacity was 4 tons when built, but later LNWR diagrams showed 3 tons for the short jib length of 11ft 4¾in. Some engines had a jib length of 16ft 6in. Entrance to the cab was on the left-hand side only. At times in later days similar 0-4-2STs without cranes operated in the yards.

Shunting power at the works was arranged in special areas or duties with an engine allocated to each. The furnace locomotives had to cope with day and night shifts, which in essence meant that between them they had to provide a 24-hour service. Yard engines, though normally considered on day shift, could not count on a strict eight- or nine-hour day, for they might have much yard clearance to do after the shop workers went home. The engine allocation as it was in 1913, and actually much as it was through 1909–20, is given in Table 15, based on a list prepared by the then locomotive accountant. About 500 wagons, many springless, were allocated to works yard and works-station traffic and were valued at £17,500 the lot. Additional to the engines in Table 15, the carriage establishment had an 0-6-0ST Special Tank to do its own shunting, and this engine was in departmental stock.

In Webb's time and even later there was much transport to and from the Crewe station area undertaken by works engines driven by works men; considerable delays took place around the station because all other traffic was given priority by the operating department. Long absences on these duties often caused congestion in the works yards, and Worsdell had suspicions that some of the delays were deliberate, though as long as John Rigg remained in service that was not the general attitude.

Table 15 also effectively introduces another feature of the standard-gauge works system – the two 'works cabs'. These were four-wheel boiler trolleys on which wooden canopies and partial sides and closed ends had been erected, and large tool and material boxes were carried on the end platforms. One of them, hauled by a 14in 0-4-0ST, ran every working day at fixed times between the Old Works and the far west end of the Steelworks yard, and could be used by any workman, foreman or official who had business along the route. The second cab was retained for use at managerial level and upwards, including prominent visitors; it ran only on instruction, and was used between Crewe station and the general offices and any part of the works to carry directors or leading railway officers. Both cabs, well cleaned and upholstered, were in use on the visit of King George V and Queen Mary in 1913.

In January 1920 a battery-propelled flat truck with solid rubber tyres was introduced, at first specifically for parts transfer between the main machine shop and No 9 on one hand and the boiler shop and Nos 7 and 8 erecting shops. Before the end of the LNWR more of these battery trucks and a few powerful petrol-engined trucks were obtained, and a few more simple runways were made for them at the far west end. The largest type could take a 3-ton concentrated load. At the end of 1919 the use of a works cab for personnel and mail to and from Crewe station was discontinued; in its place a Ford chassis was bought and a simple Wolverton-built body put upon it, to give a road bus service between the main office block and the station.

The great works re-organisation of 1925–27 was based on a completely different transport system to suit the tightly-programmed work flow. Rail transport was cut down, and 10 or 11 steam locomotives working to more strictly scheduled trips and duties were sufficient in place of the previous 17 or 18, but the works cabs were retained for passenger and light freight haulage and were controlled still more closely as to timings. One of the cabs came to be concentrated on marshalling and handling the inward and outward traffic in spares and materials from and to the various Western Division sheds. From the east end of the works the shed wagons and special stores vans were run on a daily service along the main line.

Rubber-tyred trucks running solo or pulling one or two trailers dealt with most of the inter-shop transport from 1927, and many concrete runways were laid down along the main traffic arteries through the yards and on several shop floors. Many of the inter-shop journeys were made to fixed schedules.

Transport supplements from 1927 were a transporter and several outside gantry cranes. The main transporter, carrying loads up to 1½ tons, ran the 500ft between erecting shop south and the main machine shop block to the finished parts store located in the old No 8 shop, and moved the loads well clear above the standard-gauge locomotives and wagons in the vicinity. It ceased operation in the early 1930s. Gantry cranes ran along the stacking yards to the south of the erecting shop and alongside the south wall of the wheel shop. The latter also had cross conveyors from the tyre mill through the shop.

The 18in gauge tramway was abandoned in the Old Works and Steelworks when the re-organisation was complete, except for the new layout put into the steel plant in 1925 which was worked by *Billy* until the end of 1930, when a 20hp four-wheel single-geared diesel locomotive was bought from Hudswell Clarke and worked until the plant was closed in 1932. This engine, named *Crewe* and numbered 5519, was in departmental stock. It was laid aside 1932–35 and was then sent to Horwich, where the works tramway was still in operation. It was the first diesel locomotive owned by the LMSR.

As time went on through the 1930s and 1940s the long-established pattern of Crewe works shunting changed. The 2ft 6in 0-4-0STs did little work after the re-organisation, but the class did not become extinct until 1942. The old 14in shunters disappeared gradually, though the last one (No 3084) worked until 1947, and the two last 0-4-2ST crane engines went during the same year. During the years of World War II much use was made of old Webb 0-6-0 coal engines and one or two of the Whale conversions of them to 0-6-0ST, but Midland Jinties and Horwich-built 0-6-0STs also took turns. Almost the last of the old-timers to go was the 0-6-0ST Special Tank No 3323, which was withdrawn in 1954 after over 40 years of service in the Crewe works area. With the economy drive in the war years most of the shunters came to be fired with a mixture of 50 percent coal and 50 percent coke, and all works engines had the grate area reduced by cover plates and the valve gears were modified to give a maximum cut-off of 50 percent. Under Bond the rubber-tyred tractor transport was improved and the working tightened up to help the wartime activities;

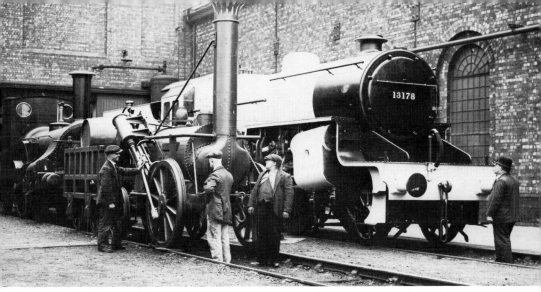

LMSR "Horwich Crab" 2–6–0 claimed as the 6000th locomotive built at Crewe emerging from the new erecting shop south, and, alongside the south wall of Webb's last erecting shop, is photographed with the Crewe single *Columbine* of 1845, and the last of several wooden and inaccurate models of *Rocket* made at Crewe; this one ended its days outside Clapham railway museum

Aerial view in 1927 of the then new three-bay erecting shop south, and beyond it the Webb erecting and machine shops of 1903. To the left of the new shop is the lower section used as a machine shop. In the foreground are the Park Place huts of 1919, and between them and the works is the Chester main line. On the large square estate beyond the works the right-hand road is Frank Webb Avenue

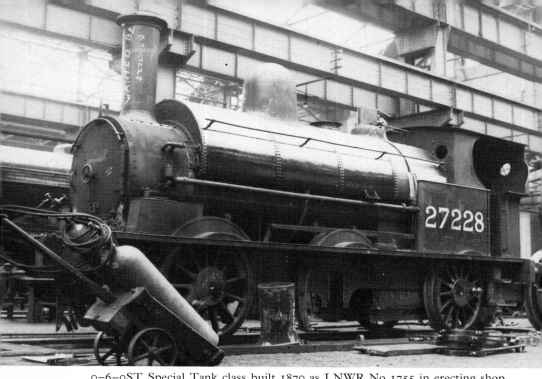

0–6–0ST Special Tank class built 1870 as LNWR No 1755 in erecting shop south for repair in the early 1930s

Lifting an unrebuilt Claughton 4–6–0 off its wheels on one of the stripping berths to the west of the traverser in erecting shop south when that shop first came into use in 1927

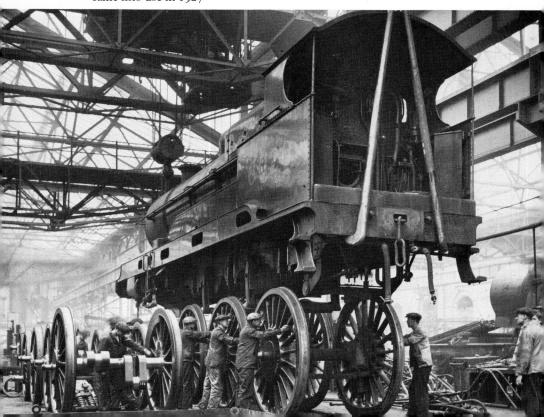

and one new feature was four daily scheduled 'pick-up goods' trains in each direction, comprised of a tractor with two trucks that ran the whole length of the works and made 26 intermediate stops. By this time the biggest tractors had 25hp engines and took trailing loads of 25 tons over the runways.

Today internal works transport is but a shade of that 60 years back — a little-recognised works advantage of diesel and electric traction. Apart from a couple of diesel standard shunters dealing with complete locomotives and large components, rubber-tyred trucks fill all needs, and the immediately obvious difference at the works compared with LNWR times is the stunning silence. Today's workers and towns-people have no conception of the noise in the Steelworks yard and old Chester tracks when up to a thousand loose-coupled wagons and a hundred dead locomotives might be in the yard area and shunted incessantly by a dozen to a dozen-and-a-half steam locomotives.

12

The Mechanics Institute

An essential part, indeed for long a centre, of Crewe railway and town life was the Mechanics Institute, which at its beginning was no more than a bare newspaper room. In its prime it turned out Whitworth Scholars and Whitworth Exhibitioners almost as a normal product (from the first in 1872 to forty-two by 1903 and fifty-three by 1909), gave sound technical training in theory and practice to thousands of apprentices and workmen for a span of three generations, and for many years provided the scene for social and civic amenities.

Almost co-incident with the opening of the works in 1843 the GJR established a small temporary news room for the use of employees and their families, and at the Crewe Banquet the founding of a library was announced. Adjacent to this, by the end of 1843, the company had already built a committee room for the use of magistrates. In the Spring of 1844 the news room and a library against the school in Moss Square were organised under two separate committees of workmen reporting to the directors, but when what were considered as revolutionary newspapers (*Northern Star* and *Weekly Dispatch*) were circulated the board insisted that these papers be given up. One result was that the patronage fell and over 30 members resigned, which was a measurable percentage, for as all workmen at that time could not read the total membership was not large.

Library and news room were brought together as one organisation at the end of 1844 under the chairmanship of Trevithick but some of the men endeavoured to run a mechanics institute, and in September 1845 with the encouragement of Trevithick the two bodies amalgamated under the title of the Crewe Mechanics Institution. To the very end, however, in conversation this was always known as 'the Mechanics Institute.' At the inaugural meeting the declared aim was recorded as "to supply to the working classes of Crewe the means of instruction in Science, Literature and the Arts," and one of the many rules permitted members' children from eight years of age upwards to become members, though they were not allowed to attend lectures. Religious and political discussions were barred. Practically all the cost of founding, housing, furnishing and running the premises was borne by the GJR, and members paid a subscription of only 10s 0d [50p] a year in quarterly instalments. Non-railway persons could become members at 50 percent extra subscription.

Soon after the formation of the LNWR in 1846 the whole scheme was confirmed by the new board, which financed construction of a building at the corner of Earle Street and Prince Albert Street as permanent quarters. In later years all jubilee and centenary celebrations were based on the opening of the new building in 1846. From this time until he left the works in 1857 Trevithick gave consistent sympathetic and influential support as a private individual and in his positions as chairman of the Institution and Northern Division locomotive superintendent, though no more than in the works did he insist on an orderly system of management, or on specific instruction to members' needs.

These premises contained not only the news room and library, which together aggregated only 88sq yd of floor area, but also a large assembly room and several classrooms. By 1848–49 evening classes were being run for reading, writing, arithmetic and mechanical drawing, but more use seems to have been made of the building at that time for public entertainments, concerts and dancing. During the next ten years classes in commercial and further technical subjects were added, though at first with small attendances. A gymnasium was added in 1854 where simple physical training exercises were given to the younger members, but by 1860 this had been converted to a coffee room. Before Trevithick left, a small work room was started and primary instruction given in turning, drilling, machining and fitting; for the more scientifically-minded a telescope was presented by Alexander Allan in 1849, and 10 volumes of the *Encyclopaedia Britannica* by Hardman Earle in 1854.

Much of the technical instruction was given by works officials. Wayte, the chief draughtsman, gave a course on mechanical drawing in 1852 but had only eight in the class. Possibly among the eight was Webb, then an apprentice of one year's standing. Webb himself was an instructor in mechanical drawing from the late 1850s until 1862, when his position as works manager made his presence in the classrooms undesirable. In 1855 the LNWR board donated £20 a year for prizes, and that sum remained until the end of the company. In later years a few more prize-money bequests were made by individuals, including £8 a year under the will of Bartholomew Kean, for many years the Crewe storekeeper.

Almost from the beginning the Institute membership went up and down sharply in accordance with the works employment. It rose to 700 in the busy year of 1848 when around a thousand men were working in the locomotive and carriage shops, but fell to only 235 in the lean years of 1850-51; it then rose gradually to a peak of 1,170 in 1854 and dropped to 900 in 1857. From the beginning of the big works expansion in the early 1860s the membership never fell below one thousand.

From its early days the Institute was controlled by a committee of three members elected by the railway, nine by members from a list of 12 submitted by the railway, and nine by members from among themselves. This gave the railway a controlling interest, but dissentient voices in the town conveniently neglected that the whole Institution and the property, the technical education in the town, and several civic services were for many years financed largely by the railway.

From the 21 members were elected three sub-committees, the first charged with the running of the news room and library, the second with the classes and the letting of the hall, and the third with the public baths, horticultural exhibitions and various games and amusements. The chairman or president was always the railway locomotive superintendent, or in later years the divisional mechanical engineer or works superintendent of the LMSR or BR. Of course these men represented the railway interest, but they equally represented the members. Every one maintained a good balance, and from the members' point of view all were influential by reason of their direct access to the railway board, and for many years their chairmanship of the annual meeting of the Institution was almost a sacred duty.

From the erection of the 1846 building the assembly hall was used as a 'town hall', and gradually it became known locally by that name. It could be hired for public meetings of all kinds on sanction being given by the relevant sub-committee. For a dozen years after its formation in 1860 the Monks Coppenhall (or Crewe) Local Board met in rooms in the Institution building, and after borough status had been granted to the town the council met in the Institution's rooms from 1877 to 1898 despite the savage political war with LNWR officers in the late 1880s.

The running of the public baths erected by the GJR in 1845 not far from the original water pumping house was put by the LNWR under a sub-committee of the Institution. There were eight baths with hot and cold water and a shower, plus a turkish bath. Though the building was primitive the facilities were almost outstanding for the time and environment, but for many years, at 1½d [0·5p] a bath, the average was only six visitors a day, possibly because the baths were inconvenient of access. A visit involved a walk over unlighted waste ground from near the town end of Mill Street, and later from the then newly-built Lockett Street. With the great development of the southern annexe of the Old Works in the 1850s these baths were closed in 1862, when access to them from any direction involved crossing several railway tracks. At that time Institution control came to an end. A new bath house, under direct railway control, was built at the north end of Mill Street and lasted well into LMSR days. In its early years it was often known as the Porcelain Baths.

Apart from the capital investments of the railway company in the building and its furnishings and equipment, and numerous railway monetary grants for one specific purpose or another, the Institution was maintained by members' subscriptions, class fees, and the letting of the hall. Probably at the instigation of Trevithick, the LNWR board in 1850 allotted to the Institution the £70 profit of a one-day excursion to Bangor. In later years a small settled income from the LNWR resulted from half the fees of all premium apprentices at the works being held at the disposal of the Institution at the company's headquarters at Euston, and this continued up to 1930. In Trevithick's time the whole premium was sometimes given to the Institution, but there were very few 'premiums' until 1862, when the intake was widened. The Institution was free from all manner of taxes until 1872 when Poor and Local rates were levied, while from 1882 a property tax had to be paid.

In 1863 the hall of 1846 was enlarged and further classrooms built, but early in 1869 a fire destroyed a substantial part of the whole building. The LNWR board financed rebuilding on an enlarged scale and paid out about £3,500 on new construction. The foundation stone of the new building was laid on 7 August 1869 by Ramsbottom. Formal opening of the new premises was on 18 April 1871 with Ramsbottom in the chair, and with a distinguished company which included that remarkable character Lord Houghton (Monckton Milnes) who performed the opening ceremony, Sir William Fairbairn (then aged 82), the Dean of Chester, and all the leading locomotive department officials.

The new building included a bowling alley, a coffee room (later made into a proper refreshment room), and a new gymnasium; the library and news room then covered 266sq yd and the library housed 3,600 books; classroom area was increased by 100 percent to about 400sq yd, while the Town Hall was larger and higher. A new fitting-and-machine shop was included and had entirely new equipment. A contemporary description of the building recorded: "The exterior is of brick coated with cement, and it is somewhat in keeping with those unique rows of workmen's cottages for which the town is noted." From 1870 the subscriptions were due monthly instead of quarterly, and about the same time 'occasional' tickets were issued that were much used for social, refreshment and newspaper-reading purposes by persons coming into Crewe for the day.

In 1880 an extension was financed by the LNWR at the suggestion of Webb, and another eight classrooms were added; the bowling alley was closed and a few small machine tools put into a new small mechanics shop that was open from 2.00pm to 9.00pm. This general extension arose because of the increase in interested membership that had begun with the works expansion through the 1860s and had been accelerated after the introduction of the 54-hour working week in 1872, after which membership rose gradually to over 2,000. A temporary widening in the range of interests occurred after W. M. Moorsom, while still a pupil of Ramsbottom, had brought his Cambridge friend James Stuart in as an outside lecturer. Stuart was a leader of the University Extension movement. This extra interest soon petered out, and from around 1878–80 the Institute's own classes concentrated more and more on practical technical education suited to job-holding, the 'Arts and Literature' part of the foundation tending to disappear.

Early in 1879 a coffee tavern (*The Euston*) was opened in one corner of the site as a separate unit, and was open for 17½ hours a day. It was a success financially, and helped the Institution's funds. With the spread of the Steelworks and increase in the number of men employed there and living in the West Street area, a branch coffee room, news room and games room were opened in Goddard Street by Webb in 1885, but did not have the patronage expected.

Machine tools in the Institution shop were mainly treadled, but around 1890, when electric power was beginning on a small scale, Webb saw to it that a gas engine and dynamo were provided so that all the machine tools could be driven and the building lighted throughout by electricity. From the time of this installation a full-time mechanic was in attendance to give fitting and machine-tool help and instruction and supervision in members' free time, apart from the classes. In such time members could make models or apparatus of their own, and under these conditions Beames, as a pupil, did much of the work on his still-existing model of the compound *Jeanie Deans*, while Darroch (later an assistant to the works manager) did the same with his model of a 4-cylinder compound 4-4-0. Happily it can be recorded that in each case some of the work was under 'foreign order'.

In Webb's last full year of office, 1902, a further extension was made to the buildings, which from then occupied more-or-less the whole triangle bounded by Earle, Prince Albert and Liverpool Streets. Shortly before that a plaque to Sir Joseph Whitworth was put on one of the inside walls. In 1903 a new physical laboratory was opened by Webb, and this complemented the chemical laboratory dating from the 1890s. The Institution had portraits painted at different times of Trevithick, Ramsbottom and Webb which were hung in the rooms, but Whale would not agree to have one of him painted and hung.

After the Technical Instruction Act of 1889 the status of the Institution in regard to education very gradually began to change through outside opposition, and it is possible that some of this arose from the political war between town and railway. The Government Board of Education and the Cheshire County Council both sought over years to gain some say over the Institution's educational activities, for a high reputation was being gained outside by the number of Whitworth Scholarships and Exhibitions obtained, beginning with W. Firkin in 1872.

In view of what the railway had done and paid for over half a century, and its ownership of all the property occupied, a satisfactory further development would have been difficult if some of the control were to move into public hands. In 1907 the Board of Education withdrew grants it had been making for certain subjects. The Cheshire County Council then offered grants in return for representation on the Institution's council of management, but this was refused. After a good deal of unpleasantness over some years, in 1912 all educational work was passed over to the County Council and the borough of Crewe.

A curious episode marked this period. Bowen Cooke sought to increase the Institution's educational status and collaborate more with official bodies. He appointed H. L. Guy from Cardiff as a full-time head of the teaching staff; but before Guy could take up office in the 1910–11 session he was offered a Royal Scholarship by the Government Board of Education, and the railway released him from his engagement. At the end of his year's scholarship he came to Crewe, but as the head of the municipal technical school! This school, at the corner of Flag Lane and Richard Moon Street, had been opened in 1897 as part of the borough council's educational scheme. As the Institution's technical education side was simply merged with the municipal school, Guy got both things. He went on to become a prominent member of the Metro-Vick staff, finishing up as secretary of 'the Mechanicals' and with a knighthood. Following the transfer of technical education some of the classrooms were converted to a social club that was opened in 1912, and this was the last change in the Institution under the LNWR.

Under railway Grouping the LMSR continued to support the remaining part of the Institution, which was then controlled by a committee of 31, made up of three, 14 and 14 members. In 1927 the LMSR financed an enlargement of the lending library and the founding of a reference library. On 23 June 1929 another fire caused extensive damage estimated at around £20,000; the main hall, staircase and several classrooms were gutted. Rebuilding on improved lines was completed in 1931, again at the expense of the railway.

At the beginning of April 1936 the library and reading room were leased to Crewe Corporation at a nominal rent for use as the public library, but the Mechanics Institution continued as a corporate body, and on 6 September 1946 Sir Robert Burrows, deputy-chairman of the LMSR, unveiled a 'centenary' tablet on the wall of the lounge in the social club. The buildings deteriorated steadily from the 1950s, and after a compulsory closure order by the borough council the buildings were abandoned on 30 September 1966 and the Institution came to an end as a legal body. The buildings were demolished around 1970; today there is no Mechanics Institute, no trace of the old buildings, no tradition, and only the old memories of very old men.

13
Epilogue

In the old days before the station came within the town boundary there was a local saying: "The place which *is* Crewe is not Crewe, and the place which is not Crewe *is* Crewe." A septuagenarian's walk through the town in 1980–81 justified either part of this epigram, for not only were many streets, buildings and works changed almost beyond recognition, if they existed at all, but the whole atmosphere bore scarcely a trace of the giants of old or of their workers – at least those of the LNWR.

The Old Works is now cleared away entirely except for one wall, and not neatly but roughly. In 1980 this site was occupied by industrial workers' caravans and rubble, and for a time on the site of the smithy stores was a short wireless mast. The north wall along what was Forge Street remains, and in it can be seen the wired-up aperture of the workmen's entrance and the ramp down to works ground level, which at the northern end was always below street level, the Brassey excavation of 1840–41 being carried no further than strictly necessary for Locke's works plans. One can appreciate also how little thought was given in those days to the convenience of the workers, for the houses at the west end of Forge Street were barely 25yd from the thump of the first steam hammer.

Of the original Crewe village bounded by Forge Street, Liverpool Terrace, Earle Street, and the present Market Street, nothing remains except the east end of Christ Church (in which services are still held), the gutted shell of the nave and the cleaned-up tower, the back purlieus of Sandon Street, and, delightfully, the building of the veterans' club at the bottom of Prince Albert Street, a club founded in 1919 by Bowen Cooke as the LNWR Veterans' Club and now that of British Rail. This building was erected well over a century back on the parade ground of the old Rifle Volunteers, which lay back to back with the original clothing factory built for Compton. The remaining space is taken up by the well-run and not untasteful modern public library, the law courts and police station, and a car park. At the south end of

Prince Albert Street, above where the chief mechanical engineer's coupé and the works fire engine stood, the old pay office was used through some years for dancing instruction to children, but is now leased for other purposes. Below it the old Chester line trace is densely overgrown with shrubs and trees, as is the whole of that line as far as the old general office.

The chief mechanical engineer's official residence, Chester Place, dating from the early 1860s and wherein Edward VII while still Prince of Wales was once entertained to luncheon, is long since demolished. It was not inhabited after Beames retired from railway service, but for some years was used by the Crosville Club. Two of the large semi-detached houses for higher officials of the locomotive department, Deva Villa and West Bank, have also gone, and a car park plus the offices of the Crosville bus company occupy much of their ground and that of Chester Place. Only two of the old official houses, remained in 1981, The Grove and Windycote, both unoccupied and derelict.

Hard by the car park are the little gems Dorfold, Betley and Tollitt Streets. Condemned some years ago, public pressure led to them being reprieved. This was after the streets had been bought from the railway by the town council, and the estate was then sold to a private developer who, after renovating the houses, sold them singly to private purchasers. All are now well painted and well kept, and all are occupied. These streets are prohibited to motor vehicles except for access, and that access is only via the back lanes that are connected along the bottom by a cross lane against the north wall of the old railway general office block, lately in the occupation of Data Processing Instruments Ltd but now empty. These three short *culs-de-sac* are the last examples of the old GJR and LNWR cottages with entrance porches set back to back.

Though the eastern end of Delamere Street is now altered entirely, the original houses west of the Catholic church remain, and, again, are well painted and well kept. Even more so is Lewis Street off the west side of Flag Lane, for in addition to the fine condition the old windows have been replaced by larger modern lights that go well with the structures. Early in 1980 the few remaining 'gaffers houses' in Victoria Street were renovated and converted into flats and bed-sitters, and, for houses of 1850–54 build, are in good order. The same cannot be said of the area around Richard Moon Street, streets and houses that date from the 1870s. Here the old Bessemer Hotel stood forlorn and boarded until its demolition in January 1980. To the east of it the recreation ground and the southernmost two dozen houses in Ramsbottom Street continue in good order; all the rest are demolished or derelict, and in the north-west corner eye-searing cheap dwellings have been erected.

The feature of Richard Moon Street today is simply a bi-ennial one – the first one thousand in the queue for opening time on 'open day'; they shuffle along beneath a profusion of two-bolt tie-plates holding together the walls of the old signal shop and brass foundry. Goddard Street remains, but bereft of everything other than the hall of the old railway brass band (now the railway club), the works dining room, the football field, two LNWR boundary stones, and, at the corner of West Street, that wag's naming – the Brunel Hotel.

Flag Lane, so long the boundary between the Deviation Works and the Steelworks, was greatly widened before World War II, and the stone bridge spanning old and new Chester tracks was entirely renewed with wide roadway in April 1937 as recorded by a plaque on the west parapet. Along Wistaston Road and Victoria Avenue the great slag tip and its 'nightlights' have disappeared by being spread and levelled since 1962 from the 70ft height to around 20ft and are now grass-grown and shrub planted. The last 'tip' of slag was in 1960, but practically none had been deposited after 1950. The gasworks ceased production in 1969 (it had been sold when the national gas boards were formed), and gradually the plant and site have been cleared, but the trace of the rail approach from the Chester line can still be seen, densely overgrown, at the Victoria Avenue end.

Most surprising of all, Coppenhall Hey hall and cottages still existed in 1982, largely hidden by undergrowth between the cooling ponds and the works southern car park. The only access this century has been off Victoria Avenue, but until the lengthening of No 8 erecting shop and the old boiler shop in 1898–99 a lane led from it northwards to West Street near St Barnabas church. One of the cooling ponds has been drained and partially filled, and the other no longer seems to be fished as was common in years gone by.

Within the works gates are still to be found some unusual historical records. In the present electric and fabricating shops the original roof beams and trussing were of wood, but in the 1898–99 extensions the trussing was of light steel rods and the extensions can be traced by them. The present main machine shop, when new in 1903, also had the wooden roof beams and light steel trussing, which was a definite transition stage in structures. Several other shops retain the wooden roof beams of the 1866–70 type, and the old tender shop even has the wooden trussing of 1874. In the present maintenance shop the old beam recording the ceremonial opening in 1882 still takes its share of the loading. Many of the shops still have the old cast iron circular-

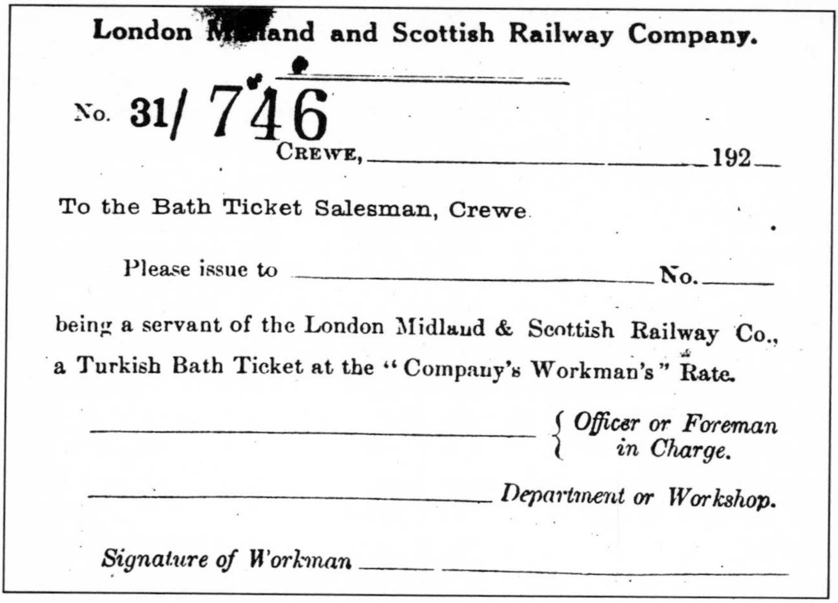

London Midland and Scottish Railway Company.

№. **31/ 746**

CREWE, _____ 192__

To the Bath Ticket Salesman, Crewe.

Please issue to _____ No. _____

being a servant of the London Midland & Scottish Railway Co.,
a Turkish Bath Ticket at the " Company's Workman's " Rate.

_____ { *Officer or Foreman*
                            {   *in Charge.*

_____ *Department or Workshop.*

Signature of Workman _____ _____

Fig 46 LMSR bath-house ticket of the 1920s

section columns, and in the present copper shop and the wheel shop
these are still surmounted by the original cast iron lattice or open-work
girders, a form that may well have been used from around 1866, for
they were always a prominent feature of No. 4 erecting shop in the
Old Works, though the Deviation shops of 1866–68 and some in the
Steelworks had the interlaced circle type of cast girder that dated in
new applications from 1861–62.

Some shops such as the present electric shop and fabrication shop
have had the cast iron lattice longitudinal beams replaced by deep steel
girders resting on the old columns and on the original brick walls, and
the electric shop, in particular, shows a historic combination of
wooden roof beams, light steel rod trussing, old cast iron columns, and
modern steel longitudinal girders. Only the wheel shop, steel foundry
and main machine shop retain the functions they had prior to the
1925–27 reorganisation.

In the fabrication shop (the old boiler shop) the location of the
rivetting tower erected in 1890–91 can still be seen, and on the east
wall are the remains of the wooden frame supporting the wall engine
installed in 1870. A yard or two away, in the north-east corner of the
shop, is a horse-shoe high up on the wall that is reputed to have been
there since the shop was opened in 1870, though at first with the hoof
attached; it has survived all whitewashings and structure renewals.

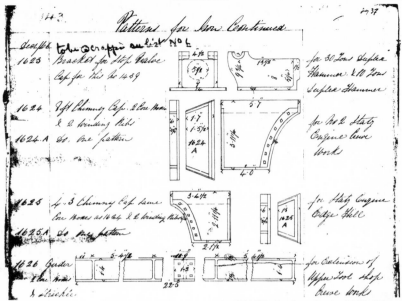

Fig 47 Cast-iron chimney-top support, cast in the Old Works foundry in 1868; the type that can still be seen on the Deviation Works 200ft octagonal chimneys

The paint shop of 1877–78 still stands with its 16 wooden doors with semicircular tops, but for years has been used only as a general store. South of it, as far as Flag Lane bridge, the ground is roughly cleared. The big water tower in Flag Lane was demolished in 1980. Eagle Bridge remains; though used as a footway between the works and the apprentice training school and electric locomotive depot, its main function is to pass locomotives into and out of the works, for a result of the great clearance has been that no *direct* access has been retained between the Chester main line and the works, locomotives coming in having to reverse a few yards down the old gas works track, go round the service station, up the gradient on to the old carriage works viaduct, over Eagle Bridge, down past the old pig bank, to make final reverse and then run two-thirds of the works length to reach the big traverser.

Crewe North steam locomotive sheds are razed entirely, and the weed-grown and brick-strewn area, on which the only new building is the lone Waverley Court, is used mainly by loco-spotters, for Lockett Street, Railway Street, and the east side of Mill Street are all down and give easy access to the ground. The South Brook still flows under Mill Street just north of Brook Street, but it is in a culvert from there until well east of the main north and Manchester lines. The gravelled back court of the Warrington Timber Co occupies part of the old mill pool.

At the north end of Mill Street the old LNWR hospital building was for long in the occupation of Trax Textiles, but was demolished in 1982. It carried to the end its date stone of 1900 and its number, 181, in Mill Street.

Until 1982 the structure of the whole great curved row of the old chain, testing, millwrights and joiners shops forming the major part of the Deviation Works, and dating from 1866–68, remained intact, but a beginning has been made in demolition at the eastern end, including the old power house and tall chimney, was demolished. The remainder of that works, though vacated by Dunlop, is still at the moment of writing under lease to that company and cannot yet be taken down; and so towering against Flag Lane bridge is still the last of the old LNWR Crewe-type hexagonal chimneys about 200ft high, with brick top supported on iron castings from the original Old Works foundry (see Fig 46). This and the western half of the Deviation buildings, along with the Dorfold Street group and the few houses in Victoria Street, are almost the only visible marks outside the Steelworks walls of 'Old Crewe'.

Appendix: Crewe Men

Development and daily running of Crewe Works depended entirely on the men, in high positions and low—perhaps above 100,000 of them in all over 140 years The most important of them are noted below in the approximate sequence in which they achieved influential positions. A list of Crewe chiefs and managers from 1840 has been given already in Table 1 (Chapter 2).

Joseph Locke (1805–60)
Locke was sole chief engineer of the GJR from 1835 to 1846, and though engaged mainly on construction and civil engineering he had the top-level surveillance of the mechanical engineering side. He was the man who suggested Crewe as the site of the locomotive and rolling stock works, who drew up the first plans and estimates, and supervised the organisation of the factory. He also recommended Buddicom as locomotive superintendent of the GJR in December 1839, and Trevithick as Buddicom's successor in 1841, and he was the sponsor of what became known as the 'Crewe-type' locomotive. After the formation of the LNWR in 1846 he was not closely connected with Crewe or with the new company, though he remained an LNWR shareholder. He was one of the four great railway engineers of early days, George and Robert Stephenson and I. K. Brunel being the others, and he was noted for his "far-seeing and strong common-sense." Locke became a Member of Parliament and president of the Institution of Civil Engineers. He died suddenly at Moffat, Dumfries-shire, on 18 September 1860. A Marochetti statue of him was erected in 1866 at Barnsley which, though not his birthplace, was where he grew up.

Locke's plans for Crewe Works were barely adequate for the GJR and its foreseeable future in 1840–41, for already he had surveyed a trunk route from Lancashire to Scotland (Edinburgh and Glasgow) and knew the GJR was likely to become a big system. Further, his acquiescence in the building of Forge Street, Moss Street and other streets immediately north of the works prevented any extension in that direction, and left but a small amount of ground south of the original Chester line for what could only be inconvenient extensions. Crewe Works and the layout of the town nucleus and its approaches were perhaps the least far-seeing of all Locke's railway construction, and with the formation of the LNWR the difficulties were intensified. After consolidation of all three locomotive divisions of that railway were approved in principle in 1855 a great works extension on a new site was axiomatic, but by the time the first real extension was put in hand in 1864 Locke had passed on.

William Barber Buddicom (1816–87)[7]

Buddicom took up office as GJR locomotive superintendent at Edge Hill, Liverpool, on 12 January 1840. He left on 31 August 1841 to begin private locomotive building in France, he later went on to railway construction in Italy and elsewhere and eventually became a very rich man. He was never in charge of Crewe works, but supervised the early estimates, lists of necessary machine tools, Brassey's ground clearance and other details; under pressure from Locke, he was the originator at Edge Hill of what became known as the Crewe type locomotive.

Francis Trevithick (1812–77)

He was a son of 'the Cornish giant' Richard Trevithick, but hardly knew his father, for Richard was much away from home and was not there at all from 1816 until the end of 1827. Francis had his early training in civil engineering under Locke from 1832, and was appointed resident engineer of the GJR at the Birmingham end of the line in 1840. As from 1 September 1841 he became locomotive superintendent of the company at Edge Hill, and like Buddicom without any previous experience of locomotive work. He elaborated the plans for Crewe works and had charge of the erection and equipment; also he had the conduct of the whole locomotive department and then that of the Northern Division of the LNWR, including running. Under him the Crewe-type locomotive was developed from Buddicom's prototype *Aeolus*, and he was content to build nothing else until he left Crewe in 1857.

He was a man of friendly, gentle, easy-going temperament, unwilling to hurt anyone or put them in unpleasant situations, and he had none of the size and immense physical strength of his father. Naturally he was popular among the Crewe workmen and their families, among whom he was known colloquially as 'Trevvy', and it seems too that his wife was equally gentle and kindly. Trevithick was unwilling and unable to run the works and the whole department on the organised and disciplined base necessary with the growing size of the Northern Division, and he shied away from responsibility (see Chapter 4). He was diffident even in pressing for a rise in his own salary as his responsibilities grew, but in 1852 his remuneration was increased from £750 to £850 a year in line with that of McConnell of the Southern Division, who had fewer engines in his care. Trevithick's relations with his works chief foreman, Allan, deteriorated as time went on, until after a serious contretemps that came before the Crewe Committee Allan's resignation was accepted in August 1853; Trevithick was so unhappy at this and the previous atmosphere that he applied for the same job in Scotland that Allan got, and was on the short list with him.

Trevithick took a leading part in the establishment of the Crewe Mechanics Institute, and he gave it and other Crewe activities such as the cricket club consistent support. For years a portrait of him by Sidley hung on the walls of the Institute, and after it was destroyed by fire in 1869 the same artist painted a replica, which was said to have been better than the original.

Trevithick's supersession as Northern Division locomotive superintendent, and the events leading up to it, have been related in Chapter 4. In August 1857 he was presented with £500 worth of plate by the workmen and Crewe townspeople, and Locke was chairman at the presentation dinner. In the same month Locke rose at the annual meeting of the LNWR and protested against

Above: Ivatt Class 2 2–6–0s (Nos 6403 and 6401) and 2–6–2Ts (Nos 1200 and 1202) outside the Crewe paint shop after completion in 1946
Below: Spare parts store in the north bay of the old No 8 erecting shop after the 1925–27 re-organisation. Connecting rods for Joy valve gear engines, and open coupling rods 8ft 3in centre-to-centre for 0–4–0ST, are in the racks
Bottom: Heavy machine shop (originally No 5 erecting shop) with frame structure and cylinders of BR Class 9 2–10–0 assembled and ready for transfer to erecting shop south

One of the 0–4–2T crane engines built in the 1890s, working in LMSR days near Flag Lane rail entrance to the Steelworks. Behind is the Flag Lane water tower and to the left is the mortar mill.   (*LGRP*)

Below: New stores building to the left and the progress office to the right

Bottom: HST power cars under erection in the main erecting shop in 1975

Trevithick's dismissal. In his earlier years Trevithick seems to have been fond of outdoor life, and in *The Railway Times* of 25 January 1845 the notorious *Veritas Vincit* warned the GJR directors "to send forth an edict to Mr Trevithick to put aside his dog and gun and more assiduously apply himself to the interests of the company." *VV* had also insinuated in an earlier issue that Trevithick really had no ability at all, and that Locke realised this. Nevertheless, the responsibilities shouldered by Trevithick grew enormously from 1841 to 1854; thereafter more dissatisfaction with his standards of management became evident among board members (see Chapter 4).

After leaving Crewe Trevithick returned to Cornwall and became factor of the Trehidy estates, of which his Grandfather had been mineral agent in the 18th century. He maintained his friendship with Ramsbottom and Webb, and on at least one occasion in the 1870s he re-visited Crewe and the works. He wrote, and in 1872 had published, a biography of his father. He died at Penzance on 27 October 1877 and was buried there. In the 1887 jubilee celebrations at Crewe he was described as "a man much admired and esteemed at Crewe."

Richard Stuart Norris (1812–78)
Norris was born at Bolton and was employed on early GJR surveys by Locke. In 1836 he became chief draughtsman in that engineer's Liverpool office, though he was considered as on the GJR payroll from December 1833, and so in length of service was the senior of all men who had to do with Crewe. After the GJR was opened he was appointed resident engineer of the Northern Division, and as such had charge of the erection of early Crewe houses and streets, also of the town and works extensions. In the early 1850s he was made both engineer and superintendent of the Northern Division, with headquarters variously at Warrington and Liverpool. Towards the end of his active career he came somewhat under the strictures of Richard Moon, as did various other old-timers. He retired from railway service in 1862 after the ND–SD locomotive consolidation, and settled near Kenyon Junction, where he died on 26 January 1878.

Alexander Allan (1809–91)
Allan was born at Montrose and served an apprenticeship with a millwright, Gibbs, at Lochside. In 1832–33 he was at Stephenson's Newcastle works as an artisan, and then went to Forrester's new locomotive works at Liverpool, where he claimed to have worked on *Swiftsure* for the L&MR. He spent some 12 months in Ireland 1835–36 for Forrester in charge of the re-erection and preliminary running of locomotives supplied to the Dublin & Kingstown Railway, and on his return he became a foreman at the Forrester works. In February 1840 he was selected by Locke and Buddicom as foreman of the Edge Hill shops of the GJR and took up his duties in March; he came to have oversight also of the locomotive fitters at the Birmingham end of the line. He moved to Crewe in 1843, and though his official title to the end of his time on the GJR was chief foreman of locomotives he was in effect the works manager. Though a stronger disciplinarian and a more decided character than Trevithick, and a capable works man for the time, there is no record of him (or Trevithick) making any real effort to implement Locke's aim to have standard locomotive parts. Allan, too, came under the lash of *Veritas Vincit*

for viciousness as well as incompetence, but then most railway men did; John Herapath in *The Railway Magazine* described him as "the intelligent foreman at Edge Hill."

Allan was well thought of as chief foreman by the members of the Crewe Committee, and in 1847 he came to an arrangement with them for regular increases in salary up to 1852, when he was earning £500 a year. After a passionate action following a row with Trevithick, and which led to him being strongly reprimanded by the Crewe Committee, the position for all parties was eased in the same month by Allan getting the vacant locomotive superintendency of the Scottish Central Railway, to begin in September 1853. On the SCR he introduced Crewe-type passenger engines and other types of 0-4-2 goods engines. While on that railway he was allowed to act as consultant to the Inverness & Nairn Railway and to provide drawings and specifications for 2-2-2 and 2-4-0 Crewe-type engines for that railway and its successor, the Inverness & Aberdeen Junction, of which his nephew, William Barclay, was locomotive chief. These engines were built by Hawthorn of Leith.

When the SCR was absorbed into the Caledonian in 1865 no place was found for Allan. The next year he became manager of the Worcester Engine Works and held the position during the four years of that firm's locomotive-building activities. The works closed in 1870, and about the same time Allan is believed to have been in an accident near Birmingham that partly disabled him. He went to Scarborough in 1872 and lived there until his death, acting from time to time as a consultant and making one or two inventions. He was responsible for several railway inventions from 1847, but only his straight-link valve motion of 1855 had any commercial success. In the mid-1840s he evolved a balanced slide valve that was fitted to two LNWR engines, and according to F. W. Webb, writing many years later, the only reason for failure was the lack of rigidity of the valve chest cover. Allan was an original member of the Institution of Mechanical Engineers in 1847.

A letter of Allan's to the *Crewe Guardian* in 1882, following an account of the new iron foundry in Crewe Works, purported to give the early history of the Crewe-type locomotive, and its reproduction in *The Engineer* for 25 May 1883 has been accepted by generations of railway writers, and still is. Only from this publication in *The Engineer* did the great but quite erroneous 'Allan tradition' arise, yet the letter was full of the mistakes and confusions of old age, if nothing more, and gave a view much perverted from that shown by contemporary documents and drawings.[11]

Thomas Hunt (1816–97)

Allan was succeeded at Crewe by Hunt, who took the title of chief indoor assistant to Trevithick. As a 14-year-old he stood on the bridge at Parkside to watch the opening procession on the L&MR. In 1832 he began work on the St Helen's & Runcorn Gap Railway, but in April 1833 he transferred to the Edge Hill shops of the L&MR under John Melling (senior), and almost his first job was to help in re-tubing *Rocket*. In August 1834 he went with Melling's son John (junior) for whom he had worked on the St Helen's line to the Dublin & Kingstown Railway to finish his apprenticeship there, and he stayed with the DKR as a journeyman and foreman until April 1839, when at the age of 23 he was appointed to take charge of the locomotives of the North

Union Railway in place of Musgrave, on the understanding that he would stay at least two years. In 1840 he began to balance the NU Bury 2-2-0s by putting counterweights in the wheels to eliminate pronounced fore-and-aft movement that was breaking intermediate drawbars and drag boxes. Hunt remained in charge on the NU until in 1846 the line was taken over by the LNWR and LYR. He then came onto the LNWR payroll as in charge of shops and engines that had come into the LNWR fold, and a few months later he was given the oversight of all LNWR engines working over the whole length from Parkside to Carlisle.

On coming to Crewe from Preston to succeed Allan his salary was raised by £50 to £450 a year, and he continued as chief indoor assistant to the Northern Division locomotive superintendent until September 1861, when he resigned to take up the post of locomotive superintendent on the Tudela & Bilbao Railway, then under construction in Spain to 5ft 6in gauge. He had to decide on the locomotive designs and place the contracts for construction. After one batch of Crewe-type 4-4-0Ts by Fairbairn he switched to 4-4-0Ts that later became the parents of the well-known 'Met tanks', working on the design in collaboration with Beyer Peacock.[12] To one of the TBR Beyer tanks he fitted a power bogie.

Hunt returned to England in 1865 and joined the North of England Railway Carriage Works at Preston. Thereafter for some years until 1875 he was in Sheffield. In 1878 he joined Beyer Peacock on the sales side; he seems to have been based mainly on London, but made several trips abroad. For seven years from 1883 he was a director of the Beyer Peacock private company. He died at Heaton Chapel, Stockport, on 27 May 1897. One of his sons, H. Robert Hunt, was locomotive chief of the Isle of Man Railway 1876–86.

Little of Hunt is known except that he was a nice man, though in his time at Preston he was described by one of his drivers as "wide awake and sharp-eyed." Ernest F. Lang, recalling his own early years at Gorton Foundry, wrote of ". . . the elusive personality of Mr Thomas Hunt. Tall, spare, and slightly bent, with strong features and pointed beard, a striking and dignified figure, he carried an air of mystery in our imagination as he came and went and re-appeared at Gorton Foundry, and no one knew precisely what he did beyond being a kind of business diplomat for external affairs, for which in appearance he was marvellously well suited." He retired from Beyer Peacock in 1890.

Why Hunt left Crewe is not known, but by his going he committed professional suicide. Though he seems to have administered his charges well at Preston and Crewe he showed some lack of judgment in relation to outside matters in 1858–61. In addition to his Spanish adventure his patent in 1859 for an outrageous boiler like McConnell's and Beattie's at their worst was ill-timed, for coal burning without smoke was coming towards simple solutions on the Midland, and his own chief, Ramsbottom, was on the point of applying the first simple two square 7in holes, with dampers, in the throat plate.

Hunt had got on well with the rather stringent and astringent Quaker board of the North Union and with Trevithick. The LNWR Stores & Locomotive Expenditure Committee and the Crewe Committee thought well of him, and when he resigned gave him a gratuity of three months' salary. He knew his predecessor, Allan, well, having to do with him for a year on the DKR, and having frequent contact with him from Preston. Possibly he found the increased tempo under Ramsbottom unsettling and wearing after 14 years more-or-less his own boss at Preston followed by four years under Trevithick's easy hand, and he may not have been a strict enough disciplinarian for the new times; no evidence has been discovered that he did not get on well with Ramsbottom personally. Indeed, the two had a strange hidden affinity. Not only were they merely two years different in age, but as septuagenarians they came together again as fellow directors of the old Beyer Peacock private company. For the last nine years of their lives they lived only eight miles apart, and Hunt died four days after Ramsbottom.

Charles Wayte

Wayte is the first Crewe chief draughtsman to be recorded by name. He joined the GJR in 1845 and by 1852, if not earlier, he had become principal draughtsman at a salary of £2 a week, raised to £125 per annum at the end of that year. He was one of the early teachers at the Mechanics Institute. Trevithick thought well of him, but he resigned in September 1854 to go out of the railway world.

William Williams

He was appointed principal draughtsman at Crewe as from 1 January 1855 at £156 a year. He is believed to have been the Williams who invented the Stephenson link motion at Forth Street in 1841 and who came to Crewe from the South Eastern Railway. He died unduly early in February 1859, before which he had charge of the design of Ramsbottom's DX 0-6-0 engines, the conversion of *Cornwall*, and the early work on the 2-2-2 Problem class.

John Ramsbottom (1814–97)

Ramsbottom was possibly the most remarkable engineer ever to be connected with Crewe works. He was born at Todmorden, the son of a small cotton spinner who owned the first steam-driven mill in the valley. John had little in the way of schooling, being trained by and worked for his father, but he schemed-out and made other machinery for the district, and at the age of 20 took out a patent in conjunction with his uncle, Richard Holt, for the improvement of power looms to weave two pieces of fabric at one time. His first 24 years were spent in his birthplace, after which he went as a journeyman on textile machinery to the Manchester works of Sharp Roberts, where he came under the influence of two outstanding men, Richard Roberts and Charles Beyer. From them probably came his appreciation of accurate measurement and its application to batch production. Eight of his testimonials from residents of the Todmorden area dated 1839 still survive, and every one mentions the reliability of his character.

At Sharp Roberts he must have been drafted early onto locomotive work, and there he attracted the notice of Beyer, who had the locomotive side in his hands. Some three years later a recommendation from Beyer helped Ramsbottom to get the job of locomotive running foreman, under the engineer, of the newly-opened Manchester & Birmingham Railway, though he had no experience of railways at all. He took up this position in May 1842, and was promoted to take charge of the locomotive and rolling stock department of the MBR at £170 a year in November 1843 when that section was separated from the chief engineer's department.

He retained that position when the MBR was absorbed into the LNWR, and when the lines between Manchester and Leeds were opened in 1849 the engines also came into Ramsbottom's charge as part of the new North Eastern Division stock—his salary was advanced to £500 a year from £300, and in 1853 was stepped up to £850. The LNWR board thought so well of him that in 1856 he was given charge of the rail rolling mill at Crewe, though his headquarters continued at Longsight, Manchester. During his time on the NED he took out nine patents, including the split piston ring (1855), safety-valve (1856), feed pump, turntables, hoists for raising and lowering locomotives, and a coal hoist.

Under the circumstances related in Chapter 4 he was made locomotive superintendent of the combined Northern and North Eastern Divisions of the LNWR in 1857, and in 1862 became the first all-line locomotive superintendent at a salary of £2,000 a year, increased to £3,000 as from 1 January 1864 and to £5,000 from 1 January 1869, a reflection of the greatly increased responsibilities, including the steel plant, he was holding and the amazingly good job he was making of them. These salaries set the pace for the 19th century chiefs at Crewe; Cawkwell, the LNWR general manager from 1858 to 1874, never had more than £3,000 a year, nor did his successor, George Findlay, ever rise to the £5,000 level in the next 18 years. Ramsbottom's salaries also began the enormous gap between the remuneration of No 1 in the locomotive department and those of the various Nos 2, none of whom had more than 20 percent of the chief's salary. This big gap continued to the end of the LNWR and in later years caused trouble in the line of succession. Much of the work done by Ramsbottom at Crewe has been detailed in Chapter 5; extensions of it included the mechanical ventilation of Edge Hill tunnels at Liverpool in 1871 when endless-rope haulage was replaced by locomotive power, the solution being based on a Ramsbottom patent of March 1869.

Largely through the enormous amount of work that he did for over a dozen years, and the strain of accomplishing it to the satisfaction of himself and Richard Moon, he began to wear out in 1870, and the stress became more intense in the summer and autumn by his presidency of the Institution of Mechanical Engineers, though he gave no presidential address, and by the death of the then Crewe works manager. In September 1870 he told the board he would have to retire at the end of twelve months, and his absences became more prolonged in 1871. For some years after the end of September 1871 the LNWR board retained him as consulting engineer at £1000 a year.

The complete release from the immense day-by-day administrative task and the large extensions of Crewe Works and the locomotive department made the cure. By 1875, at 60 years of age, he was back to full health and vigour, and remained a hale and hearty man with firm lines for another 20 years. He took up outside consulting work, though he was already wealthy from his large salary and patent royalties. Altogether he took out 40 patents, but only three of them came after his retirement from Crewe. Nine were related to steel and steel-making; six, over 14 years, were to do with fluids. The first of them in 1851 resulted from his suggestion to the LNWR board in January 1849 of "fitting a cheap apparatus in the nature of a gas meter, to record mileage and speed run by each engine."

In 1883 he was appointed consulting mechanical engineer to the LYR, where in collaboration with Barton Wright, the locomotive superintendent, he planned the new Horwich works and specified its equipment. On the death of Lord Houghton in 1885 he was elected a director of the LYR and became chairman of the locomotive committee, in which position he greatly influenced and supported his old apprentice John Aspinall, who had succeeded Barton Wright. He resigned only in 1896 on account of age. Also in 1883 he became a director of the Beyer Peacock private company, formed some years after the death of Charles Beyer had terminated the original partnership. Here he strengthened the close relations he had maintained with Gorton Foundry from its inception in 1855.

One cannot record that Ramsbottom was a nepotist, and he promoted no one above his capacity; yet he had a strong family feeling and helped his sons, cousins and nephews into jobs, but thereafter left them to make their own way. His sons, John Goodfellow and George Holt, were trained at Gorton Foundry in preference to Crewe from 1880 and 1884. Both remained with Beyer Peacock until 1900–02, attaining increasingly responsible positions. Ramsbottom's younger cousins, Frank Holt (1825–93) and Charles Holt (1830–1900) also were in locomotive work. The former began an apprenticeship with Sharp Roberts and Sharp Bros before Ramsbottom left, and later went to Crewe, and while there was put in charge of the South Staffordshire Railway locomotive working as Trevithick's representative while the ND had oversight. Later he was for a short time in India, and then was with Beyer Peacock, R. & W. Hawthorn, and the Midland Railway, and was works manager at Derby until he died. He was credited with the initiation of steam sanding. His brother Charles was works manager at Gorton Foundry from 1877 to 1900. Robert Ramsbottom Lister, son of one of John Ramsbottom's sisters, was taken on as an apprentice at Gorton Foundry in 1869 and remained with Beyer Peacock all his working life, being chief draughtsman 1890–1900 and works manager 1900–04. A second nephew, Frederic John Ramsbottom Sutcliffe, became a Crewe apprentice in 1860, and as a result of his experience at the original 'melts' he went into the private steel industry and became well known.

John Ramsbottom's principal characteristic was supreme competence. He was a completely objective man, and though well aware of his worth he was not egotistic. His manner was pleasant; he had no vanity, and no one laughed more heartily than he at Wodehouse's quip at the farewell Crewe dinner in 1871 that the new home of Mr Ramsbottom had hitherto been the property of a Mr Sidebottom and was situated at Broadbottom. Cusack Roney in 1868 described him[13] as "the earnest, persevering, never-tiring John Ramsbottom." He had the ability to pick good subordinates from the choice available, and once he had trained them to his ways and became confident that they could stand the pace, he did not trouble them from day to day, and he saw to it that they had regular increases in salary. From his humble beginnings he rose not only to pre-eminence in the world of mechanical engineering, but also one day entertained the Prince of Wales (later King Edward VII) to luncheon in his house near the works after Edward had made a tour of the shops in January 1866. This was at a time when there was more social protocol than in later years, and before Lord Richard Grosvenor (later Lord Stalbridge) had joined the LNWR board and brought a succession of distinguished visitors to Crewe.

On his retirement Ramsbottom was entertained formally by the LNWR board at Euston Hotel. Among those present at the dinner were the Lord Mayor of London, the Duke of Buckingham, who (as the Marquis of Chandos) had been LNWR chairman 1855–60, a critical period in Ramsbottom's career, Charles Beyer and Sir Joseph Whitworth. In 1873 Ramsbottom donated £1,000 to Owens College, Manchester, to found a two-year scholarship for LNWR locomotive department employees under 21 years. Another event of his time at Crewe was the naming of a new street after him; in 1872 Webb named one of the new express 2-4-0s in his honour.

Ramsbottom was a founder member of the Institution of Mechanical Engineers, and when he died at Alderley Edge on 23 May 1897 only two founder members remained: his friend Peter Rothwell Jackson of the Salford Rolling Mills and Richard Williams of Wednesbury. A year or two after his death a memorial window was put into the then new chancel of Christ Church, Crewe. Ramsbottom's estate was proved at the large sum of £144,372, but he made no bequests outside the family, nor was he known to contribute to organised charities. The silver plate given him by the company when he retired was much prized, and he left it specifically as a family heirloom.

John Rigg (c. 1812–80)

Born at Littleborough in the Pennines, eight miles distant from Ramsbottom's birthplace. The earliest record of his railway work is on the Manchester, Sheffield & Lincolnshire Railway, on which eventually he became running shed foreman at New Holland. In 1852, partly on the recommendation of Isaac Watt Boulton, Ramsbottom appointed him running foreman of the NED at Longsight. According to Boulton, Ramsbottom shortly afterwards was worried about engine and crew working for heavy Whitsun week-end traffic and Rigg said to him: "Leave it all to me. I feel quite at home with it, and all will come out right." It did, and from that time Ramsbottom trusted him fully, in 1857 taking him to Crewe as outdoor assistant (running) of the enlarged Northern Division. His starting salary at Crewe was £250 a year. From 1867, when Thomas Wheatley, the outdoor assistant of the Southern Division at Wolverton, went to the North British Railway, Rigg also had oversight of the SD running department, but retained his office at Crewe, the central point. His final salary was £800 a year. For some weeks in 1871 while Ramsbottom was absent through illness, Rigg acted as deputy locomotive superintendent. He retired in 1877, and from then until his death in February 1880 he had a railway pension of £400 a year. Rigg was a practical man and capable of rising with the job as its scope increased. He must have been inventive, for in 1865 he designed a corridor coach with lavatory accommodation. He was also a shrewd and astute business man, fond of the bawbees. He came to own considerable property in Crewe, and long before his retirement from the LNWR he was financially interested in cheese-making, brick-making, engineering, and fustian-cutting establishments in the town. He took a leading part in the affairs of Crewe through the time of the Monks Coppenhall Local Board.

George Wadsworth

He was the locomotive accountant at Crewe through Ramsbottom's time there and for many years of the Webb régime. He had entered the service in 1852; by 1857 had found found favour with Moon, and was appointed to succeed Bell as locomotive accountant of the Northern Division. By 1865 he was acting as locomotive accountant for the whole line, still with his office almost next door to Ramsbottom's. He retired in 1885. He was a member of the old Local Board and was chairman of its finance committee, and he was one of the original members of the town council on the incorporation of Crewe as a borough in 1877. On both bodies he acted very much as an LNWR representative.

Thomas Stubbs (1836–70)

Stubbs was born at Carlisle and joined the NED at Longsight as a boy draughtsman in 1852. At the end of 1857 Ramsbottom transferred him to Crewe drawing office, and on Webb's elevation to works manager in September 1861 Stubbs became head of the drawing office at £140 a year, later increased to £170. When Webb left LNWR service Stubbs became chief indoor assistant (works manager) as from 1 July 1866, and his salary was raised to £300 a year; by March 1869 it had increased to £600. He died on 16 September 1870 after a three-week illness, and as a mark of the opinion the board had of him his salary up to the end of the year was paid to his widow and young children. His obituary recorded that he had filled his last position with great satisfaction. He must have been a remarkable man for Ramsbottom to appoint him chief draughtsman at 25 years of age and works manager at 30, especially as he seems to have had no period in the works as a youth. Probably Stubb's death had a big effect on Ramsbottom, who was just beginning to feel the strain of over a dozen years as chief, and had given in his notice scarcely ten days before; he must have viewed Stubbs as well able to look after the works with no more than nominal supervision. When Stubbs became works manager he was given George Radcliffe as his special assistant for the rail mill, then still in the southern annexe to the Old Works, but Radcliffe rose little higher under Webb.

H. W. Kampf

Began as a boy on the LBR at Wolverton in March 1841, and later became a draughtsman under McConnell. From 1857 until his retirement he was senior in length of service of all the locomotive department officers. On the reshuffle following the consolidation of the ND and SD he was transferred in April 1862 to Crewe as a draughtsman, and on the promotion of Stubbs in 1866 he became head of the office. After the death of Stubbs, Kampf more-or-less had to take over the works management also, particularly during Ramsbottom's absences in 1871. After Webb's provisional appointment to succeed Ramsbottom no important positions were confirmed until near the time of the actual change, and then only with Webb's concurrence. For some reason Kampf must have been unacceptable to Webb for permanent promotion to works manager or retention as chief draughtsman, and soon after Webb took over as chief Kampf was transferred back to Wolverton by the terms of a Locomotive Committee minute of November 1871: "Ordered that Mr Kampf be appointed indoor assistant at Wolverton at £250 p.a. and

Right: BR diesel-electric locomotives under repair in the main erecting shop

Below: Clearing the site for shop to accommodate the large number of unclassified diesel repairs in the mid–1960s. This shop is now the electric equipment erecting shop. View looking east

Bottom: Modern single-phase electric locomotives under construction in the main erecting shop

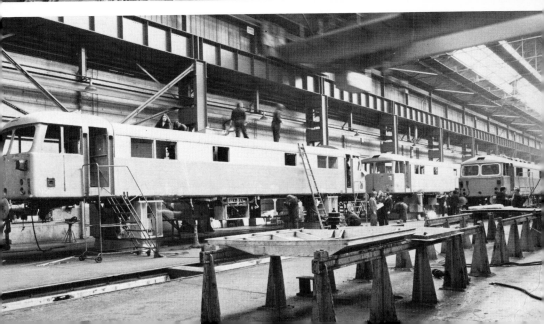

Above: Tiny at work on 18in gauge cross-track in the tender shop at the Steel-works. *Below: Midge*, of 1870 build, with one of the standard tramway wagons

Bottom left: Pet, the second-built tram engine, of 1865. This view is in the paint shop, and to the right is the front of *Cornwall*. *Bottom right: Billy*, of 1875, with hydraulically-operated wheel brakes

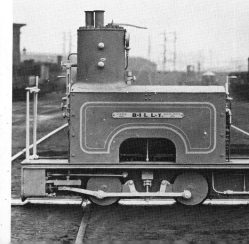

Above: The first BR standard locomotive, No 70000 *Britannia*, with *Cornwall* outside the Crewe paint shop, January 1951

Below: Stanier Princess Royal Pacific No 46211 *Queen Maud* built at Crewe in 1935, after repair at Crewe in March 1959, after running nearly 1,500,000 miles; outside the signal stores   (*K. R. Pirt*)

Bottom left: Coupled wheel pair of George V 4–4–0 with clean break through one tyre. Wheel shop to right and steel foundry and spring mill to left, *circa* 1930.
Bottom right: Early rubber-tyred truck acquired for works internal transport, 1919; battery-propelled Lansing make that operated at the Steelworks

Top: John Ramsbottom F. W. Webb C. J. B. Cooke *Centre:* H. P. M. Beames R. A. Riddles R. C. Bond *Bottom:* George Whale W. W. H. Warneford J. N. Jackson

be paid a bonus of £250 in consideration of the efficient and meritorious services he has rendered at Crewe since Mr. Stubbs's death and during Mr Ramsbottom's illness." Kampf handled carriage work under Bore and the decreasing amount of locomotive work at Wolverton, but after the latter came to an end he was transferred in November 1877 to Carlisle as locomotive foreman; under Webb he got no further, and finished his 48 years of service in 1889 at that place.

Francis William Webb (1836–1906)

F. W. Webb was the giant of Crewe, possibly because of the long period of 30-odd years as the chief, and partly because of the way in which he made his presence felt daily not only in every section of the locomotive department but in every shop in Crewe Works. He had immense capacity as an organiser, as an administrator, as a cost accountant, and as an inventor; unlike Ramsbottom he was an egotist, and tended to become more so as the years went by. He used the words 'I' and 'my' rather than 'we' and 'our', and in contradistinction to the generally impersonal approach of Ramsbottom. All his adult life he lacked the warming and stabilising influence of a family life and so was an incomplete man, though perhaps not a lonely one as some writers have averred. Eventually he became imperious and irritable, and at the very end unstable, though not all of these traits came from the man himself without outside influences. Though he drew everything into his personal orbit, and insisted on full credit to himself in outside relations, he was by no means ungenerous during his life, and he followed this by ample provisions under his will, though the bequests were to charitable institutions as much as to individuals.

A curious feature of Webb's quick rise to high position (he was only 35 years old when he became No 1 in the LNWR locomotive department) which has never been noticed in the numerous written accounts of the man and his work was the extent to which he was favoured by untoward events. The early death of William Williams led to Webb's appointment as chief draughtsman at the age of 22. Two-and-a-half years later the injudicious resignation of Hunt at the age of 45 led to Webb's being stepped-up to works manager. Finally, after he had been away from the LNWR for four years, the untimely death of Stubbs at the age of 33 and the concurrent decision of Ramsbottom to retire in a twelve-month brought something of a crisis for the future direction of the department. No one of sufficient status and experience being on hand, the possibility of getting Webb back appealed immediately to both Moon and Ramsbottom.

In all these events that fell his way Webb had already shown himself capable of stepping into the shoes of the man above him; he had the advantage that of all possible candidates with LNWR connections he alone had what in those days was known as 'a gentlemanly upbringing.' This was still of importance to the board in 1870, in a tradition that had begun in 1839 on the GJR, and Moon was known to hold that an LNWR officer was first of all a gentleman and secondly an LNWR man.

Webb was born on 21 May 1836 as a son of the Reverend William Webb, for over 50 years rector of the parish of Tixall, Staffordshire. He was among the first in a long line of sons of the church who rose to high positions in the locomotive world (Patrick and James Stirling, H. A. Ivatt, Bowen Cooke,

Vincent Raven, A. C. Stamer, Nigel Gresley, *et al*). He became one of the early premium apprentices at Crewe in August 1851, and his time ended towards the close of 1856 when he was in the drawing office. Trevithick then reported to the Northern Division sub-committee that "Frank Webb, draughtsman in his office, is out of his apprenticeship, and that he is an exceedingly respectable young man and his services are very valuable. Resolved that it be recommended to the Executive Committee to retain Webb's services at £2 a week wage". Frank was the diminutive by which he was always known to his few intimate friends and his brothers, and happily that name was chosen for the street at Crewe named after him when he had retired; it shows that in his own time his human attributes were recognised.

He continued as a draughtsman, and under Williams did the design work for the conversion of *Cornwall* to a 2-2-2 with a DX boiler, and much of the drawing work on the first DX design. The general arrangement drawings of these two types, signed by Webb himself as the draughtsman involved, still exist. On his promotion to principal draughtsman in February 1859 his salary was advanced to £140 a year. On his next step, to chief indoor assistant, in September 1861, he was advanced to £180 and two months later to £220, probably because the new shops and re-arrangements had increased his responsibilities. In three further stages he was advanced to £600 in 1864, a threefold increase in three years.

After giving some four months' notice, he left LNWR service on 30 June 1866 to become manager of the Bolton Iron & Steel Co, a concern owned by the Hick and Hargreaves families, and which had installed a Bessemer trial converter as early as 1860. He was capable of holding this appointment because under Ramsbottom he had taken a large part in the planning and establishment of the Crewe Bessemer steel plant and as works manager had responsibility for its operation. By the summer of 1866 he was one of a handful of men in England with 18 months' experience in the day-by-day running of a commercial Bessemer plant, and so was very valuable to the Bolton owners. Moreover, he had become much interested in steel production. Above all, he was ambitious. There was then no sign of Ramsbottom wearing out, and at 52 the latter could be expected to go on another 12 or 15 years leaving Webb, then only 30 years of age, little opportunity for further advancement on the LNWR.

During his period as Crewe works manager 1861–66 Webb began his inventive career, which became so extensive and continuous, and was tied for so long to patents; but the LNWR board, ever-mindful that the patent-royalty business had been a contributory cause of the disappearance of the Melling family and John Gray from the GJR and L&MR 25 years earlier, paid no fees to officers of the company for the use of any of their inventions, though the patentee was allowed to collect fees elsewhere as he could. Bowen Cooke wrote in 1892 that "owing to Mr Webb's ingenuity the LNWR is now possessed of over 50 patents." By the time of his last invention in January 1903 Webb had almost 80 patents, of which 15 were joint with A. M. Thompson, the LNWR signal and telegraph superintendent.

Webb's first two inventions, in the mid-1860's were the steel-headed rail and the curvilinear slotting machine, both of which have been referred to in Chapter 5. Ramsbottom appreciated Webb's talents, and on Webb giving notice of going to Bolton the Locomotive Committee minuted on 8 June

1866: "The Committee concur in Mr Ramsbottom's suggestion that a gratuity be presented to Mr Webb, being partly in recognition of the curved-surface shaping machine and the steel-headed rail, both of which inventions, as Mr Ramsbottom informs them, are due to him, and they Recommend that the sum of £500 be presented to Mr Webb, subject, however, to his executing such a document as Mr Blenkinsop [LNWR solicitor who had succeeded Swift] may advise for the purpose of securing to the Company in a more formal manner the free use of such of Mr Webb's inventions as they are now employing." Something of Webb's many inventions has been given in Chapter 6.

When in September 1870 Ramsbottom gave the needed twelve months' notice of his retirement, and Stubbs died almost at the same time, Moon contacted Webb at once, and after a preliminary interview confirmed the offer to Webb in a letter dated 8 October 1870[14] reading:

"I took the opportunity as agreed of naming to our Special Comm^{te} what had passed with reference to your rejoining our Comp. as Locomotive Superintendent.

Ist that the salary should be £2,000 for the 1st year and £3,000 afterwards. We thought that the notice had best be as in the case of Mr Ramsbottom, twelve months, and that the number of pupils if you take any, for your own comfort as well as ours, should be limited to four.

You know the regulations of the Co. as to patents and other matters, so that I need not trouble you with them here.

I do not know what rent Mr Ramsbottom pays for his house, but you can have it on the same terms as he has had it.

I mentioned to the Comm^{te} that you could not leave the friends with whom you are at present for about 6 months, but that you may possibly arrange to leave then at an earlier period. We shall be ready for you whenever you can make arrangements to join us, and perhaps you will let me know after seeing your friends.

The Special Comm^{te} unanimously agreed to my proposal, and Mr Chance, the Chairman of the Locomotive Comm^{te} desired me to say that it has his special concurrence.

Hoping that you may have a long and promising career."

Moon wrote again to Webb on 18 November 1870 after having had Webb's reply, to say it was agreeable that he should finish at Bolton on 30 June 1871 and then rejoin the LNWR. At this last date Ramsbottom's notice had not expired, and as he was in rather better health the board agreed that Webb should make at LNWR expense a short tour of the USA to study steel-making and locomotive practice. He was back by the end of August and took over officially on 1 October. Thereafter for over 30 years he was undisputed 'King of Crewe', with unswerving support from the two LNWR chairmen, Moon to 1891 and Lord Stalbridge thereafter, though by the end of 1902 Stalbridge realised that Webb would soon have to go because of his age and the friction with the then general management and operating department.

Webb proved capable of handling the whole locomotive department and Crewe Works through an increase of 60 to 100 percent in size and capacity, with an eye on efficiency and economy that was unsleeping. He took an actual practical part in every aspect of the works, but tied almost every advance to himself. If he accepted suggestions or ideas from outside, for example the Pintsch gas-lighting system, he modified every one to make it a Webb idea, with the sole exception of the Joy valve gear. That exception itself is a pointer to Webb's underlying humanity, susceptible to the warming, genuine influence of "dear old David Joy" – the only man to whom he would every pay patent royalties.

The foibles to which Webb in his later years became attached, and the obstinacy with which he clung to them, were solely in locomotive design matters and never in works practice or management or on the organisation and supervision of the whole locomotive department; in fact they were confined to compound locomotives and continuous brakes. He pressed none of his other inventions beyond the trial stage if they were not then successful.

Webb's early work on electricity generation and electric shop drives has been noted in Chapter 6, but at 60 years of age his mind was still progressive enough to see much further. Speaking at the jubilee of the Crewe Mechanics Institute on 29 January 1896 he said: "In 10 to 15 years from now trains moved by electricity will run from all the large centres of the country at a rate of speed which can hardly be realised, probably 100mph." On the same occasion he said also that he was prepared to run trains by electricity; and that the time might come when trains would run daily from London to Carlisle without stopping. About this time he suggested to Stalbridge the construction of an electric train, but this idea was not sanctioned; the eventual authorisation he got shortly before he retired to electrify the Newport Pagnell branch experimentally was just allowed to lapse under Whale.

As Webb grew older he became more difficult in manner and less tolerant of suggestions. From the late 1890s this was bound up increasingly with the mutual antipathy between him and Frederick Harrison, the LNWR general manager from 1893. They were both self-opinionated men, and the younger Harrison resented both Webb's independence of him and his much higher salary, for by then Webb was receiving £7,000 a year, at least 40 per cent more than Harrison's salary. From around the turn of the century Webb's then new 4-cylinder compound 4-4-0s were unable consistently to keep time with the ever-increasing loads and speeds, and Harrison lost no opportunity of spotlighting the deficiencies, not only by the introduction of the so-called '17-rule' in October 1901 but by repeated complaints to Stalbridge, many of which Webb refuted.

Webb's mind undoubtedly softened after he had passed the climacteric of 63 years, but almost to the end of his time at Crewe the softening showed more in greater irascibility and in a less obvious tiredness, though at times he feared he was becoming penurious. Only in the last week or so did a loosening of the mind occur. In November 1902, perhaps after a time of depression or foreboding, and after a period when strong opinions had been expressed to Stalbridge by Harrison and Turnbull (the operating superintendent) as to the thousands of minutes time a month they claimed were lost on the principal express trains by Jubilee and Alfred 4-4-0s, Webb told the board he would soon have to retire, and the directors minuted: "Mr Webb having desired to be relieved from the duties of chief mechanical engineer, the directors wish to record their very great appreciation of the devoted and exceptional services he has rendered to the Company since his appointment in 1871."

According to the terms of the appointment 12 months' notice was needed. Not until the board meeting of 22 April 1903 was a successor named and other consequential staff changes sanctioned, still without any date mentioned for the changeover; but in May Webb became ever more fey and had to go about a week before the end of the month just about the time of his 67th birthday. Whale first attended a Locomotive Committee meeting the day after the board sanctioning his new appointment, and Webb was with him. Webb's last attendance at a Committee was on 8 May 1903, and again Whale was present.

Webb's last public acts seem to have been the opening of a new physics laboratory at the Crewe Mechanics Institute in April, and attendance at the annual dinner in London of the Past and Present Crewe Men on 5 May. On 30 May the *Crewe Chronicle* recorded that a few days before he had been taken seriously ill and that he was at Colwyn Bay. He improved almost at once, but had a relapse and was taken to Coton Hill mental hospital in Staffordshire. After a few weeks he recovered sufficiently to buy a house at Bournemouth, to which he was taken by Dr Atkinson, where he remained under care until his death on 6 June 1906. Neither Stalbridge nor Whale was at the funeral, and Crewe was represented by A. R. Trevithick.

For many years there has been a story that in his last few months Webb became so unbearable that Whale and Bowen Cooke went to Euston and insisted to the directors that Webb would have to go. This is not really credible; Cooke was by no means in disfavour with Webb, and the opposition of Harrison and Turnbull did not need any risky supporting action by two officials responsible to Webb, however much the two parties were in agreement.

A likelier version of the last sad days at Crewe is that of one who was a 'Crewe Premium' at the time. According to this, Webb had been one day away on business at Manchester, and on his return to his office in the late afternoon W. Horabin, then assistant chief clerk, brought in some letters for signature. He thought Webb's usually abrupt manner had become rather peculiar, a feeling that changed to astonishment when Webb asked him if he would like his overcoat. Horabin managed to stammer out "Well, sir, it would be a bit big for me", for Webb was not too far off 6ft and portly, whereas Horabin was short. On getting outside Horabin reported to George Ellis, the chief clerk, and they sent a messenger to Webb's brother Canon A. H. Webb, at St Paul's vicarage. The canon came over and persuaded Webb to go home with him, and the works did not see him again.

After Webb's retirement his compounds made him notorious, but the deprecatory writings would not have appeared and continued without inside passive support. His principal work was almost deliberately forgotten. Enthusiasts tend to regard locomotive design as the acme of a chief mechanical engineer's work; actually that forms but a small part of the whole. In his day Webb was famous for, and got his high salary because of, his handling of the main activity—the vast extension of the whole LNWR locomotive department including Crewe Works and the running division, the organisation and daily administration. At the next shareholders meeting after his retirement (August 1903) Stalbridge said: "His name will always be joined to that of Crewe, as he has, almost from its very beginning, been the mainspring of the greatest of our manufacturing departments."

After Webb's death several malignant obituaries appeared in the technical and transport press, none of which would have seen the light of day if offence at Euston or Crewe had been expected. Unfortunately the not ungenerous obituary in *The Engineer* was followed by vitriolic correspondence against the dead man and his compounds. None suggested, and no biographical notice then or since has hinted, at the tragedy of a man of very great capabilities and deep sensitivity who never found the understanding environment that could have unfolded his full potentialities as a human being, and softened or eliminated the final breakdown.

Webb had a most human side that came out from time to time in the works and at public gatherings. His reaction to the Shrewsbury porter's tip, and his tolerant view of the night-shift barber's shop in the millwrights are well known. Ten weeks before he left he spoke feelingly at the Mechanics Institute prize-giving of the hope "That we may all meet together here again next year." In his Crewe mayoral address in November 1886 he said of his apprenticeship days: "I lodged first with a barber, Richard Shermen, at the corner of Mill Street . . . Those were happy days . . . The roller now in the possession of the Crewe cricket club is one I moulded with my own hands, and it was not a 'foreign' order, either." Even at the height of the town's political trouble it was recognised that "If Mr. Webb was left alone he was a gentleman, but he was susceptible to influences brought to bear on him," a contemporary view quite different from that put forward by several 20th century writers who were not born when Webb retired.

Webb's will was dated 22 May 1903 and must have been drawn up some time previously, for it contained numerous bequests well thought out; it was signed just at the time of the breakdown, and almost concurrently Webb had given £5,000 to the Crewe Cottage Hospital, knowing that organisation needed the money at once. The will was proved at £211,542, the purchasing equivalent of a couple of million today, and not subject to savage death duties or capital transfer tax. Webb left £10,000 to found a nursing institution to give free attendance to the poorer people of Crewe, and gave £9,000 to various church purposes in the town. He endowed a bed at University College hospital preferably for the use of LNWR employees; left £1,000 each to the men's convalescent home at Rhyl and the Railway Servants Orphanage at Derby; £2,000 each to University College, Liverpool, and Owens College, Manchester, to found scholarships for LNWR employees and their sons; £1,000 to the Institution of Civil Engineers for Webb prizes for railway engineering papers; £30,000 each to his brothers Canon A. H. and Colonel W. G. Webb; £5,000 to his nephew W. W. G. Webb (who was an assistant at Crewe); £5,000 each to his friends Dr. J. Atkinson of Crewe and G. R. Jebb of Birmingham; £3,000 to his Crewe friend and solicitor A. G. Hill (son of the man who presented the steel works ground); £5,000 to his godson Henry Robertson (grandson of one of the first partners in Beyer Peacock); £300 to George Ellis and £200 to W. Horabin. The residue, in the end amounting to about £70,000, went to found the Webb Orphanage at Crewe for the children of deceased LNWR employees. This institution was opened at the end of 1911. Webb asked that the orphanage board should consist of his executors, and the chairman, vice-chairman and locomotive superintendent for the time being of the LNWR; Beames and others continued to act as the last-named representative long after the LNWR ceased to exist.

As befitted his position, Webb took much part in Crewe civic affairs. He did not become the first mayor of the borough in 1877, that office falling to the company's doctor James Atkinson, but he was mayor for two years November 1886–88, following Whale, who was chief magistrate in 1885–86. This was at the time when the local political war (see Chapter 6) was rising to its climax; when that came to a head Webb stepped down from civic work, but he continued as a county magistrate and an alderman of the Cheshire County Council. He was given the freedom of Crewe in 1900 at the time the 4,000th Crewe engine was completed. Gardening was another of his interests, kept up not only at Chester Place but also at his country home, Stanway, near Church Stretton, where he went many week-ends, the legal possession of which he retained until his death; in general from 1871 to 1903 he lived very simply at Chester Place with only two domestics.

Thomas William Worsdell (1838–1916)
Was the eldest son of Nathaniel Worsdell, coaching superintendent of the GJR and the Northern Division of the LNWR from 1838 to 1860, and thereafter for 20 years general storekeeper at Crewe. After a few months at Crewe as a boy, T.W. served an apprenticeship at Brimingham with an uncle who made small engines and machine tools, then he returned to Crewe and was put in the drawing office by Ramsbottom. He left again in 1860 and was for some years with a small engineering firm in Birmingham. In 1865 he went to the USA and within a year or two had become one of the Pennsylvania Railroad's master mechanics at Altoona. After Webb was nominated to succeed Ramsbottom, Worsdell applied in June 1871 for the works manager's job at Crewe, but was told by Moon that no appointment would be made until Webb's return. Webb actually saw Worsdell in America, but not until 10 November 1871 did the Committee confirm the latter as works manager at £600 a year. However, Worsdell had arrived back in England during August, and with the consent of Ramsbottom had been much about the works in September, making notes and generally weighing-up the position. He was manager at Crewe during a period of great expansion at the Steelworks end, and as with preceding and succeeding managers his initial salary was gradually increased, to £800 by the end of 1876. Due possibly to restless character, or simply to the realisation that there was no rising future for him on the LNWR under a man only two years his senior, he applied for the locomotive superintendency of the LYR in October 1875 and got on the short list. He gave three months' notice in November 1881 to become locomotive chief of the Great Eastern Railway in February 1882, where he made his first applications of 2-cylinder compound locomotives and took out his first patent, No 999 of January 1885, for such power. He did not stay long at Stratford, for in May 1885 he moved to the corresponding position on the North Eastern Railway. His experience at Crewe enabled him to bring the Gateshead shops to a high level, and it was through him that the first definite classes and the excellent construction of later NER locomotives were due; probably his Altoona days led to the NER double-window cab. Possibly his asthmatic condition, intensified by the climate of the north-east, led him to resign due to ill-health in September 1890, but he was retained by the NER as consulting mechanical engineer for the years 1891–92 at £1000 a year. He retired to Arnside on Morecambe Bay, and died there on 28 June 1916.

Charles Dick (1838–88)
Born at Broughty Ferry, he served an apprenticeship from 1854 to James
How at Monifieth Foundry. After short times as a workman in the marine-
engine shops of J. & G. Thomson on the Clyde and of James Jack & Co at
Liverpool, he was taken-on in the Crewe erecting shops in August 1860 after
walking to that place from Liverpool in search of work. In 1862, while a
chargehand erector, he attracted the attention of young Webb at the evening
classes of the Mechanics Institute where he won a prize. Webb brought him
into the office as a temporary tracer and draughtsman, and in 1863 he became
an established member of the drawing office staff at 8s 4d [42p] a day. He
succeeded Kampf as chief draughtsman on 15 December 1871 at a salary of
£160 a year raised in steps to £225 at the end of 1874 and, as he himself wrote,
with heavy work and long hours. Under his charge were developed the
designs of the Webb Precursors, Precedents and coal engines. In February
1877 he was appointed manager of the signal department at Crewe; he had
manufacture, installation and maintenance in his care, with much outdoor
work along the line in all weathers. G. P. Neele, the LNWR traffic
superintendent, paid him compliments for his signal work in *Railway
Reminiscences* (1902).

In February 1882 he succeeded Worsdell as works manager, though the
appointment was still styled indoor assistant. He died on 2 June 1888 of chest
and kidney complaints at the age of 50, but in essence he was worn out by the
work and its responsibilities following his hard and often penurious youth. In
reporting his death to the Locomotive Committee Webb said "he was a very
able and faithful servant of the Company." A grant of six months' salary, less
amount paid on sick leave, was given to his four children aged 23 to 14, for he
was a widower. Dick came to take much part in Crewe local affairs. He was
deputy mayor to Webb in the Jubilee year of 1887, and presided at the public
dinner to celebrate the Queen's Jubilee and Crewe's railway jubilee, for Webb
as mayor of the borough was away at the national thanksgiving service in
Westminster Abbey. He was treasurer of the Mechanics Institute 1875–81.
After Dick's death a shelter was erected in the then new Queen's Park in
memory of him; he himself had supervised the layout of the park. Webb and
Dick always got on well together and were much of an age. One of Dick's
letters preserved long after his death shows him to have been human and
unaffected, and gives a good first-hand account of Crewe in the mid-1880s.[15]

Walter Norman
Succeeded Dick as chief draughtsman. He had joined the LNWR locomotive
department in June 1864. During his time as chief he had design oversight of
the Cauliflower 0-6-0s, Experiment and Dreadnought compounds, and the
office work involved in the conversion of DX engines into Special DX. He
resigned to join the West Australian Land Company and left at the end of
May 1888. Had he withheld his notice another month he might have been on
the cards for promotion after Charlie Dick's death.

Bartholomew Kean (1818–87)
Kean was locomotive storekeeper for many years until his death in the Crewe
jubilee year. He took much part in Crewe civic affairs and was one of the
town's independent aldermen. He joined the GJR service in April 1846 and

was one of the few men who entered the service before the formation of the LNWR who found much favour with Moon. He was one of the few Catholics who attained responsible positions in the works.

William Adamson

Began at Wolverton in 1854 and by the 1862 consolidation was a foreman. He was transferred in that capacity to Crewe in 1864, and later became foreman millwright and later outdoor superintendent responsible to Webb, a position he held until his retirement. His successors in the last-named job were A. H. Hignett who retired at the end of the century, and then E. C. Bickersteth, son of an LNWR director, who lasted until after World War I.

Henry Douglas Earl

Appointed works manager on the demise of Dick, he had begun as a premium apprentice under Ramsbottom in March 1869 and in June 1874 went into the drawing office. In June 1875 he was made an assistant manager at the Steelworks end, and later also came to have charge of the construction of new shops at the west end. He continued as works manager from 1888 until the Webb-Whale changeover in 1903, when he was made wagon superintendent with headquarters at Earlestown in the circumstances related in Chapter 7. From 1 May 1910 he became carriage superintendent at Wolverton and retired in May 1916. During his period as Crewe Works manager were planned and built No 9 erecting shop and adjacent machine shop, the rail mill was remodelled, the Brett drop-stampers were introduced, and Webb's great expansion in the use of electricity throughout the works was carried out under his supervision. Contrasted with Worsdell and Charlie Dick, Earl did not let the exigencies of the works manager's job get him down, nor apparently did he allow Webb's increasing autocracy to disturb him unduly. At one time he was a town councillor, but after losing his seat at the height of the political war in 1889 he took a quieter part in town affairs. One of his sons, F.D., became assistant works manager and, in LMSR days, outdoor superintendent.

Kenneth Macrae

Succeeded Wadsworth as locomotive accountant in 1885 and retired in 1909. He was a town councillor and alderman, and in those capacities was always a strong 'company' man in civic affairs.

Dr James Atkinson

Was the first mayor of Crewe on its incorporation as a borough in 1877. He was the railway surgeon from 1866, succeeding Edwards the first 'company' doctor in Crewe. Atkinson was a personal friend of Webb, and by many was believed to be the latter's *bête noir* in regard to town matters, and he always put the railway's importance very strongly in the council. He and Webb were largely responsible for setting up the railway hospital in Mill Street. His daughter married the Reverend Walter Bidlake, for some years vicar of Christ Church. Atkinson retired in 1909, being followed as company doctor by Dr J. Lawrence, the last LNWR doctor, who retired at the end of 1922.

John Nicholson Jackson

Was appointed chief draughtsman on trial in June 1888 after Norman's departure, and was confirmed in that position in December at £225 a year. He was born at Lancaster in 1852. After being in general and marine engineering at that place and Birkenhead he entered Crewe shops in February 1875 and was taken into the drawing office in 1876. At the 'general post' in 1903 he retained his position and his salary was increased from £350 to £450, he remaining as chief draughtsman under Whale and Cooke until he retired at the end of 1919. In his time as office chief were designed all the Webb compounds from the Teutonic class onwards, all the Whale types and all Cooke's engines.

Thomas Edward Sackfield

Jackson's locomotive assistant from 1893, he supervised locomotive design from then until his retirement in 1924. He won a Whitworth Scholarship in 1879 at the end of his Crewe premium days. This gave him three years at Owens College, after which he returned to Crewe drawing office, where he eventually became a well-known personality among Crewe premiums and pupils who spent a period in the drawing office; they were much helped by the small but large-moustached Tommy. One of his especial cares was the model room and the laying-out of valve motions, and he was prominent on important dynamometer car trials. He was a successful teacher of evening classes at the Mechanics Institute from 1882 to 1917. A year after his retirement he was elected to the town council and took a good part in civic affairs.

George Whale (1842–1910)

Whale became chief mechanical engineer in succession to Webb, officially as from 1 July 1903 but actually from some five weeks earlier. The first known drawings signed by him were locomotive weight and wheelbase sheets dated 25 May 1903. He was born at Bocking in Essex, and educated at Lewisham grammar school. In November 1858 he entered Wolverton as a premium under McConnell, and was transferred to Crewe as a locomotive draughtsman in 1865 at 9s 0d [45p] a day. He was made an assistant to John Rigg in 1867, and when Rigg retired ten years later Whale was appointed Northern Division running superintendent. He held that position for 22 years until on the retirement in 1899 of A. L. Mumford, his Southern Division *confrère*, he was made running superintendent of the whole LNWR, though still responsible to Webb.

Friction between the two men tended to increase from that time, partly because Whale was now accountable for *all* locomotive failures and troubles instead of half of them, and partly because Webb's new engines did not measure up to the constant increase in performance required by the forward policy of the Harrison management. Whale had good relations with the traffic people, who gave him encouragement in the awkward situation. Harrison was never known to visit Crewe in Webb's day, but two or three months after Whale took over Harrison spent a full day at the works and office. The trouble with Webb bit into Whale deeply despite his easy temperament. After his accession he would allow no good word to be written of Webb or his products, nor would he name a locomotive after him as Webb had done for Ramsbottom.

For many years Whale had a fine dark beard, but he removed this about the turn of the century, and during his time as chief mechanical engineer he was clean-shaven. He was a comfortable good-tempered man who did not tick-off his subordinates with others present; by the same token he did not stick up unduly for his own drivers and fitters in inter-departmental matters. One result was that he was well liked by the traffic officers. He retained all his characteristics until the winter of 1907–08 when an internal complaint led to a first operation; this made him more easily ruffled, an irritation that increased when his doctor took him off cigars and other items of good living to which he was partial. His ill-health increased, and in January 1909 he told the board he would have to go at the end of June, but because of his absences his successor was more-or-less in charge for the last few weeks. He had a second operation a month or so after he retired, and never fully recovered from this. He died at Hove on 7 March 1910, leaving a widow and two sons, one of whom was in the LNWR civil engineering department. As chief mechanical engineer Whale's salary was £3,000 a year plus half the fees of pupils not exceeding six at a time at £150 a year each. He took-over Webb's four remaining pupils who still had some time to go, but his total remuneration was little more than half of Webb's final figure. He was the first of the 'poor' chief mechanical engineers, his estate totalling £15,600 at his death. During 1907 he was one of a party of LNWR officers who visited the USA to study railway practice, but no innovations came to the locomotive department from this trip. Something of Whale as a chief mechanical engineer has been told in Chapter 7.

Arthur Reginald Trevithick (1858–1939)

Became works manager at Crewe on the accession of Whale at a salary of £800. He was one of the several sons of Francis Trevithick, and was born at Crewe, though after his father had left LNWR employ. He was educated at Cheltenham and then went to Crewe as a premium a few months before his father died. On completion of his time he went over to the running side, and in the late 1880s was foreman at Preston. On the retirement of Kampf in 1889 he was made locomotive foreman at Carlisle with an increase in salary from £170 to £250. Carlisle was always considered a special case; the foreman had more authority than elsewhere, having Whitehaven and Tebay under him as sub-sheds. In essence he was district locomotive superintendent, with a repair section under him that gave intermediates and a few general repairs to small engines. Carlisle (Upperby) erecting and repair shop was 450ft by 50ft; there was also a small tender shop, a fitting shop, smithy, and a weighing machine to check axle load and weight distribution on repaired engines. All these were in direct descent from the old Lancaster & Carlisle shops. For this section the chief at Carlisle was responsible to the Crewe works manager, for maintenance and running to the Northern Division running superintendent.

Trevithick was of strong build; unlike his gentle father, he was of firm and decided character, and was a boxer of local repute. He was known to bundle out of his Carlisle office and kick downstairs three recalcitrant Springs Branch drivers who were prevaricating about return times of working during the upset in operation caused by the 1893 coal strike.

At the end of 1899 he was brought back to Crewe as assistant locomotive works manager under Earl at a salary of £500. He was one of a party of LNWR officials that made a tour of the USA early in 1903, and shortly after his return he succeeded Earl. He was then given as locomotive works assistant J. Homfray who had succeeded him at Carlisle. Thus the Pen-y-darren Trevithick-Homfray locomotive collaboration of 1803 was followed exactly one hundred years later by a similar association at Crewe, but whether J. Homfray was a direct descendant of Samuel is not clear. Though he was not inclined to stand much nonsense, Trevithick was a fair and just manager, and little in the way of labour troubles occurred in his time at Crewe, though trade union friction throughout the country was then rising.

On Whale's retirement Trevithick was expected to succeed, but the board preferred Cooke, as related in Chapter 7, and Trevithick was much upset, as Earl had been before him. In 1910 Trevithick was appointed wagon superintendent at Earlestown, and in 1916 he went to Wolverton to succeed Earl as the last carriage superintendent of the LNWR. He remained there as divisional mechanical engineer under the LNWR/LYR merger of 1922, and his continuance under the LMSR was announced, but as he was approaching 65 years he retired as from formation of the Group, and died at St Ives just at the outbreak of World War II.

Charles John Bowen Cooke (1859–1920)
Chief mechanical engineer from 1909 to 1920, he was like Webb a son of the church, his father being rector of Orton Longueville, Hunts. His two brothers were in holy orders. Cooke became a premium apprentice at Crewe in 1875, and in 1878 was accepted as a pupil by Webb. At the conclusion of the two-year pupilage in 1880 he became a junior assistant to Mumford, the Southern Division running superintendent, and remained an assistant of rising grade until in 1899 he succeeded Mumford. In 1903 his position was confirmed, and in a sense enhanced in that he now reported direct to the chief mechanical engineer without the intervention of an all-line running superintendent. In February 1909 he was selected to succeed Whale as chief mechanical engineer as from 1 July, but actually handled many matters before that date, a situation helped by the fact that from 1903 he had his office at Crewe; previously he had been located for many years at Rugby.

Cooke, usually known as Bowen Cooke as if that were a hyphenated name, was a tall well set-up man who was generally liked on and off the railway, and was normally open and generous in his nature, with courtesy and good manners. However, he often showed an initial reserve to outsiders, and he had also a 'strong' streak in him that was felt by one or two running assistants who, on contretemps occurring, came under his permanent displeasure when they felt they ought to have had support. One result of his long period of responsibility in the SD running department was that he could depute authority, and in personality he turned out to be a good chief mechanical engineer in troublous times. He grew in professional stature during his last appointment, but the organisation and equipment at Crewe did not really progress during his tenure. His principal work for the LNWR was the introduction of superheating and its application to mainline passenger and freight engines, but for four long years his main occupation was to try and meet wartime demands. Despite his physique, the difficult years of World War I told upon him, though perhaps no more than the troublesome 18 months after the armistice, when a year (1918–19) as mayor of Crewe added to his duties. After some months of off-and-on ill health he died at the home of his daughter and son-in-law at Falmouth on 18 October 1920, and was buried at St Just-in-Roseland.

Before he entered Crewe as an apprentice Cooke had a year's education at Neuwied, on the Rhine. Memories of this time were with him always and were reflected in his close interest in German engineering; on at least one occasion he referred to his admiration for the Bavarian Maffei four-cylinder 4-6-0s and how they influenced his thoughts on the Claughton design. Not unnaturally, as years went by, he tended to be annoyed at continued remarks that the Claughtons were based on the GWR Stars, particularly as the exchange had been initiated by the GWR; he was wont to say one might as well describe the Claughtons as enlarged Alfreds with the compounding eliminated and an extra coupled axle added. Of the locomotive exchanges that were a feature of Cooke's first 15 months as chief mechanical engineer, those involving *Polar Star* and the NBR Atlantic were initiated by the other companies. The Caledonian *Cardean* brief trials were a West Coast joint venture, and those with the GNR Atlantic and the LBSCR 4-4-2T seem to have been initiated by Cooke. Cooke was a great locomotive enthusiast, and his book *British Locomotives* was a standard from 1893 until World War I.

Walter Wyndham Hayden Warneford.
Works manager at Crewe from 1910 to 1916, he was yet another son of the church, and a 'moonraker' to boot, having been born in Wiltshire in 1866. His father was a canon of Salisbury cathedral. He began as an apprentice at Miles Platting works of the LYR in 1882, but in 1883 transferred to Crewe as a premium, and then as a pupil of Webb. In March 1889 he became an assistant at the steel plant, then assistant manager having charge of 'the melts' and the iron and steel foundries. This appointment he held until his promotion to works manager. A dapper little man, he looked diminutive alongside Cooke's 6ft. They worked together without any obvious friction, but were never wholly *en rapport*. In April 1916 Warneford was made wagon superintendent at Earlestown and retired soon after the formation of the LMSR. His only son lost his life in the 1914–19 war, and he was a relation of the VC, Lieutenant Warneford, who brought down a Zeppelin in France in 1915.

George Ellis
Was chief clerk to Webb through the last half of the latter's time. He continued as chief clerk to Whale but died in 1904, being succeeded by William Horabin, hitherto his deputy. Both men were beneficiaries under Webb's will, but Ellis did not live to get his portion. Horabin lived on until 1940.

J. Reddrop
Was appointed chemist as a young man barely 20 years old by Ramsbottom in 1866 as related in Chapter 5, and held that position until about the time Webb retired. He was succeeded by F. G. Tipler who died in 1920 after 42 years of service with the company.

T. Ormand
Succeeded Macrae as locomotive accountant in 1909 and retired in 1921. He entered LNWR service as a boy of 14. He was succeeded by J. A. Platt, the last locomotive accountant of the LNWR.

Thomas Edward Goodeve

He followed Warneford as steel plant manager in 1910 and became assistant locomotive works manager in October 1911, remaining in that position until LMSR days. He entered LNWR service in 1896 at the age of 20, and by the time Webb retired he had charge of the testing shop and experimental section. On Whale's accession he became an assistant to the works manager.

Hewitt Pearson Montague Beames (1875–1948)

Beames, who followed Cooke as chief mechanical engineer, had a strange and frustrating last quarter to his career. An Irishman by birth, he became a Crewe premium in 1895 after a period at Crawley's, the military crammer. He was taken as a pupil by Webb in 1898, but just after being made a junior assistant to the Crewe Works manager he obtained leave in January 1900 to go off to the Boer War in Paget's Horse. After 18 months in South Africa he returned to Crewe in his old position, and from 1902 to 1909 he was an assistant to the outdoor superintendent. He became personal assistant to Cooke in January 1910, and this lasted until October 1914 when he joined the Royal Engineers and later went to France. He was recalled to Crewe in April 1916 and made works manager and chief assistant to Cooke, an unusual appointment, for at that time he had no previous managerial experience at all nor the control of any large number of men. In June 1919, whilst retaining the works managership, he was appointed deputy chief mechanical engineer, a formal position unique in LNWR history.

In November 1920 he was appointed chief mechanical engineer, but this position he held for little more than a year, because from 1 January 1922 the LNWR and LYR were merged, though retaining the title of the LNWR. George Hughes, chief mechanical engineer of the LYR from 1904, was made chief mechanical and electrical engineer of the enlarged system; running was taken away from the chief mechanical engineer and given to new superintendents of motive power, but the carriage and wagon departments came under the cme. Beames then simply became divisional mechanical engineer, Crewe, though his salary was not reduced. Through 1922 he had as colleagues, equal in status but not in remuneration, the divisional mechanical engineers at Wolverton (Trevithick), Earlestown (Warneford), Horwich (Shawcross) and Newton Heath (Gobey). On the formation of the LMSR on 1 January 1923 Beames continued as mechanical engineer, Crewe, and it was in that capacity he had the responsibility of the big works reorganisation, he himself being responsible for the idea of 'the belt', following a visit to the USA.

With a revision in LMSR organisation he was appointed in December 1930 to Derby as deputy chief mechanical engineer to E. J. H. Lemon, the chief, though he continued to reside at Chester Place, Crewe, the official residence of the LNWR chief mechanical engineer. When Lemon was promoted to vice-president as from 1 January 1932 he was succeeded not by Beames but by W. A. Stanier from Swindon. Beames continued to act as deputy chief mechanical engineer to Stanier until his retirement at the end of September 1934 at the age of 59. The larger side of his nature was shown by his letter to Stanier in 1931: "I am very disappointed, but there is no one I would rather serve under than you." Also he wrote warmly to Riddles in 1946 congratulating him on becoming an LMSR vice-president, and again later when Riddles became a member of the Railway Executive. After his accession to high place during World War I Beames took more interest in civic affairs, and he was also president for years of the Webb Orphanage and of the Crewe Mechanics Institute.

W. Savage

Son of a Wolverton man, he was a well-known Crewe figure for years. He came to Crewe when the family was transferred there in 1868 when he was ten years old. He began as a Crewe apprentice in 1872 and afterwards was in the drawing office for some years. He won a Whitworth Scholarship in 1881 and then went into teaching until 1892, when he returned to Crewe as foreman of the brass foundry and testing department. He became foreman of the steel foundry and of 'the melts' in 1896, and in 1916 was made assistant manager at the Steelworks end. He retired in 1921. From his return to Crewe until his retirement he was an effective teacher at the Mechanics Institute.

J. Ryder

Became assistant manager for the steel department in 1921 and remained there until he retired in January 1932, though from May 1931 he was graded as steel plant manager. He began at Crewe in 1886 and was in the laboratory and test room until sent for special work to the steel plant in 1916.

F. Arnold Lemon

Succeeded to the works management in December 1920, and had the longest spell of any man in that position. When Beames went to Derby early in 1931 Lemon became known as the Crewe works superintendent, a title that lasted through to the days of BR. Lemon was born at Castle Cary, Somerset, and began as a Crewe premium in the mid-1890s. Afterwards he was for some years in the running side, including a period as foreman at Birkenhead, and 2½ years in charge of the Dundalk, Newry & Greenore Railway. He became assistant works manager at Crewe in 1916, and in that position was much occupied with the changes brought in 1919 with the 47-hour week. As works manager he had to take a leading part in the re-organisation of 1925–27 and handle the disruption brought by the general strike in 1926. For many years he was an effective chief, but through the 1930s increasing deafness became a handicap, and with the more onerous duties arising out of World War II, coupled with an unsuitable assistant works manager, he resigned at Stanier's suggestion in 1941. He died at his birthplace in the late 1950s.

Robert A. Riddles

Riddles can be accounted one of the greatest Crewe-trained men. Though he never held the highest executive position at Crewe, he went on to become a vice-president of the LMSR and was the first and only Member for Mechanical & Electrical Engineering of the original British Railways Executive.

He was a premium apprentice at Crewe works from 1909 to 1913, and while attending the Mechanics Institute classes he took a course in electrical engineering, feeling there would be a future for electric traction. After service in the Royal Engineers through the 1914–19 war, in the course of which he was severely wounded, he returned to Crewe and was put in charge of the

Park Place 'city' (see Chapter 8). In 1920 he became 'bricks and mortar assistant' at Crewe with special charge of the new large erecting shop then under way, but also with oversight of engine shed and other locomotive department structures. When work on the erecting shop was stopped, Riddles was put in charge of the small progress department, and was sent to Horwich for a month to study LYR methods of engine shopping. The progress (really production) department then began to develop, particularly when the support of Beames was gained after Riddles had proved a case for economy, more authority being granted to Riddles to plan work through the shops and see that it was done. Along these lines he came to have much say in the details of the big Crewe re-organisation of 1925–27 which, through his ideas supplementing Beames's introduction of 'the belt', was taken much further than the proposals for which Hughes had got board sanction in 1924.

On the completion of this scheme Riddles was sent to Derby to initiate a similar system, in this case with the advantage that he could begin on the base of the Midland's good methods of engine shopping and the active support of the then Derby works manager, H. G. Ivatt. When this work was done he returned to Crewe as principal assistant to Arnold Lemon when J. V. Denning was sent off to Bow works. In 1933 Riddles was transferred to Euston as locomotive assistant to Stanier, and in 1935 was promoted to principal assistant to the chief mechanical engineer.

After a period from 1937 in Glasgow as Mechanical & Electrical Engineer (Scotland) of the LMSR – he was the first to have the double title – during which he was seconded to take the Royal Scot train and streamlined locomotive to the USA on exhibition, Riddles was in September 1939 brought into government service in charge of the production of transport equipment in the Ministry of Supply, but after Dunkirk he was appointed Deputy Director-General of all Royal Engineer equipment, which then included locomotives as well as an enormous range of products from jerry cans and Bailey bridges to the initial work on the Mulberry harbours. In this capacity Riddles specified and saw through the Austerity 2-10-0 and 2-8-0 types, and the Ministry orders for wartime Stanier 2-8-0s.

In 1943 he was recalled to the LMSR as stores superintendent, a move designed to give him chief officer status from which he could be promoted further. Possibly the higher direction of the LMSR at that time realised what was more widely appreciated only later: that by the time he left the Ministry there was no railway job Riddles could not hold down with competence, drive and imagination. In the event he was promoted to vice-president in 1946, and in September 1947 was nominated to the nationalised Railway Executive preparatory to the working initiation of British Railways on 1 January 1948. He retired in the autumn of 1952, not wishing at over 60 years to have yet another re-organisation pushed on him with the direct takeover of the railways by the British Transport Commission.

On BR Riddles was responsible for the initiation of the well-known 'interchange trials' of 1948, and for all the BR standard steam locomotives, when he laid down the lines to be followed in the design and construction of each class. He also ensured efforts to standardise workshop procedure and administration, and in this he accepted Crewe practices as the model. He also had full charge of electric traction, with an electrical engineer (first Cock and then Warder) under him. At the end of his railway career his was the suggestion that initiated the trials of 50-cycle traction on the Heysham–Morecambe line, a suggestion prompted by the feeling that *this* was the real means for the future rather than further efforts on existing dc systems and diesel traction, and this was a fitting *finale* to his early studies at Crewe. After a few years in retirement he became chairman of Stothert & Pitt, of Bath, and held that position for eight years. In 1981, as with his great predecessors Ramsbottom, Webb, Whale, Cooke and Stanier, a locomotive was named *Robert A. Riddles* after him, but in accordance with the time and with the thread running through his career, this was a straight electric.

Roland C. Bond (1902–80)

Became works superintendent at Crewe in 1941 in succession to F. A. Lemon, and was the first 'manager' since Charlie Dick who was not a Crewe-trained man, but unlike Dick he was railway-trained, having begun at Derby as an engineering apprentice in 1920.

After two years in India for Vulcan Foundry on the GIPR electric locomotives he returned to the LMSR and was made assistant works manager at Horwich in 1931; he was transferred to the corresponding position at Crewe in 1933 when Riddles went to Euston. In 1937 he was given charge of the design and erection of the joint LMSR/LNER testing station at Rugby. With the coming of the war this work was stopped at once, and Bond was sent to Glasgow to replace Riddles as Mechanical & Electrical Engineer (Scotland), but in March 1941 Stanier sent him to Crewe as works superintendent, where he handled the difficult wartime period with a competence that gained him a reputation as a works man that has not yet died out. He maintained the old tradition of being chairman of the Mechanics Institute and of the Webb Orphanage. On the death of Fairburn (who had succeeded Stanier as LMSR chief mechanical engineer) in 1945 Bond was sent to Derby as Mechanical Engineer (Locomotive Works) to the new chief mechanical engineer, H. G. Ivatt, and was soon appointed also as deputy chief mechanical engineer. In this capacity he brought to conclusion the LMSR limits-and-fits standards initiated while he was at Crewe.

With the formation of British Railways Bond was appointed Chief Officer (Locomotive Construction & Maintenance), reporting direct to Riddles. On the further reorganisation he became the chief mechanical engineer of British Railways in 1954, and in 1958 succeeded John Ratter as technical adviser to the 'general staff' of the BTC. In 1962, after the Beeching reorganisation, he retained that position to the new board until in 1965 he was appointed general manager of the new BR Workshops Division, a fitting end to the professional career of the leading British locomotive works man. He retired in 1968.

James Rankin (1895–1947)

Rankin became the Crewe works superintendent in February 1946, and revived the Charlie Dick tradition in being an 'outsider', for he was born at Kilmarnock and trained there at the Andrew Barclay locomotive works. After service in World War I he was taken-on in 1920 as a locomotive draughtsman by the Midland at Derby and was later a works inspector there. In 1928 he became a junior assistant to F. A. Lemon at Crewe, and after periods at Horwich and Derby became works superintendent at the latter place in May 1941 after a time in acting rank. Unfortunately he died on 24 December 1947 after less than two years as works chief at Crewe.

Tom F. Coleman

Became chief draughtsman at Crewe in 1933 after a long period on the North Staffordshire Railway and seven years as chief draughtsman at Horwich. At Crewe he succeeded F. M. Grover, who had followed the celebrated J. N. Jackson. Coleman moved on to Derby in 1935 as chief draughtsman at LMSR locomotive headquarters, from which position he retired in 1949. Both at Crewe and Derby he was closely connected with the design of Stanier locomotives of all types, particularly the streamline Pacifics, and for 15 years he was a well-known personality in the British locomotive world.

Dr Harold Moore

Dr Moore the first and only LMSR 'company doctor' at Crewe, being appointed on the formation of that company and retiring only when the company came to an end. He died in 1954. He was a man of fine but unassuming character, with a reputation for never being taken-in by feigned illness or injury. Early in his tenure he got what was for the time up-to-date radiographic equipment for the railway-owned hospital. There are still men at Crewe works today who claim happily that they were treated by Dr Moore.

Irvine C. Forsyth

Rankin was succeeded by Forsyth as works superintendent in 1948. Forsyth was a delightful Derby-trained man who had been in the running department from 1925 to 1946, when he was transferred to Crewe as assistant superintendent. He was in charge when the first changeover to diesel construction and repair was made; soon after the last steam locomotive was built he was transferred to headquarters, and finished-up as chief production manager of the Workshops Division. He died at Crewe in 1979.

Ellis R. Brown (1905–77)

Before nationalisation he was an LMSR man; he was assistant to Forsyth and succeeded him as works superintendent, but he was translated to Derby headquarters at the end of 1962 as production manager (locomotives) of the Workshops Division. He was followed by J. C. Spark, hitherto an LNER and ER man.

J. J. C. Barker-Wyatt

Appointed works manager on 1 November 1964, he succeeded Spark, after experience on several Regions of BR. He had charge of the final concentration, when the Old and Deviation Works were closed and vacated, and the iron foundry cleared and altered to suit other purposes; he also had to cope with the appalling influx of 'unclassified' diesel work that plagued Crewe (and other BR works) for several years. In his turn he, too, was transferred to Workshops Division headquarters in September 1967, and was succeeded by George Oldham, a Crewe-trained man who had had a period at Doncaster. On his retirement in 1974 he was followed by C. H. Garratt, who was moved on in 1977 and made way for the present works manager, F. O. de Nobriga.

Two men, neither of whom was ever 'at Crewe' in the accepted sense, must be mentioned here.

Sir William A. Stanier (1876–1965)
Sir William had a pronounced influence on Crewe over the 12 years (1932–44) he was chief mechanical engineer of the LMSR, largely because of his intense personal interest in workshop equipment and practice and in engineering production, as touched on in Chapter 9.

Sir Richard Moon (1814–1899)
Though not an engineer, Moon had a great and long-term influence on the town and works. In early life he wished to go into the church, but his father would have none of it, and he entered the family commercial business in Liverpool. He was elected to the LNWR board in 1851 and within a year he had become most active in the company's affairs. According to one who worked with him for years "he looked at the whole business as an industrious and vigilant merchant caring for his own property". Through his efforts gradually the board acquired more control over the various departments and brought them into proper relation by regular supervision through active committees, though only after Moon became chairman in 1861 could full effect be given to his principles, for he had opposition from both directors and officials. For the 30 years from 1861 all his activities were directed to the LNWR.

As related in Chapter 4, he was the man who backed Ramsbottom, pushed him, and was perhaps partly responsible for his breakdown in 1870–71. In his prime through the 1850s and 1860s Moon had little use for the veterans who entered railway service in the 1830s; Norris and Bell as well as Trevithick incurred his displeasure. He pushed and supported Webb, but Webb did not break down until long after Moon's day. The two men shared a common zeal for ordered management and economy, also an austerely religious outlook coloured by their love of organisation. Moon sponsored Ramsbottom's and Webb's big increases in salary for, uncommon among railway directors of his day, he was always willing to pay big money to get men of real ability. Moreover, he sanctioned regular increases for lesser fry if their chiefs put up proposals. He always ensured that adequate and timely finance was available for the big expansions at the Steelworks, and he was always willing to consider the manufacture of extraneous articles.

All his photographs show a grave and unemotional man, but he had a happy family life. David Stevenson recording[16] that he was "a man of grave aspect with a pleasant smile, enhanced by its rarity; always approachable by those of his officers in whom he believed." In 1840 he married Eleanor Brocklebank, of Cumberland, and had six children. He was created a baronet in the 1887 Jubilee honours, but the baronetcy is now extinct. Like Ramsbottom he endowed a scholarship for LNWR men at Owens College. Soon after Lady Moon's death at the beginning of 1891 he gave up the LNWR chairmanship and did not remain a director. He died on 17 November 1899 and was buried at Bingley, near Coventry.

Crewe apprentices
Crewe apprentices were an essential part of the works and of the far-flung 'Crewe tradition'. The first 'premium' on record was William Woods, for whom Lord Delamere paid a fee of £15 to Trevithick in 1846, but Trevithick's most celebrated premium was Webb. Until 1862 not many

premiums were admitted who did not have already a connection with the LNWR. After the amalgamation of the locomotive divisions, premiums were taken from outside, the whole intake of apprentices and pupils being widened and more regulated in three general categories: trade apprentices, premium apprentices, and pupils.

Ordinary trade apprentices normally were sons of Crewe or other LNWR employees, and were trained for only one branch, such as turners, fitters, machine men, moulders and so on. Successive entries soon formed a family tradition, and in present BREL days fourth and fifth generation men are known in the works. Several Crewe registers of the Ramsbottom and Webb periods survive[17] which show the monthly inflow and outflow of workmen, with reasons for leaving, previous employment, into which shop they were taken, and so forth. These form a good background for Crewe families and works environment.

From the early 1860s there was a Crewe foremen's tradition as well as the workers' and apprentices' family traditions. These men had absolute authority within their own spheres and were accustomed to strong mutual support. Many of them lived alongside each other in Delamere and Victoria Streets, known colloquially as 'Gaffers' Row.' Well-known foremen of the later Ramsbottom and earlier Webb years were George Dingley of Nos 3 and 4 erecting shops, Kemp of the steel plant, Martin of the joiners, Roberts of No 1 shop, Braidwood of the fitters, Hymers of the iron foundry, Beazley of the painters, William Ellis of the boiler shop, Williams of the tender shop, and Antrobus of the copper shop, In the later years of Webb and up to 1914 were Henry Cooper of the boiler shop, who was in the service for over 59 years and who died two weeks after his retirement in 1911, Joyce of the west-end erecting shops, Lindop of the Old Works fitting shop, and later Henry Powell of the wheel shop, a well-known locomotive model maker who won the 1948 championship cup at the Model Engineer exhibition with a 7¼in-gauge Stanier Pacific. A Locomotive Foremen's Pension Fund was begun in 1890 and started with over 200 members including running-shed foremen.

Premium apprentices came from wider social circles and geographical limits. For a sum usually of about £200 paid by instalments to the company, they went through a five-year apprenticeship and were paid normal trade apprentice rates. They were taken through a variety of shops and could attend some day classes at the Mechanics Institute, but they did not always get into the drawing office, and their footplate experience was limited to a few footplate passes. As a rule half the premium payments were credited to the Apprentice Fee Account of the company at Euston; the other half was available to help the finances of the Mechanics Institute. In the last quarter-century of the LNWR around 30 new premiums were admitted each year.

Pupils usually were accepted from the ranks of the premiums, either at the end of apprenticeship or after three years. They were not pupils of the company but of the chief mechanical engineer, who had free choice as to whom he took. Occasionally pupils were taken without previous apprenticeship, but then generally direct from a university or perhaps after some experience at another works. Such pupils were taken until the mid-1930s. Pupilage lasted two years at a cost of around £150 a year, of which half went to the company and half to the chief mechanical engineer. From the later years of Webb the number of pupils at one time was limited to six, and they were given still wider opportunities than premiums, and invariably had periods in the drawing office and on the footplate, in addition to weekly footplate passes. A 'prize' for second-year pupils was a fortnight's *locum* in the summer, when they acted for shed foremen on holiday.

Neither premiums nor pupils were guaranteed LNWR jobs at the end of their time, and those without influence usually went elsewhere at once or after a few months working as journeymen at Crewe or some shed. Even those who stayed did not always go high, perhaps just to foreman level, though some of them were Whitworth Scholars and Exhibitioners.

Among the many Crewe premiums and pupils who later became celebrated in the locomotive and railway world, and who are not covered earlier in this chapter, were James Crawford Park (1856–61), locomotive superintendent of the GNR (Ireland) from 1881 to 1895; Wilson Worsdell (1866–67), chief mechanical engineer of the NER 1890–1910; Sir John Aspinall (1868–72), locomotive superintendent of the GS&WR (Ireland) 1882–86 and the LYR (1886–98), and general manager (1899–1919) of the latter; H. A. Ivatt (1868–72), locomotive superintendent of the GS&WR (1886–96) and GNR (1896–1911); R. F. Trevithick (1867–72), locomotive superintendent of the Ceylon Government Railways and of the western section of the Imperial Japanese Government Railways; Roger Atkinson (1870–73), superintendent of rolling stock, Canadian Pacific from 1896; H. A. Hoy (1872–77), chief mechanical engineer of the LYR (1899–1904) and general manager of Beyer Peacock (1904–10); Edgar Worthington (1875–78), for 22 years secretary of the Institution of Mechanical Engineers; F. C. Lea (1878–80), celebrated Professor of Mechanical Engineering at Sheffield University; George Hughes (1882–87), chief mechanical engineer in turn of the LYR (1904–21), LNWR (1922) and LMSR (1923–25); T. O'B. Otway-Ruthven (1889–93), chief mechanical engineer of the Nigerian Government Railways; F. R. Collins (c. 1890–94), later chief mechanical engineer of the South African Railways; Nigel Gresley (1893–94), later chief mechanical engineer of the GNR (1911–22) and LNER (1923–41); Donald Fraser (1895–97), later locomotive superindentent of the Canton–Hankow Railway; Eric A. Robinson (1890s), later managing director of the Superheater Co; J. G. B. Sams (1897–1902), locomotive superintendent of the Jamaican Government Railways and running superintendent of the Kenya & Uganda Railways; H. F. Cardew, chief mechanical engineer of the Nizam's Railway; R. E. Bury (1897–1902), grand-nephew of Edward Bury, the early locomotive builder, and who became chief mechanical engineer of the Mysore State Railways; A. W. Sutherland Graeme (1898–1903), one of Webb's last pupils, and later chief mechanical engineer of the Federated Malay States Railways; H. G. Ivatt (1904–08), later chief mechanical engineer of the LMSR and the LM Region of British Railways; Sir Reginald Terrell (1908–11), who became an MP and a director of signalling and other companies; Kenneth Cantlie (1916–20), technical adviser to the Chinese Minister of Railways and later the overseas representative of the Locomotive Manufacturers' Association; and Donald H. Stuart (1920–22), assistant chief mechanical engineer of the Burma Railways.

The Past and Present Crewe Association, a very loose body for long known as the Crewe Premiums' and Pupils' Association, began in the early 1880s at a suggestion, it has been said, made by Aspinall to Webb. The first dinner was in 1884 at 'the Cri' in Piccadilly Circus. In 1981 was held the 74th annual dinner. Gatherings usually have been in London, but occasionally from 1919 in Crewe, at the Crewe Arms Hotel. Few were more entertaining than the 1919 dinner, after a four-year gap, when Gresley and Aspinall sang to the refrain of *The Holy City* J. A. Bowes's poem *Crewe Steam Shed*. When the 1927 dinner was held at Crewe so that members could see the re-organised works, the doyen was Sir John Aspinall, who had begun his time at Crewe 58 years before. At the 1980 dinner in London the doyen was R. A. Riddles, who had begun at Crewe 71 years earlier. For many years prior to World War II the secretary was Reggie Terrell; today it is Andrew Steel, who after service at Crewe is now in the BR mechanical department at York.

References

1 *The Social and Economic Development of Crewe 1780–1923* W. H. Chaloner, 1950
2 *Locomotive Profile* No 15, 1971
3 *Rail Accidents* Mark Huish. Proc. Inst. Civil Engineers, 1851–52
4 PRO. Rail 1008. Chairman's letter
5 *Locomotive Profile* No 15, 1971
6 PRO. Rail 1008–101
7 LNWR General Stores & Locomotive Expenditure Committee, 18 February 1862
8 *Working & Management of an English Railway*. G. Findlay, 1889
9 *Round the Works of Our Great Railways*. C. J. B. Cooke, 1893
10 In discussion of Stroudley's paper *The Construction of a Locomotive Engine*. Proc. Inst. Civil Engineers, Vol 81, March 1885
11 *Locomotive Profile* No 15, 1971
12 *Locomotive Profile* No 10, 1971
13 *Rambles on Railways*. Cusack Roney, 1868.
14 PRO. Rail 1008. Chairman's letters.
15 *The Autobiography of Peter Taylor*, 1903
16 *Fifty Years on the LNWR*. David Stevenson, 1891.
17 PRO. Rail 410/1905

Index